SUBVERSIVE ARCHAISM

THE LEWIS HENRY MORGAN LECTURES
presented at the University of Rochester

Rochester, New York

Duke University Press Durham and London 2021

SUBVERSIVE ARCHAISM

Troubling Traditionalists and the
Politics of National Heritage

MICHAEL HERZFELD

Designed by Courtney Leigh Richardson
Typeset in Garamond Premier Pro and Din by
Westchester Publishing Services

Library of Congress Cataloging-in-Publication Data
Names: Herzfeld, Michael, [date] author.
Title: Subversive archaism : troubling traditionalists and the politics
of national heritage / Michael Herzfeld.
Other titles: Lewis Henry Morgan lectures (Duke University Press)
Description: Durham : Duke University Press, 2021. | Series: The
Lewis Henry Morgan Lectures | Includes bibliographical references
and index.
Identifiers: LCCN 2021012724 (print)
LCCN 2021012725 (ebook)
ISBN 9781478015000 (hardcover)
ISBN 9781478017622 (paperback)
ISBN 9781478022244 (ebook)
Subjects: LCSH: Nation-state. | Nationalism—Social aspects. |
National characteristics—Political aspects. | Authority—Social
aspects. | Marginality, Social—Political aspects. | State crimes. |
Political crimes and offenses—Greece—Crete. | Political crimes
and offenses—Thailand—Bangkok. | BISAC: SOCIAL SCIENCE /
Anthropology / Cultural & Social
Classification: LCC JZ1316.H47 2021 (print) | LCC JZ1316 (ebook) |
DDC 322.4—dc23
LC record available at https://lccn.loc.gov/2021012724
LC ebook record available at https://lccn.loc.gov/2021012725

This book is for
RAVINDRA K. JAIN,
anthropologist, guide, and friend,
my first graduate teacher in anthropology,
who taught me by example how to ask usefully awkward questions
and how to listen carefully to the answers.

Contents

Preface and Acknowledgments

This book is based on the 2018 Lewis Henry Morgan Lectures, which I delivered at the University of Rochester, Rochester, New York, on 10–13 October. The invitation to give these lectures is a great honor and an extraordinary intellectual opportunity. Bob Foster, in conveying the invitation to me, requested that I look back on my earlier work, causing me to recall his generous 1999 invitation to serve as discussant on an American Anthropological Association panel about regional anthropologies. This book, which is based on the Morgan Lectures but has entailed considerable refinement of the argument, continues that commitment to a critical and comparative approach, grounded in local ethnography but alert to its entailment in wider, cross-regional dynamics.[1] It seems to have been my anthropological fate to end up, in two different countries, in tiny, obscure places that both became foci of spectacular conflict with hard-fisted state power.

In neither place was I expecting anything of the kind. In Crete, I thought I was going to study kinship and marriage, just as an obedient Oxford-trained anthropologist should. In Bangkok, I was seeking to understand the impact of historical restoration and conservation on local historical memory, a theme that I had explored in urban settings in both Greece and Italy.[2] In Crete, I instead ended up studying competitive masculinity and its relationship to the nation-state. And in Bangkok I found myself studying what initially seemed to be an unimportant community that then turned out to be a source of enormous aggravation to the municipal (and implicitly also the national) authorities; its predicament became an international cause célèbre—minimally if at all, let me hasten to add, as a result of my own intervention. The sad end of that community is also an illustration of what happens when an already hostile bureaucracy, restrained to some extent by the rules of the democratic game, passes into the rougher hands of a military dictatorship. In a society that treats virtue as innate and represented at its purest in the monarchy, marginal people—the poor, the provincial, migrants, and squatters—must also contend with implicit assumptions about their karmic predestination to failure. Such assumptions politically shore up the material causes of their marginality.[3] By comparison, the Cretan villagers were rather lucky. They live and participate in a lively democracy, their village still exists, and today, with a charming blend of cheek and dignity, they forcefully rebut calumnies that represent them as un-Greek and cheerfully challenge voyeuristic tourists seeking the thrill of criminality. But neither story is a happy one.

For a long time I was puzzled by the Thai authorities' hostility toward the tiny Bangkok community. Its residents, though poor, were staunch royalists; although they tactically stood aside from the clashes between the so-called Yellow (conservative-royalist) and Red (pro-Thaksin leftist) Shirts, yellow shirts far outnumbered red in the residents' everyday dress. Given their political leanings, it was perhaps understandable that the left-populist government of Thaksin Shinawatra would be hostile; long before political violence flared on the streets, the residents had mostly appeared to be loyal to the conservative Democrat Party, although their allegiance was by no means stable. But that the military regime should so enthusiastically finish off a project of destruction that its own favorite bogey, Thaksin, had relentlessly pursued seemed counterintuitive— until I realized that the residents' cultural and political conservatism made their presence, as a self-constituted and self-regulating democratic polity in miniature, potentially embarrassing to the central authorities regardless of who was in charge of government.[4]

Related issues arose in the Cretan village. Gripped for years in the caressing armlock of astute political patrons from the largely pro-Western center-right of the parliamentary spectrum, patrons who happily exchanged access to basic resources for the bloc votes of large clans, the community also resented a larger and more influential neighbor's greater access to this patronage network.[5] The villagers also resented the simple necessity of playing the patronage game at all, seeing it as a violation of their formal and ethical rights as citizens. Having to bribe doctors to perform routine operations or promising votes in exchange for a hospital bed struck them as outrageous but unavoidable affronts to democratic principles. But they also knew how to work the system within the limits of their competition—and occasional cooperation—with their more powerful neighbor.

By the time I revisited the village in 2013, my earlier work about it, *The Poetics of Manhood*, had appeared in Greek. Shortly thereafter, in a television interview, I criticized the police action and the resulting and nationally uniform infamy suffered by the village.[6] The warm reception accorded by the villagers to both of these productions amplified an already embracing friendship and led easily to new field research.[7]

My gratitude to the people of both communities for accepting and even encouraging my interest at what were extremely difficult times for them is enormous. I am greatly indebted to Harvard University's Asia Center and Weatherhead Center for International Affairs for financially supporting my research during the four years preceding the completion of this book. That research allowed me to look back critically on my earlier work, an aspect of the book that has also necessitated an embarrassingly heavy burden of self-citation; in mitigation, I suggest that the citations do at least save the reader from a much longer volume![8] At the same time, I have been greatly inspired by many other scholars' research; I especially thank Bronwyn Isaacs and Trude Renwick for their willingness to let me cite their unpublished but extremely important and interesting findings. Phill Wilcox was graciously willing to do the same with her doctoral thesis, but happily it has meanwhile been transformed into a book and is cited in that form. Warm appreciation goes to the organizers of the events held around the 2018 Morgan Lectures at the University of Rochester, Robert Foster and Daniel Reichman, who co-chaired the entire event and provided hospitable intellectual leadership and inspiration, splendidly backed up by their colleagues Kristin Doughty, Kathryn Mariner, John Osburg, and Llerena Searle. The indefatigable Donna Mero ably managed all those practicalities that abound at such moments. I am deeply grateful to my five discussants (Katherine Bowie, Douglas Holmes, Andrew Alan Johnson, Deborah E. Reed-Danahay, and Thomas Gibson) for combining incisive critique with kindly understanding of my conceptual confusions and to the six Morgan Fellows (Chuan Hao [Alex] Chen, Zebulon Dingley, Rocío Gil, Kelly Mulvaney, Emiko Stock, and Courtney Wittekind). They all brought usefully provocative responses to my emergent ideas. Four others later added generous and helpful comments: Naor Ben-Yehoyada, Giuseppe Bolotta, Gregory Feldman, and Konstantinos Kalantzis. The manuscript also benefited greatly from the anonymous reports solicited by Duke University Press. At the press itself, Ken Wissoker's warm enthusiasm for this project has been matched at various stages in the book's preparation and production by the meticulous collaboration of Jena Gaines, Ellen Goldlust, Kate Herman, Lisl Hampton, and Joshua Gutterman Tranen. I was accompanied to Rochester—and throughout much of the fieldwork in both locations—by my partner, Cornelia (Nea) Mayer Herzfeld, whose subsequent critical reading of this work brought clarity and focus and whose skilled blend of provocation and support is the glow that pervades my life and writing.

Foreword

ROBERT J. FOSTER AND DANIEL R. REICHMAN

CO-DIRECTORS, LEWIS HENRY MORGAN LECTURE SERIES

Michael Herzfeld delivered the Lewis Henry Morgan Lectures at the University of Rochester in October 2018, continuing an annual tradition that began in 1963 with Meyer Fortes's inaugural lectures on kinship and the social order. Professor Herzfeld presented a public lecture on the evening of 10 October and it was followed by a daylong workshop during which members of the Department of Anthropology and invited experts discussed several draft chapters of the manuscript that became this book. Formal discussants included Katherine Bowie (University of Wisconsin), Thomas Gibson (University of Rochester), Douglas Holmes (Binghamton University), Andrew Alan Johnson (Princeton University), and Deborah E. Reed-Danahay (the University at Buffalo).

Herzfeld offers a fresh take on a familiar question: Does the hyphen in *nation-state* separate or join the two words? This question points toward the historical contingency of nation-state formation—to nation building or nation making as a never-completed process. Over the past two generations, scholars of the nation-state have accordingly turned their attention to struggles between state agents and their various rivals to control the narrative of nationhood on which the legitimacy of the state rests. The capacity to represent, in all senses, the people who comprise the nation presumes control over this narrative, which defines the character and heritage of a discrete and distinctive collectivity.

Herzfeld's notion of subversive archaism directs our attention elsewhere. What if the struggle does not mainly concern the definition of the nation but rather the political structure in which the nation is embedded? That is, what if the challenge to the state's legitimacy focuses on the nation-state itself as a peculiar form of polity rather than on any particular narrative of nationhood or definition of *ethnos*? And what if the challenge, moreover, appeals to a vision of polity regarded as an older and more homegrown alternative to the liberal bureaucratic state?

The original title for the Morgan Lecture event in Rochester was "What Is a Polity?" While that title has changed, Herzfeld pursues this inquiry throughout this book, laying out the high intellectual and deep ethical stakes involved. What, indeed, is a polity? In answering this question, Herzfeld exposes the underpinnings of the modern nation-state by examining challenges to state sovereignty that emerge from other meaningful "forms of social aggregation." Ethnographically, the book focuses on two of Herzfeld's long-standing areas of expertise—Greece and Thailand—but there is no doubt that his arguments have comparative implications for people and places around the world.

Herzfeld's detailed and sensitive comparison of the fates of two small communities suggests that the challenge of subversive archaism is as serious as it is, on the face of it, improbable. The Cretan village of Zoniana, with its segmentary clan system, and the Bangkok enclave of Pom Mahakan, the materialization of the kingly Siamese cosmopolity (*moeang*), both arouse what Herzfeld terms an "anxiety of unmodernity" among the bourgeois bureaucrats of their respective nation-states. These communities are inconvenient relics of what he describes as "a different ethos and a different age," constant and uncomfortable reminders of "the historical fragility of the very idea of the nation-state." While they might serve the state now and then as a useful internal Other against which a unified modern nation can be mobilized, their moral claims present an irreducible affront to the state's legitimacy. As a result, they live dangerously. Circumstances of political and economic change, such as the ones Herzfeld describes in this book, can trigger violent state actions to bring these alternative polities in line with the prevailing global model of an imagined national community.

Through the concept of subversive archaism, Herzfeld develops a theory of social movements in which people resist the power of the bureaucratic state by strongly identifying with the state's dominant traditions, ideals, and values. Rather than challenging state power from the outside, subversive archaists consciously (sometimes aggressively) claim membership in the "authentic" national community to resist bureaucratic incursions on their lives and livelihoods. In so doing, they assert, as Herzfeld phrases their attitude, that the state "is not the only acceptable or most venerable form of polity." Following the lead of his Zoniani and Chao Pom interlocutors, Herzfeld advises us to expand the meaning of polity beyond that of a formal structure of governance to include a way of life or mode of social existence: "the consensual community reached by people acting with full awareness of constructing a distinctive social environment." The polity is thus an "ethical space," sometimes evanescent, entailing certain forms of urbanity and civility; it is as much cosmological as political.

Herzfeld's inquiry recalls that of Lewis Henry Morgan in the nineteenth century into the relationship between forms of governance and the forms of urbanity and civility they encompass. Morgan set out to understand the emergence of the territorial nation-state through a social evolutionist lens, tracing the origins of the state (he called it *political society*) as it replaced kin-based social orders, which he called *gentile society*. In *Ancient Society* (1877) he argued that the territorial nation-state emerged historically from societies that were ordered by membership in clans (*gens*), phratries, and tribes. As private property and urban settlements began to develop, "government upon territory and upon property" replaced government of "aggregates of persons" (272). Morgan looked to the ancient Athenian polis to find his own answer to the question "What is a polity?" It is only fitting that Herzfeld begins to answer this question through an ethnography of modern Greece, where tensions between the *politia*, the police, and the people often hinge on the power of bureaucratic rule of law versus personalistic attachments to localities and kin groups. Harkening back to Morgan's discussion of the Greek patrilineal clan or gens, Herzfeld notes that the residents of the village of Zoniana in Crete continue to use the term *yenia* for patriline.

This is of course not to say that Morgan's evolutionist conclusions hold any weight today. The very forms of urbanity and civility that Morgan celebrated as *progress*—the manners and mores of "civilization"—are what Herzfeld's subversive archaists contest or reject outright. In Bangkok, the informal urban community of Pom Mahakan resisted eviction by the Thai state by invoking state-sanctioned traditionalism and norms of upstanding citizenship. They asserted their identity as authentic and respectful Thai citizens in order to avoid being trampled on the path to progress, emphasizing their autochthonous origins and the historical continuity of their settlement. Ultimately, they failed. In Crete, residents of no-longer-remote Zoniana dealt more successfully with attempts by police to curtail sheep stealing and subsequently the illicit cultivation of cannabis by some villagers, although one violent episode in 2007 brought the armed force of the Greek state down on the whole village. Zoniani asserted their autonomy by appealing to nationalistic ideas of roguish masculinity, heroic rebellion against authority, and pride in enduring local and quintessentially Greek traditions. In both of these cases, subversive archaism counteracts marginalization by making claims to cultural centrality.

Ethnography from around the world has shown how the territorial nation-state is under stress. Centrifugal forces of globalization and transnational capitalism pull outward at the boundaries of state and society, while the centripetal forces of populist ethnonationalism and myriad localisms pull inward. As Herzfeld's work brilliantly demonstrates, comparative ethnography can help us understand both the particularities and the commonalities of this phenomenon as it is experienced by people in very different historical and cultural situations. Not all subversive challenges to the nation-state that appeal to heritage imply an attractive alternative polity; some, like the neo-Nazi groups of Europe, are decidedly uncivil and manifestly racist. In both Zoniana and Pom Mahakan, however, people asserted their right to exist as a moral community—to something more than the rights of the sovereign individual. While bureaucratic states continually attempt to encompass these forms of sociality, local people reach back into the past in order to authorize their claims on the future. Morgan, who looked to ancient societies as inspirations for a more democratic future, would have understood.

1. THE NATION-STATE OUTRAGED

Subversion at the Heart of the Nation-State

In the grand sweep of human history, the nation-state is a newcomer to the galaxy of social arrangements. Nevertheless, it has achieved global supremacy. Even though it is now facing competition and infiltration by corporate financial powers, it has already successfully broken the back of most forms of social aggregation at any level higher than that of the nuclear family.

In this success, however, lurks an ever-present danger. The nation-state is built on foundations that are antithetical to its design, its official ideology, and the way in which it operates. Although it has always presented itself as a centralized and unified entity, numerous suprafamilial social arrangements, ranging from the extended family household to the large organized clan as well as regional separatist movements, threaten its stability from within. Those fractures are especially visible to anthropologists who, through intimate interactions in local communities, encounter perspectives that are invisible (or simply unacceptable) to those at the apex of state power. In a world increasingly inundated with talk about heritage, these local complexities often appear in the form of stories and attitudes that contest official renditions of heritage and commandeer official language for very different representations of the past.

The state's problem lies in the history of its own emergence from revolt and warfare. Nation-states typically produce official narratives emphasizing cultural, social, economic, and political harmony and unity. They deploy an array of carefully selected, emblematic cultural products, collectively dubbed *heritage*, as legitimating evidence of the nation's deep past and as a mark of the state's benign tutelage. Yet many states today are conspicuously lacking in harmony. Multiple levels of potential and actual factionalism challenge the rhetoric of national unity. Anthropologically well-documented accounts of these dynamics concern Jordan, Libya, and South Sudan.[1] By contrast, many older nation-states, especially in Europe, have more or less successfully buried the external markers of historical conflict in top-down historical narratives. Yet even their triumphal stories rest on unstable ground. The emergence of rightist populists claiming to be adhering to "tradition," "heritage," and, in the United States, "strict constitutionalism" and the "right to bear arms" suggests the persistent resilience of a slumbering but powerful volcano. The nation-state, for its part, cannot simply ignore or shut down such outbursts of traditionalism, because to do so puts its own legitimacy (and its revolutionary credentials) in question. Most nation-states therefore survive in part by allowing a measure of play to such inconvenient forms of heritage and culture.

These potentially awkward traits usually appear as officially prohibited but pragmatically licensed naughtiness, concealed within what I call *cultural intimacy*: the space of those cultural traits deemed embarrassing in larger (and especially international) public contexts but evoking "rueful self-recognition" and companionable familiarity among complicit insiders.[2] Benedict Anderson famously argued that nationalism drew its strength from the promise of collective immortality. But this is only half the story—the half the official state narrates.[3] The other half is represented by the lawbreakers. For the most part, the nation-state draws its resilience from a measure of permissiveness with regard to relatively minor but commonplace infractions of law, and most bureaucrats recognize and deal with that reality every day of their working lives.

Arguably, no nation-state can exist for long without that built-in tolerance. Officials often look the other way when minor infractions or unseemly behavior remain relatively discreet but will not countenance anything that too brazenly challenges their moral authority.[4] When a Tea Party insurrection turns into a well-organized militia, or when an eccentrically disobedient cleric's challenge to the state's religious orthodoxy gathers adoring crowds, it is high time for the bureaucracy to be alarmed. States may be more tolerant of tax evasion or unlicensed gun-toting than they are of well-organized challenges to official cultural doctrine.

The threat to the nation-state is that of an insubordinate "way of knowing and seeing"—and using—national heritage.[5] Heritage commonly first appears as a state-generated discourse. Nation-states invest enormous resources in constructing a homogeneous repertoire of collective heritage, which functions as a palpable, ubiquitous representation of national unity. Museums, theatrical displays, music and dance repertoires, and a stream of explanatory rhetoric all conduce to its factitious uniformity. But that is where the state faces its greatest internal vulnerability. In ransacking vernacular sources, the state risks a knowledgeable local rejection of its totalizing interpretations. Traditionalizing citizens may challenge the bureaucrats' self-ascribed cultural authority.

That may not in itself explain why bureaucrats sometimes respond with disproportionate violence. But it does explain why traditionalism alone does not suffice to protect communities when, for whatever ostensible reason, the bureaucrats decide to use force. Bureaucrats conventionally see themselves as embodiments and agents of modernity, and thus of a rationality they (wrongly) assume to be universal. Why, they wonder, can these absurdly retrograde citizens not understand that their customs are disgusting, archaic, and impediments to progress? Why do these throwbacks persist in holding the nation back, both internally and in the eyes of the world, with their defiance of the law and their persistent harping on the antiquity of local traditions? Why do they reject a modernity that could liberate them from unhygienic living, grinding work, and lifestyles that mire them in a dilapidated past? Why do they not gratefully accept the state's firm guidance on the evolutionary path to development?[6] And why are those wretched anthropologists so intent on encouraging them in their antiquated ways and even in their defiance of legal authority?

Such attitudes are common throughout the world. They are usually expressed as irritation, frustration, and petty acts of spite, and occasionally erupt in headline-catching confrontations. But they rarely result in massive violence. In this book, however, I am concerned with those rarer cases where violence ensues, and especially where at least some of that violence is conducted by state agents. The violence highlights stakes that may not emerge so clearly in less dramatic contestations. By offering a comparison between seemingly very dissimilar cases, I also propose to discommode the universalizing language of heritage.[7] Local groups with distinctive cultural styles reveal the liability that the nation-state accepts in deploying the concept of heritage as its conceptual banner. Rebellious citizens can point to historical antecedents in their local cultural heritage that not only are older than the state itself but also represent alternatives to its disciplined modernity.

Violent responses expose the fragility and contingency of the state's cultural claims. They usually occur in contexts where other factors—unhelpful publicity, shifts in political patronage, unlawful activities by some community members, sudden moves by a few local hotheads—precipitate confrontation. They end with humiliation and, in extreme cases, destruction. They also bring the nation-state's problem into clearer focus: how to assimilate rebellious holdouts who challenge the state's right to impose uniform law and order and to define and represent the national culture? A comparison of cases will show why the state does not always welcome citizen-generated traditionalism and indeed, on occasion, tries to discredit and destroy it.

Merely One among Many: The Nation-State as a Variety of Polity

The global ubiquity of nation-states creates the illusion, backed by their rhetoric, of absolute permanence. The rhetoric, however, is often belied by historical experience, while the coherence of state authority is repeatedly undermined by the necessity of reconciling contradictions among its laws and by the pragmatic cynicism of everyday bureaucratic and political practice. When formal arrangements break down in smaller or weaker states, more powerful states pounce, crying, "Corruption! Failed state!" In so doing, they—unintentionally, we may assume—reveal the historical fragility of the very idea of the nation-state.

The claims of the nation-state to eternity and universality parallel the very similar claims of European logic and rationality described by Stanley J. Tambiah in his Lewis Henry Morgan Lectures.[8] Typified by Weber's view of the bureaucratic state as the ultimate incarnation of that rationality, these claims are themselves the paradoxical signs of a narrowly European and colonial source.[9] A child of Victorian evolutionism and of European global colonialism, the modern nation-state has always sought to present itself as the logical culmination of political development. The recent acceleration of information flow, however, has fostered increasing speculation about possible alternatives.[10] If universal literacy and print capitalism enabled the rise of nationalism, as Benedict Anderson argued, their current electronic incarnations now undermine the nation-state's pretensions to permanence and permit the resuscitation of older political visions.[11]

Political formations do not necessarily disappear even when they seem to have been displaced. Whereas some authors (notably James C. Scott) have viewed these upsurges of older identities as always egalitarian and often threatened with extinction, there are exceptions.[12] Such cases sometimes exist in a tense symbiosis with the nation-state, which they eventually transform and which they often strip down for some of its more attractive accessories.[13]

I focus primarily on examples from Thailand and Greece. In addition to partially shared relations with colonialism, there are, as Scott has pointed out, similarities between the relations linking mountain-dwelling farmers and pastoralists with the urban and coastal centers of state government in both Southeast Asia and the Mediterranean.[14] I hope, however, that the ethnographic cases will allow us to move beyond any hint of geographical or environmental determinism and will provide a broader vision of how alternatives to the nation-state emerge from the shadows of the past. A further issue concerns the romantic appeal of resistance to the state, since that romance—or at least its precursor in struggles for national redemption—is part of the state's self-vision. For Pierre Clastres, "archaic" societies often lack the economic greed and hierarchical structures of modern industrial society. He and Scott both offer genuinely romantic visions of what a society could be without the economic interests that dominate our own.[15] Both positions consequently suffer from a too-easy binarism of tribal and nomadic versus urban and sedentary, thereby ironically reproducing the colonial logic that ruthlessly marginalized virtually all such social groups in political reality and, as Johannes Fabian points out, in the anthropological imagination as well.[16]

Clastres and Scott have admirably increased awareness about both the brutality of domination and the possibility of an alternative political ethics. But mention of their work sets the stage, in contrastive fashion, for my chosen focus on something related but different: the proactive, agentive, and often astute production of an idiom of social and cultural archaism for explicitly political ends within the framework of national identity.

Subversive Archaists and the Nation-State

The subversive archaists of this book are not "insurgent citizens" in James Holston's sense of people seeking a collective identity outside that of the nation-state and rejecting the myths in which national identity is grounded.[17] Far from being Scott's perpetual refugees from civilization and literacy, moreover, they often display an impressive command of official rhetoric, heritage-speak, and bureaucratic formalism. Nor are they ideological anarchists—"the most misunderstood and vilified of political actors"—or Luddites.[18] They do not constitute revolutionary movements. They represent recursive eruptions of ideologies and practices that may, as in some populist movements, be radically conservative.[19] They look remarkably like what they oppose. Above all, they do not spurn the trappings of national heritage. On the contrary, they exceed the traditionalism of the state. They are intensely loyal to the nations of which they are members, and they are often the first to volunteer their lives for national causes. They try to work with the state, or to infiltrate it, and they are hurt when the state rejects their advances.

Their often intense loyalty does not make them less annoying to those in power. Take, for example, the "whiskered lunatics" of Lawrence Durrell's disparaging account: warlike men willing to sail in puny boats from Crete and Rhodes to join the national independence struggle in Cyprus.[20] Such men, for whom state bureaucrats have no more patience than the British novelist contemplating the chaotic decay of imperial rule, do not patiently wait to be called up. They claim to know better how to *be* loyal members of the nation than do the pen-pushers ordering others to sacrifice their lives. They fight the state's modernism with self-conscious and aggressive displays of loyalty to national ideals, traditions, and history; their traditionalism—as also, in many cases, their dramatic masculinity—both amplifies and parodies official representations of national heritage. We will meet some of them again in these pages.

Subversive archaists do sometimes take up arms, although their predilection for violence is also often exaggerated or misrepresented. In one of the two principal cases, a democratic state—Greece—was dealing with a place where a police officer lost his life and where frequent blood feuds titillate the sensationalist national press and challenge the state's monopoly of retributive justice. The other state, Thailand under a military-controlled government, faced resistance that was not violent but was nevertheless far from passive. The Thai authorities countered the community's claims to represent national tradition and heritage by accusing it of generic turpitude despite strong evidence to the contrary. In both cases, carefully articulated campaigns of vilification presaged a resolute intent to break the archaists' will.

A Global Range of Cases

Perhaps the most famous example of subversive archaism, one in which bureaucrats have often suffered humiliating failure or been caught in embarrassing complicity, is the phenomenon known in Italy as *mafia*. While there is some question about the historical accuracy of treating mafia as an organization, or even as a loose constellation of organizations, *mafiosi* are unquestionably real people and recognized as such, and they have proved highly adept at playing the state at its own rhetorical games.

The seemingly unending confrontation with Italian state power has precipitated a pattern of disrespect for central authority articulated as the localist ideology of "Sicilianism." *Sicilianismo*, which elevates the mafia code to the status of a morally justified alternative to state law, nicely illustrates subversive archaism. It provided a convenient culturalist defense of mafia activity past and present.[21] It purports to justify insubordination against officialdom in the name of cultural purity and pragmatically translates into conspiracies of silence even among those who oppose the activities of the mafiosi.[22]

Italy, with its locally celebrated tradition of compromise between law and social reality, offers many other opportunities for subversive archaism. Tradition justifies all, as when a former *malavitoso* (underworld thug) in Rome told me in a hurt voice that he and his mates were simply misunderstood defenders of the (archaic) values that led them to protect women from harassment in their district.[23] Italian officials and subversive archaists often engage in forms of complicity that have become a tradition in themselves. The intricate reciprocities between Italian politicians and Sicilian mafiosi, for example, often long defer official reprisals.

Mafia criminality is nevertheless abhorrent to much of the Italian population, especially middle-class urbanites in the northern and central areas, as well as to the local anti-mafia movement.[24] That the state has reacted with reciprocal violence is less surprising than that this response was so long deferred, especially when we consider the Italian state's decades-long feud with alleged bandits in Sardinia. But the delay itself reflects the complex reciprocities in which state actors and subversive archaists are sometimes entangled.

Both sides deny that mutuality, as they do their often-shared historical roots. Under-the-table dealings with lawbreakers are to present-day administrators what local defiance of the state in defense of religious or cultural freedom is to the creators of official national history. Attempts to revive historical examples of such defiance are potentially no less embarrassing to the state than the evidence of present-day collusion between officials and citizens. In the United States, the Branch Davidians who made a fatal last stand at Waco, Texas, were the recent embodiment of a lineage that stretches back to the emergence of the Church of Latter-Day Saints and even earlier—indeed, one could argue, to the emergence of the United States as a refuge from the religious authoritarianism of British colonial rule. Such histories recall elements of subversive archaism in the early history of the state itself. The violence conducted against these rebellious elements by the federal authorities certainly threw plentiful fuel on the already raging fires of antistate militancy and the white supremacism that lay at its core and that the insurrection at the U.S. Capitol on 6 January 2021 laid bare.[25] Those more consistently violent movements, to which I shall briefly return in the final chapter, do not themselves fit the model of subversive archaism, but they can easily exploit the excessive use of state force against subversive archaists to galvanize support for their own far less sympathetic causes.

We should consider a wide range of groups within this larger exploratory frame without conflating the diversity of their ideologies and practices in a single caricature: armed communities in the western mountains of the United States, the Old Calendarists who form obstinate and often persecuted minorities in Eastern Orthodox Christian nations, the Gush Emunim settlers whose fiery

Jewish orthodoxy and rejection of the secular state provoked a leftist Israeli government to destroy their settlements as illegal.[26] Many, but not all, are religious fundamentalists who accuse the state of sacrilege—a particularly wounding charge, given many states' self-representation as earthly manifestations of a divinely ordained and redemptive destiny.

Where the state is officially atheist, its heritage conservation policies often repressively treat all religious relics and practices as "culture." To the Chinese authorities, for example, groups like Falun Gong represent a potent threat to secular authority. The popularity of their appeal to an archaic meditational practice, *qigong*, a rhythmic exercise in breath and body control, signals more than mere rebellion or even revolution. It suggests an archaism that is inconsistent with the scientistic and modernist qigong adopted by the Chinese state; it also stands in dramatic contrast to the bodily regimentation that Susan Brownell has documented so well in her study of Chinese sports practices.[27] If we look at Chinese anger over Taiwan, moreover, we see a similar rejection of what is a self-traditionalizing entity.[28] The mainland authorities refuse to recognize Taiwan as a nation-state, which adds insult to the injury of its successful heritage program by insinuating that it is not, in fact, a Chinese state but a Taiwanese one, all the while exhibiting a Chineseness that looks more traditional than much of what is on show in the mainland. There, many cultural treasures were pillaged by the retreating Nationalist troops and are now on display in Taiwan; much that was left behind was destroyed later in the Cultural Revolution.

The state confronts serious risk when it attacks subversive archaists. Overkill can have negative and long-lasting repercussions. The state therefore usually prepares its ground well, beginning with a carefully orchestrated attack on the archaists' collective reputation. (China's long propaganda war against Taiwanese separatism may thus have ominous implications for the island's future.) Bureaucrats may feel that subversive archaists are daring them to attack. Archaists sometimes reckon that state officials can indeed be provoked into actions that cast doubt on state claims to represent national virtue. Their risk nevertheless exceeds that faced by the state, which is stronger and owns more effective means of mayhem.

Some cases concern minority populations whose claims to greater antiquity are a source of tension not only with their national government but also with the ethnic majority in general. Such a situation arose in the island zone of Soqotra, in Yemen, studied by Nathalie Peutz.[29] The Soqotrans aggressively championed their heritage as distinct from that of the rest of the country. Here, however, while the official response entailed a great deal of violence, that violence must be read in the context of a complex civil war. The Soqotrans are speakers of a minority language. Even as their national government attempts to engage UNESCO in the process of monumental conservation, it is losing much of its patrimony to the ravages of ongoing conflict. The Soqotrans, relatively unimportant geopolitically, are concerned that what they regard as their unique heritage counts for nothing in the eyes of any of the forces contending for power in Yemen today.

In one important respect, they resemble other communities that practice subversive archaism. In a world in which the possession of heritage has become a global key to recognition, they champion their distinctive traditions against the special interests of all the major warring factions. Heritage can be a two-edged sword—a prized possession expressive of national unity, but also the (highly vulnerable) target for the state's intolerance of internal difference. Peutz does indicate that the Soqotrans were often careful to disguise their opposition to the state, although it seems that this diffidence has waned in recent years as the Yemeni state itself became ever more deeply mired in disaster.[30]

The Soqotrans have had to deal with an official as well as a foreign view of their habitat as remote and inhospitable. They see themselves as the victims of a government that does not appreciate their hospitality toward the state's representatives, which the latter fully understand as a symbolic but meaningful inversion of the bureaucrats' greater power. The Soqotrans are Yemeni citizens; yet they can appeal to an antiquity that both differentiates them from other Yemenis and offers an alternative to the antiquarian claims of the nation-state.

In particular, the Soqotrans' adherence to a patrilineal clan structure was dismissed by their socialist critics as "tribalism." It was later reinstated under the Saleh regime, which also then attempted to build ties of patronage with the clans in what looked distinctly like a reversion to the social values and practices that had been displaced by the modernist-socialist state.[31] In this way, the Soqotrans suddenly found themselves in an unexpectedly advantageous position, having been encouraged by the Saleh regime to join it in strategically deploying tradition against what was left of the modernist establishment. Theirs was thus arguably, at least for a brief while, a case of *successful* subversive archaism. Their clever exploitation of ecological discourse against the state's more conventional environmentalism, moreover, recalls—but also inverts—the views of shepherds in the Sardinian village of Orgosolo; the Orgolesi (people of Orgosolo) challenge state environmentalism while representing their long-standing pastoral practices as an alternative way of respecting nature.[32]

Subversion and Complicity

The Soqotra case represents a middle ground of sorts between the subversive archaism that ultimately invites violent repression and situations in which a state may actively depend on (or at least draw benefit from the presence of) those archaists. Collusion between local outlaws and the state occurs especially when it does not take overtly organized form; unlike political patron-client collaboration, this more diffuse collusion rests on shared ideological interests rather than on reciprocal favor-trading. Notably in this regard, Fiona Greenland has shown how tomb robbers (*tombaroli*) in Italy have been engaged in long-term complicity with the Italian state in claiming that anything that comes out of the Italian soil is by definition part of Italy's heritage.[33]

The tombaroli have one distinct advantage. Unlike the bureaucrats, they can claim an embodied relationship with the very soil of the nation. Their vivid accounts of moist, earthy underground prowling gain an affectionate hearing in the culturally intimate spaces of Italian life.[34] The authorities can arrest individuals for specific offenses, but an all-out onslaught on the tombaroli could easily end in public disgust, undermining the state's popular entitlement to a share of the chthonic authority attached to all antiquities recovered from Italian soil.

State actors have excellent reason to conceal their connivance at technically illegal practices. Early in my fieldwork in the Cretan mountains, I heard from a shepherd, locally notorious for his own sheep-stealing skills, that a distinguished politician was meeting shepherds in the district capital to strategize the acquittal of their kinsmen accused of theft by bribing witnesses to retract their testimony.[35] This same politician was vociferous in his public demands for the suppression of animal theft. In 1993, he called on the Minister of the Interior to ask what measures had been taken against criminal activity in the prefecture. In a letter to a local newspaper, one commentator, after ironically wondering whether the politician and he lived on the same planet and insisting that the criminals were "'local produce' and most of them already known," observed that "no one regards any citizens as *a priori* guilty, because, the way things are now, no individual or official body dares regard anyone as a suspect, since those who are suspected [of crimes] enjoy a well-known and unexceptionable protection."[36]

The politician's distinguished career ended in disgrace when he was betrayed—a very unusual event in the tight and secretive societies of mountain Crete—after performing the same favor for someone accused of cultivating cannabis, by allegedly pressuring two police officers to withdraw their testimony. His fall lent credibility to a widespread assumption that those who publicly attacked such collusion were often, as in his case, its most culpable practition-ers. It also cast an interesting light on the temptations to which such powerful politicians were exposing police officers. It triggered a shift in the balance of po-litical power in western Crete, contributing, together with increasing revulsion against political corruption at the national level, to a general weakening (or at least muting) of local patron-client arrangements.

Subversive archaism plays on discourses of culture rather than on explicit forms of political authority, although relations with patrons may be framed as resting on traditional values. Subversive archaists often emphasize, and some-times exaggerate, cultural traits now largely obliterated or rendered illegal by modernization. Such traits can take the form of dress codes, speech forms, performances of particular types of music and drama, and rituals associated with vernacular religious practices; they may also include the bearing and use of weapons, ritualized theft, bride abduction, and strict laws of vengeance. Not all such gesticulations of cultural autonomy result in mayhem, and many are ignored as irrelevant to the modern nation-state or are fossilized by the official museum and folklore research machinery. But in a few extreme cases they can be spectacularly represented as unacceptable wrongdoing. This fram-ing can generate a potentially unhealthy or condescending interest on the part of the general public (violence voyeurism and "slum tourism"). It can also lead to spectacular repression.

Subversive archaism does not have a single political color. It is also not usefully conflated with populism, although there are certainly areas of over-lap. Subversive archaists do not necessarily reject expertise, as so many pop-ulists do; indeed, they often depend on experts—historians, anthropologists, archaeologists—to validate their readings of history. In those readings, they, too, become experts of a kind; again, some of the more articulate tombaroli exemplify this vernacularized expertise.[37] They may deliberately avoid attach-ing themselves to a currently popular bandwagon or mass movement.[38] Their insubordination is not so much an uprising of disaffected citizens as it is a claim on privileged authenticity—a claim that does not always charm the entire citi-zen body and certainly does not appeal to its bourgeois leadership.

Historical Continuities and Subversive Archaism
in Greece and Thailand

My two principal cases concern communities, one in Greece and the other in Thailand, where I have conducted ethnographic fieldwork over long periods of time. Viewed through the usual lens of area studies, Greece and Thailand seem decidedly dissimilar. They do, however, share one important feature of political history. Neither country was officially colonized by Western states, but both were constantly under pressure to conform to Western demands, demands that were cultural as well as political and economic. I call the indirect but often humiliating domination of these states "crypto-colonialism." Not all subversive archaism occurs in crypto-colonial states, but the bad odor of colonial interference in those states opens their cultural bureaucracies to criticism as bearers of foreign values and as agents of foreign interference.

All official history involves conceptual airbrushing; Greek and Thai national narratives illustrate this proclivity well. Their common ground is a principle of continuity, carefully constructed against evidence of more complex origins. Greek official historiography emphasizes a principle of "unbroken continuity" (*adhiaspasti sinekhia*) with the classical past, conserved during nearly two millennia of Roman, Byzantine, and Ottoman rule. For decades following the Greek War of Independence (1821–43), Greek scholars largely discounted the relevance to modern Greek identity of any cultural elements—Slavic, Turkish, Arab, or Albanian, or even western European—that threatened to disrupt the smooth surface of that paradigm. Their mortal enemy was Jakob Philipp Fallmerayer (1790–1861), a nineteenth-century pan-Germanist ideologue who, fearing that an Orthodox Christian anti-Ottoman alliance led by Russia would threaten German dreams of unity and independence, sought to weaken Greece's international standing. He argued that today's Greeks were largely of Slavic and Albanian stock.[39] An entire ethnological industry was marshaled to counter his claims; for any foreign scholar to be called "a Fallmerayer" remains a mark of Cain to this day. The imposition of a German king (the Bavarian Prince Otto) by the colonial powers in 1832 added to Greek resentment of foreign (especially German) interference.

The official model of Thai continuity is starkly different. It is, by contrast, centered on kingship—specifically, the ideal of the virtuous king or *thammarat* (Sanskrit *dharma raja*).[40] Despite variations over time, that concept is underwritten by a total identification of the kingship with Buddhism, a relationship now presented as unchanging but historically often adjusted to meet the demands of a modernized religious establishment.[41] It presents the current (Chakri) dynasty, which begins in 1782, as the culmination of a much longer sweep of time. Where Greek continuity rests on the premise of shared cultural (and implicitly genetic) roots, Thai continuity is retrospectively underwritten instead by a sacralized kingship. Abrupt internal changes in the present dynasty are rendered insignificant by the practice of naming each king "Rama," thereby representing them all as embodying an unchanging divinity.[42]

Official historiography thus airbrushes inconvenient exceptions and ruptures out of the narrative of continuity. In Thailand, that process not only smooths over intradynastic difficulties, sometimes even reversing official pronouncements; it also harmoniously sutures the current dynasty with its predecessors.[43] Few pre-Chakri monarchs are mentioned by name in official narratives (exemplified in the National Museum in Bangkok); the violent royal contests for power never mar the image of serene kingship.[44] Instead, limpid continuity supervenes. Notably, King Taksin, who was killed by the first Chakri ruler in the latter's power grab, is today commemorated in statuary and text as an important precursor. Such violent disruptions of the earthly kingdom in no way perturb the serene cosmology that has long treated usurpers and reprobates as legitimate wielders of power; their legitimacy historically lay, and perhaps still lies, in their status as reincarnations of deity, but could also be rehistoricized by claiming genealogical continuity with those they had overthrown.[45]

In a move to push the continuity still further back, the official narrative credits a thirteenth-century king, Ramkhamhaeng, with the invention of the Thai writing system. When a Thai and a British scholar questioned the authenticity of a stele purporting to represent Ramkhamhaeng's edicts in the earliest surviving example of Thai writing, they narrowly escaped prosecution for offending the monarchy. Such charges are probably the closest Thai equivalent to being called a "Fallmerayer" in Greece.[46]

Most scholarly opinion today views the inscription as probably genuine. Historian David Wyatt remarked that "to forge it would have required the skills of the greatest linguist the world has known [so] it is better to regard it as genuine."[47] But the debate is mainly interesting, as Craig Reynolds notes, for its political implications.[48]

Much was at stake. The stele appeared to confirm the monarchy as the bearer of cultural continuity, backgrounding the multiple ruptures between the older Siamese polity and today's ethnonationalist Thai state. Treating King Taksin as a precursor belongs to the same narrative subterfuge. That strategy, however, has sometimes backfired. During the Red Shirt uprisings, demonstrators made liberal use of the similarity of Taksin's name with that of the fallen populist prime minister Thaksin Shinawatra; some even suggested that Thaksin was Taksin's revenant ghost, seeking revenge for his death at the hands of the Chakri kings—an effective piece of subversive archaism in its own right.[49] Yet the artful removal of conflict from the imagined history of seamless monarchical continuity has been so repressive that as recently as 2015 the Bank of Thailand introduced a new 100-baht note with an image, on the reverse side, of none other than King Taksin.[50]

Sometimes the airbrushing takes dramatic form. While a military revolution in 1932 is officially recognized as the end of the absolute monarchy, the disappearance of a famous commemorative plaque—preceded by the secret removal of closed-circuit cameras by the city authorities—generated a lasting (and unresolved) furor. Even more disturbing, surreptitious moves to overturn the commemoration by substituting the names of loyal royalist officers for those of the putschists serves as a warning to any would-be democratic revolutionaries hiding in today's military.[51]

The king—scion of an indigenous monarchy—is called the "father" (*phaw*) of his people. Tracing this paternalistic metaphor back to the Ramkhamhaeng stele enfolds present-day paternalism within a chronologically deep genealogy, anachronistically associating the early Siamese kingship with twentieth-century visions of Thainess and political monarchism.[52] Measured by the king's Thainess, moreover, all other persons fall short; those who, for reasons of class, language, or personal character, fall too far short are not even considered truly Thai. The centrality of monarchy to the sense of Thai identity presents a sharp contrast to Greece, where the monarchy was always seen as a foreign institution.

In Thailand, the language of the powerful central plains became the mark of polite speech and official action. Despite vast morphological changes, the Ramkhamhaeng stele is treated as its original textual realization. The stele's 1833 discovery by Mongkut, the prince who eventually became King Rama IV in 1851, further enhanced the monarchy's role as guarantor of national continuity. Language thus joins religion and the monarchy as fundamental diagnostics of a supposedly unchanging Thai identity, projected back through a reimagined past. Conversely, minority self-abasement before the symbols of monarchy recurrently enacts the ethnic hierarchy.[53]

The association of monarchy and religion is fundamental. "Buddhism supports and validates the king's role as its patron and protector. In his role as the sustainer of the faith, the king benefits . . . ordinary people because through his efforts they are given the opportunity to make merit."[54] In short, without a king there would be no redemption, no possibility of even slightly improving one's karma. Prince Dhani Nivat, an administrator and scholar, claimed that the monarch could only legislate in accordance with strict Buddhist principles and thus could not invent law not already enshrined in sacred text. Historical evidence nevertheless suggests that long before the capital moved to Bangkok from Ayutthaya in the time of King Taksin, Siamese kings had long been in the habit of freely making laws to suit their rule. As defenders of the Buddhist faith, they were always-already invested with the aura of sanctity. Dhani's energetic promotion of the concept of the *thammarat* (virtuous king) sealed over the disjuncture between that ideal and the monarchs' legislative activism. Dhani's account of Rama I's revolt against Taksin and ascent to the throne, moreover, omits the new king's command to execute Taksin. Clearly the historiographic ends here justified the editorial means.[55] The scholarly prince—whose influence became especially strong in the early years of Rama IX's reign, when he variously served as regent and president of the Privy Council—thereby enhanced the implied continuity with the pre-Chakri past and legitimized the king's present temporal authority as already embedded in the sacredness of his office.[56] Those who hold political office are expected to defend the monarchy by whatever means are deemed necessary; today, as virulent online threats suggest, they have also incited a loyalist following into echoing that principle with vastly enhanced impact. The consequences are predictable, given a notorious pattern of impunity that persists even during relatively democratic times.[57] Some exiles' criticism of the current royalist-military power elite has ended with their abduction and gangland-style murder abroad.[58]

Historiographical seamlessness is crucial for the Thai state. Thai kingship, thus connected with antiquity, relies on three props: the Buddhist religion, the (central) Thai language with the royal diction (*rachasap*) as its culminating refinement, and the institution of monarchy itself.[59] The comparison with Greece is especially instructive here. The corresponding elements in Greek nationalism are the neoclassical-inflected formal speech of Athens, Greek Orthodox religion, and "blood" as the vehicle for the transmission of national identity. But Greek blood was a badge of Greekness that no Greek king was ever able to claim. In Thailand, kings are considered indigenous, their status firmly yoked to a vague and mythologized antiquity.[60] In Greece, the first king, a Catholic, was baptized into the national Orthodox religion and had to learn to speak Greek. The last king, Constantine II, claimed continuity—on coinage, for example—with the Byzantine emperors under the name Constantine XIII, but this gesture to history impressed no one and did not save the monarchy from abolition in 1974.[61]

Despite these differences, the principal effect of the Cold War on both countries was to solidify institutional ethnonationalism, marked in both by an explicit contrast of local religiosity with the alleged amorality of neighboring countries. It is nevertheless not coincidental that in Greece the extremes of ethnonationalism have lost political ground, whereas in Thailand they remain dominant. In Greece, especially after the fall of the military junta and the abolition of monarchy in 1974, national identity was increasingly associated with parliamentary democracy (symbolized as the resurrection of an ancient Greek tradition), while church influence gradually weakened. Greece still does not recognize ethnic minorities as such, but for the most part adopts an increasingly laissez-faire attitude toward them.[62] Thailand, by contrast, has resisted granting many minority groups citizenship and has developed an extraordinarily complex set of bureaucratic practices that affects the rights and mobility of both minority persons and migrants from neighboring countries; meanwhile, and concomitantly, the mutual institutional entailment of king, nation, and religion has steadily intensified.[63]

Common to both countries, however, is the assumption of a unified, unique, and essentialized national culture. In both, during the Cold War, minorities were seen as potential fifth columnists for the communists next door, and as a threat to the integrity of national culture. In Thailand, during Rama VI's reign, the intellectual Luang Wichit Wathakan—strongly if indirectly influenced by Italian fascism—had proclaimed the doctrine of "Thainess" (*khwam pen thai*). The dictator Phibun Plaeksongkhram (in power 1938–44 and 1948–57) assiduously cultivated the concept through the official regulation of everything from dress to music, representing as quintessentially Thai the adoption of a palpably Western aesthetic in all public appearances and performances. This unambiguously crypto-colonial precept is still invoked in most claims of adherence to tradition and heritage.[64]

Concomitantly, the monarchy came to be identified with concepts of orderly, polite self-presentation (*khwam riap roi*), which was paradoxically symbolized by the adoption of largely Western-style clothing and Western models of bodily propriety as marks of true Thainess. Indeed, a point of similarity between Thailand and Greece was this conceptual indigenization of hierarchically gendered Victorian models of sexual and personal modesty.[65] Whereas nineteenth-century Greek intellectuals fetishized the ideal democratic *polis* of classical antiquity as the origin of the modern state and as the political expression of true Hellenism, however, and consequently never evinced much sympathy for the foreign-imposed monarch, most twentieth-century Thai leaders, while modifying the existing polity in ways that brought it into line with Western models of governance, sought political and cultural continuity in the institution of kingship.

This brief foray into the two countries' respective historiographic modalities is the context for the more ethnographic perspective that follows. The two principal cases explored in this book share, each in its distinctive manner and setting, a claim to represent tradition against a nationally "authorized" version.[66] The comparison of these cases, each of which draws on the national peculiarities just discussed, animates and instantiates the concept of subversive archaism. The Thai story is of an explicitly royalist community struggling to maintain its existence even as the orchestrated national adulation for the palace had begun to fray. The Greek tale concerns a rambunctious society in the heart of the country's most consistently antimonarchist region. The comparison will lead, in the final chapter, to a larger consideration of how "national" heritage, in the post–Cold War and globalized world, has become the ground of contestation between nation-states and communities of highly varied political complexion. To understand that "vertical" articulation, we must now shift the focus from national to local cultural politics and to the challenge archaists pose to state authority.

Humiliation in the Mountains

Zoniana, a predominantly pastoral village in the west-central Cretan mountains, has long been maligned as the home of goat thieves and the site of dramatic vendettas. With a population currently estimated at between 450 and 1200, it has long been viewed as a place of resistance against and refuge from foreign invaders, whether Venetian, Ottoman, or, in the last century, German.[67] Its people harbor deep suspicions of both foreign powers and national politicians. They often see bureaucrats and politicians as traitors to an idealized, egalitarian vision of Greek life—a vision that fits foreign tourists' images of amiably freewheeling Greek rogues (Zorba the Greek comes to mind) more than it does the state's pedantic historiography. The villagers are quite capable of playing up to official discourses about history and heritage, but their renditions are often parodic and irreverent.

Tension between community and state has long rumbled below the surface. The village disposes of an impressive armory of guns. Some are a legacy of resistance to the Nazis during World War II, but the authorities allege that the villagers' performances of masculine heroism mask a less attractive engagement with traders in narcotics and weapons. There are also, however, credible suspicions that such illegal expansions of traditional activities happened only because of political encouragement and bureaucratic indifference. The police, for example, rarely conduct genuinely exhaustive searches, a dereliction that local observers interpret as evidence of official collusion. Villagers prefer to settle disputes internally and regard reporting to the police as betrayal; they especially emphasize their ability to end conflicts through a traditional conciliation ritual called *sasmos*. They also value civility. The grave courtesy with which Cretan highlanders greet visitors was already noted by the English traveler Robert Pashley in the nineteenth century and still persists, along with lavish hospitality and quick-witted engagement in political debate.[68] Zoniana is emphatically not, its reputation notwithstanding, a lair of uncouth ruffians and reprobates.

In 2007, the fragile accommodation with the authorities collapsed in violence, the trigger a police raid of which someone, presumably a police officer, had secretly warned village contacts. A group of young hotheads, vaunting their male pride in defiance of their elders' more sedate tradition of accommodation and restraint, decided to ambush part of the anticipated patrol. In the fracas that followed, a police officer was gravely wounded, eventually succumbing to his injuries several years later.[69]

The response to the ambush was immediate and crushingly disproportionate. A heavily armed and masked police detachment, a miniature army, descended on the village.[70] The team searched almost every house in the village. I was told that they arbitrarily made individual men grovel, lie on the ground, or even dance at gunpoint; berated some women for the possession of simple kitchen knives; and locked down the entire community for a month, harassing anyone with an identifiably local name who was unlucky enough to chance upon a patrol on the nearby roads.

While the initial confrontation was about the cultivation of cannabis, still illegal in Greece, the more humiliating aspects of this attack appeared to have all the elements of revenge for the villagers' defiance. Having provoked the community into collective self-defense, the police treated all Zoniani indiscriminately as criminals, ignoring most villagers' disapproval of the hotheads' actions. Villagers freely admitted that there were *some* delinquents among them; some accused these youths of betraying village values but blamed that betrayal on the temptations of sudden wealth.[71] The village survived, chastened and resentful, but with increasing recognition that the state's new attention has led to a more sustained investment in its physical, educational, and recreational resources and the hope that this, in turn, would curtail criminal activity altogether. Some, indeed, claim that today Zoniana is the *only* village in the area that is now not engaged in cannabis cultivation. Viewing Zoniana collectively as a criminal community is certainly a gross distortion.

Reputation, however, has material effects. The events of 2007 (in Greek *ta yeghonota*, the happenings) dramatically reoriented a hitherto obscure village's relationship with the nation, the state, and the world at large. They also disclosed the workings of state power, even if the exact linkages remain somewhat obscure and the police have been exonerated of complicity—an outcome that does not surprise the villagers, with their cynical understanding of how the state operates.[72] The village's fearsome reputation, pruriently cultivated by the media, still festers in the urban middle-class imagination. One woman, told by the American anthropologist Richard Grinker that I was living in Zoniana where he and his family planned to visit me, reacted with horror and demanded, "But he doesn't actually stay there overnight, does he?" A car rental agent in the coastal town of Chania first pretended to Grinker that he had never heard of the village; then, reminded that it was often in the news, claimed that it would be impossible to get there; and finally indicated with dramatic gestures and throaty exclamations that the villagers would be fierce and dangerous. Grinker, fortunately, was undeterred, and he and his family were made warmly welcome.

Destruction in the City

In the second case, this one in Thailand, the tiny urban enclave at Pom Mahakan in the heart of old Bangkok started out in the reign of Rama III (reigned 1824–51) as a royally sanctioned settlement of bureaucrats. Its origins were thus impeccable. By the early twenty-first century, however, its original denizens and most of their descendants long since deceased or departed, its image much more closely resembled that of Zoniana. It had acquired the reputation, assiduously nurtured by hostile municipal officials, of being a nest of drug addicts, wife beaters, and prostitutes. When I began working there, the city clerk, who had expressed warm support for my doing research in the city, advised me not to spend any time in that community. She consistently refused to make her own inspection, even though she passed by every day on her way to and from work. Willful ignorance thus fed the flames of calumny.[73]

The community leadership worked hard to deflect its dangerous reputation. Technically squatters—occupiers of real estate that did not legally belong to them—the residents mounted a public relations campaign to claim the moral and cultural rights appropriate to the guardians of an older vision of national identity. Their relative unity stood out in notable contrast with the squabbling of middle-class communities facing similar dislocation but apparently unable or unwilling to do much about it. Like the Zoniani, the people of Pom Mahakan saw in their very rejection by the state authorities the clearest evidence for their superior moral claims to represent national identity in its purest and most venerable form.

The residents never claimed legal possession of the site. They argued, however, that they had already demonstrated their capacity for good stewardship, protecting the site's monumental and architectural attractions from disrepair and dirt and ensuring that it did not become a lair of drug addicts and pushers. They also pursued a vision of social responsibility and community self-development. As late as December 2009, the Pom Mahakan work committee formally submitted to the entire community a budget of 10,000 baht (approximately $285) for celebrating national Children's Day (*wan dek*) that January as they had done for several years, with the specific goal of encouraging the children and youths of the community to "amuse themselves creatively far away from drugs and other such miseries."

The event, in addition to encouraging the young to grow up to be "good adults on the basis of the principles of love and attentiveness to their families (*khrawp khrua*)," was also intended to remind both local youth and the people of neighboring communities of the historical and cultural significance of Pom Mahakan. The community leaders were resolutely pedagogical, intending to inculcate into the young knowledge of their roots (*rahk*) and identity (*tua ton*) as Chao Pom.[74] In so doing, they were trying to guide their youth out of the damning category of "slum children," and to do so in a way that garnered public attention and drew legitimacy from the royal associations of this national event; the day, marked by a major speech by the prime minister, was timed to coincide with Queen Sirikit's birthday.[75] In another document issued for the same event, local pride was explicitly harnessed to official historiography: "The Pom Mahakan community is a community that has a historical background of considerable depth. It has houses that are over 200 years old that go back to the Rattanakosin era, and its long history invests it with a significant quality that is a source of pride for the residents."[76]

The Rattanakosin era is the period from the establishment of the Chakri dynasty in 1782, the construction date of the wall into which the Mahakan fortress was inserted, until the so-called democratic revolution of 1932 that ended the absolute monarchy. By invoking this resonant name, the Chao Pom were also coopting the airbrushing tactics of official historiography, absorbing into a single, undifferentiated historical period the older mandala-based polity and the radically different bureaucratic state that emerged in full under Rama V, and implicitly aligning themselves with the soon-to-open Rattanakosin museum a short distance away. In a state where continuity was defined by royal succession, the Chao Pom knew how to talk the talk.

They could also point to an impressive array of traditional crafts and skills. Some of these cultural skills, notably Thai massage and kickboxing, faded from memory with the death of their main exponents; but others—birdcage building, the raising of fighting cocks, crafting ceramic ritual objects, and selling homemade foods—continued to flourish. Some residents participated as extras in a film about pre–Rama V Siam, and continued to wear period clothing for some time thereafter; they also participated in a traditional dance drama (*likae*) that was first performed in Bangkok on the Pom Mahakan site.[77] Many also learned useful building skills, displayed in the construction and ornamentation of new houses designed to harmonize with the antique buildings. They celebrated the site's historical importance with religious rituals and well-organized photographic and documentary displays. They had also successfully collaborated with the police in eradicating drug use, without violence, during an internationally notorious time of extra-judicial killings in the name of a war on narcotics. And they had steadfastly repeated their desire to serve as official guardians of the site while continuing to live there at the city authorities' pleasure. One Bangkok governor, Apirak Kosayodhin, had even signed off on such a plan in 2004, but his sudden exit from office, apparently engineered by political enemies, left Pom Mahakan once again at the mercy of more intransigent actors in the city bureaucracy.

While the city bureaucrats repeatedly agreed to meet with the residents, it was clear from their condescending mien that most of them saw the Chao Pom as inferior rabble. They did not question whether these supposed reprobates would be evicted; the only uncertainty was when it would happen. The military assumption of full control of Thai political and civic life through the coups of 2006 and 2014 hastened an endgame that not only saw the residents scattered to other parts of the city but also destroyed outstanding examples of wooden architecture linking community life with the history of city and nation. In 2018 a quarter-century-long cat-and-mouse game ended with terminal destruction, carried out in several phases (fig. 1.1). Under the stern gaze of a group of soldiers who had established themselves on the site for a month for what seemed to be the sole purpose of intimidating the locals, a team of municipal workers grimly trudged through the remnants of the community. They carted off recognizable pieces of homes, some of which were historically and aesthetically significant examples of vernacular architecture. Reluctant recruits to this cultural vandalism against a population of poor Thais so like themselves, they glumly paraded from demolition site to garbage truck carrying pieces of timber walls past signage that ironically pointed to the community's heritage museum—itself perhaps the most explicit marker of subversive archaism—while the residents watched in grim silence or helpless tears, their lives and history disappearing in the mounting detritus.

The demolition of several fine examples of older vernacular architecture on the site looked suspiciously like an act of wanton revenge. A violation of internationally recognized norms for the protection of architectural heritage, it followed a long-standing tendency in Thailand to privilege temples and palaces over ordinary dwellings and so to conflate national with royal history.[78]

FIGURE 1.1. Dreams Destroyed: The End of the Pom Mahakan Youth Club. Photograph by author.

The failure of even the prestigious Association of Siamese Architects to save the most interesting buildings suggests that plebeian posterity was the last thing the city bureaucrats wanted to assure. On the contrary, the protracted negotiations about which buildings to select for preservation seem to have served a policy of attrition rather than of compromise. In the end, the authorities did not so much airbrush the site's despised plebeian past out of the city map as firebomb it to extinction.

Lessons from a Comparison

These two case histories, with their common experience of a traditionalism rejected by the officially constituted nation-state, but also with their significantly different outcomes, together provide perspective on the role of the state in shaping ideas about culture and heritage.[79] In both instances, under radically different political conditions, official authorities invoked national law over the residents' cultural claims.[80] Instead of accepting the communities' self-ascription as bearers of national cultural values, they treated them as dangerous sites of lawlessness and immorality. The label became a libel; the libel became a pretext.[81]

Exasperated officials and the sensationalist media alike then prepared the public for what would retrospectively appear to be justly severe responses. In Zoniana, after the raids, tourists—mostly from Greece and Cyprus, and sometimes in organized busloads—sought the thrill of seeing vast fields of cannabis and meeting the fearsome bandits in their mountain fastness, only, inevitably, to be disappointed.[82] Pom Mahakan was the target of at least one explicit attempt to engage it in "slum tourism."[83] Such activities sometimes afford residents the chance to showcase virtues such as hospitality and care for tradition.[84] But in both places they demanded tremendous demonstrations of injured dignity to counter the media sensationalism that had constituted these communities as objects of voyeuristic fascination.

In the Greek example, much of the vilification came from the media. News outlets gleefully capitalized on the idea that there was a part of the country where even the intrepid representatives of law and order feared to tread. They likened the village and its upland pastures to the alleged no-go zones in the seedier parts of Athens. While from the villagers' point of view the journalists were doing the bureaucrats' dirty work for them, the journalists' stance also suggests a generous helping of Schadenfreude at the state's embarrassment by a small village.

The initial raid, the one in which an officer was fatally wounded, took place one morning in early November 2007. About twenty armed villagers fired on a team of forty-three police officers who had come to break up a narcotics gang alleged to be based in the village. A reputable Athens newspaper, *To Vima*, with a sarcastic sprinkling of ironic ellipses and scare quotes, commented that "the 'Zoniana state' attacked the . . . weak Greek Police," adding that this was the fifth mass attack against police officers in the Milopotamos district "with the goal of making the area . . . inaccessible [*avato*] and to ensure there would be no control over the hashish cultivators."[85] But in perhaps the most significant comment in this report, the writer pointed an accusing finger at higher police officials: "Indicative of the 'autonomization' of the . . . state of Zoniana is the fact that, according to police union members, before the police operation there had been confabulations of officers with local leaders in Milopotamos in order to secure the immunity of the police from being fired on"—an agreement that the village hotheads then either ignored or subverted.[86]

The tone of this report is representative of the way in which the general public was led to understand the situation. The term *avato* provides a constant refrain throughout all the reportage, and it is clearly not intended to be more complimentary to the police than to the villagers.[87] Under the sarcastic heading "Zoniana—inaccessible for the police," another journalist described a second raid: "that [raid] also ended in fiasco. And a fiasco, what's more, that yet again exposes the district police to ridicule. The errors—as some policemen have complained—were childish, the omissions criminal." The writer describes how the cannabis had all been uprooted in advance. And despite a violent confrontation with one armed villager, who tried to ram a police car and run over two police guards with his truck, there was "not a single arrest made by the 50 policemen who were in the village!" It also appears from this report that two senior police officers quarreled because one of them deliberately intervened to prevent anyone from being arrested.[88]

We do not know—although the villagers have their suspicions—why the police would avoid arresting anyone who deliberately attacked an officer. Local politicians, with powerful connections in other communities in the area, may have pushed government and bureaucracy into a confrontation from which the state could not afford to back down. The media created the image of a massive, if very localized, conspiracy, one that deserved to be quashed—and would have been suppressed had it not been for the perhaps deliberate incompetence of the police.

In the Thai example, by contrast, the media were largely sympathetic to the residents' plight even after the military coups of 2006 and 2014—perhaps even more so, since it was probably safer to criticize the municipal rather than the national government. It is not entirely clear which of the various forces both competing and cooperating in the exercise of power—government, military, or palace—was driving the drift toward the community's total elimination. Lately, fueled by a series of top-down reallocations of urban land use in Bangkok's oldest areas, suspicion has increasingly fallen on the last of these three elements. But it was the city authorities who bore the brunt of immediate responsibility. The journalists seemed genuinely sympathetic to the community; the vilification campaign that preceded the final act mostly took place outside the mainstream media, although reporting on official accusations of community malfeasance may also have contributed to the intimation of justice served. It is clear, however, that the vilification began from official sources, as in the city official's warnings to me. The moral panic was carefully crafted, producing a misleadingly negative impression much like the claim that Zoniana was too dangerous a place to spend the night.

That members of both communities had violated specific laws is beyond contestation, but it does not render either community comprehensively illegal. Rather, well-publicized infractions furnished easy pretexts for drastic official action. The Zoniani had long engaged in reciprocal sheep and goat rustling—a ritual of masculinity that sophisticated Greek urbanites found repulsive, incomprehensible, and absurd but that for centuries had been the basis on which shepherds achieved mutual social recognition for their masculine prowess.[89] The arrival of a cash economy subverted this system and introduced new elements, including the drug trade, but many villagers remained resistant to the new temptations. As early as the 1970s, traditionally minded shepherds banded together to suppress reciprocal animal theft as it morphed into a largely commercial enterprise. Traditionalist villagers do not confuse local morality with indiscriminate profiteering.[90]

Similarly intentional misapprehensions afflict the reputation of the Chao Pom. Otherwise law-abiding to a fault, they were accused of squatting. While admitting the technical illegality of their continuing presence, however, they countered that the advance compensation for losing their homes had proved inadequate. Moreover, they had already demonstrated their ability to maintain the site far more effectively than the authorities; until the very end of their struggle they maintained a clean and tidy environment that offered a stark contrast to the litter-strewn, muddy area already under the authorities' control. Not only did the elected community president (*phrathahn chumchon*) participate in everyday sweeping and maintenance of the common areas, but section heads, in charge of clusters of households, saw to it that their areas were kept clear of unsightly garbage. Signage enjoined respect for cleanliness and forbade smoking in the vicinity of one of the most precious wooden houses.

Although the Chao Pom claimed total loyalty to the nation, they challenged the moral authority of state-codified law and criticized its inability to redress the evils of inequality and poverty. In a country with a long history of political interference with the independence of the judiciary, however, a clear distinction between moral right and legal prescription invited trouble. Judges, seeing their role as the implementation of royal virtue, were ill-disposed—as became clear in the rulings of the Administrative Court against the community—to recognize such lowly commoners' stance as a moral right. How dare such riffraff defy a municipally planned park in honor of Queen Sirikit, spouse of Rama IX? How dare they presume to construct their own floral garden in its place? (It was apparently to be quite a different matter, some years later and after the demolition of the community and the failure to generate much enthusiasm for the characterless park that replaced it, for the Bangkok municipal authorities to disguise their failure by mounting a massive floral exhibition there.)[91] The judges' further argument that a public park could not also contain private dwellings reflects the formalism with which Thai judges, as Duncan McCargo has noted, have generally viewed their role as "epitomizing virtuous rule"; that view of their duties requires judges to serve the monarchy, the exemplar of all true virtue, rather than the polity at large.[92] The vision of a regenerated Rattanakosin rumored to be favored by Queen Sirikit's son, Rama X, would especially have increased the pressure to clear the space after the 2014 coup. Royalists the residents may have been; but the insistence of such karmically inferior citizens on honoring the queen in their own way could be, and evidently was, interpreted as insolent.[93] After 2016, the residents' continuing presence became, quite simply, a nuisance to those in power at every significant level.

The residents nevertheless clung consistently to the moral high ground. They insisted, for example, that no resident should act violently against city officials or workers carrying out the officials' orders. They had also always rejected social, cultural, or religious exclusion; in response to the tsunami that hit the South in 2004 and despite their own poverty, they mounted a voluntary project to bring aid to the region's predominantly Malay-speaking and Muslim population. That stance may have subtly enhanced rather than lessened official hostility, since it challenged the perceptible historical shift to the current ethnonationalist exclusivism of the military leadership. The Chao Pom also had to contend with official skepticism about their own status as a community. The authorities regarded them as a ragtag crew of mixed backgrounds hailing from several provinces; from their own perspective, that complex origin made them a microcosm of the Thai nation—but such a pluralistic vision of Thai history and culture was increasingly unpalatable to the ever more harshly ethnonationalistic state.

Ethnonationalists reject cultural difference as much as political dissidence. Their deployment of stereotypes is insidious; the successful projection of a negative generalization can become a self-fulfilling prophecy. Nevertheless, long-sustained official harassment was less successful in marshaling public opinion against the Chao Pom than in uniting the residents and stiffening their resolve, much as frontal police aggression brought the Zoniani out in unified protest. State violence often sows the seeds of subversion, generating solidarities that themselves have a long local history and belong to the armory of archaisms the communities oppose to the cultural authority of the state. These solidarities also, as we shall see in the next chapter, frequently resemble the forms of cooperative resistance that originally made possible the emergence of the independent nation-state itself—an irony of which subversive archaists are often productively aware. We now turn to that historical backdrop.

2. NATIONAL LEGITIMACY AND THE ILLEGITIMACY OF NATIONAL ORIGINS

Mimicry and Mockery

The images and symbols mimicked (and sometimes mocked) by subversive archaists have very accessible historical origins. I devote this chapter to three important facets of those origins. These facets are especially important where the dominant ideology feeds an adversarial relation with ethnic minorities and looks on internal criticism of ethnonational politics with a jaundiced eye. Subversive archaism, with its challenge to state standards of national authenticity, strikes at the very core of ethnonational authority.

I begin with a consideration of the reuse of histories of national revolt against foreign occupation or invasion. Subversive archaists often display an uncanny knack for evoking—and claiming as their own—the heroes who supposedly dedicated their lives to national freedom and whose exploits adorn the nationalistic historiography taught in schools. In Greece, such heroes were usually local warlords or powerful shepherds; in Thailand, heroic kings who defied the military power of neighboring peoples, especially the Burmese. Whether those heroes' goals were quite as noble or efficacious as the schoolbooks insist is irrelevant now to both the archaists and the government, since both sides have a vested interest in maintaining the idea of the heroes' absolute virtue. Less admirable goals, while long the object of historians' critical interest, are not something either side, each nationalistic in its own distinctive way, willingly contemplates.[1] Scholars, sometimes funded by state bodies, often furnished the original images now firmly embedded in the official model. Their construction of the past also proves useful for the subversive archaists, who have been exposed to it by the same educational bureaucracy that now views them with hostility.

How much independence did heroic national pioneers actually achieve? My second concern here is with the hidden colonial hand behind some of the independence movements, and the ways in which it reproduces that evasive but powerful geopolitical hierarchy at the local level. Romantic tales of swashbuckling guerrillas and courageous monarchs notwithstanding, countries that achieved independence as modern nation-states under Western European tutelage remained heavily indebted to those powers. While there is important variation in the way the unequal crypto-colonial relationship was created and maintained, claims of national independence often occlude a pattern of collusion between local leaders and distant Western colonizers.[2]

Such collusion is also a template of sorts for more localized forms of patron-client relationship. It is a principal source of the contempt with which subversive archaists regard state bureaucrats, whom they view as foreign lackeys with no understanding of the true local culture. It is also the historical root of a hierarchical system of political protection at the local level—a structure of patronage that feeds the intensity of the locals' contempt for the corruption of the political and bureaucratic establishment even as they take whatever transient advantage of it they can.

Conversely, patronage—which is predicated on the maintenance of that encompassing international hierarchy—has material consequences for the way in which the state conceptualizes its relations with local communities. Just as many nation-states depend on the consent of the colonial powers, and may suffer when the geopolitical balance changes, local communities are dependent on political patrons. When their patrons lose power on the national stage, their client communities are suddenly vulnerable to exposure and attack. The inhabitants' traditionalizing—hitherto indulged by their patrons through their encouragement of the locals' claims to special status as well as through mutually advantageous personal deals—is now publicly excoriated as a betrayal of official cultural history and values. What had internally functioned as a moral structure of mutual obligation now becomes, in public discourse, mere corruption. In Greece, corruption is known as *dhiafthora*, or "erosion," a term suggestive of the eschatological concept of the corruption of the flesh (as, indeed, is the English word). In Thai, the usual formal term is *thujarit*; but in everyday speech the English-derived *khorapchan* is much more common and suggests, not without some justice, that the ill-repute of patronage and the practice itself both spring from powerful Western discourses.[3] This is a hierarchy that sets the weak up for blame by the strong at multiple levels. The pervasive presence of patron-client relations is a clear index of the extent to which the colonial powers have sunk their invisible teeth into the social fabric of both countries. Crypto-colonialism is a form of patronage that reproduces itself locally in practices that the colonial powers then all too easily mock as endemic and indigenous corruption.

When patrons prove fickle or when the patronage system itself weakens under attack from increasingly moralistic national media, subversive archaists become particularly vulnerable. In the early days of my fieldwork in Zoniana, there were already complaints about the cynical opportunism of politicians who came to the supposedly remote village to seek votes before every election, always, once elected, to disappear again until the next time; one of the few open communists among the villagers complained—in verse—that, before elections, politicians came seeking votes, but that once they had won and "it was fine for them to eat," they would forget the village completely.[4] In Thailand, a common metaphor for corruption is eating the polity (*kin moeang*). And indeed, nearly three decades later, I heard Chao Pom complaining that politicians who came seeking votes (*ha siang*) rarely kept their promises. Community leaders avoided commitments to any political party; their one chance of garnering support lay in luring the vote-seekers into a bidding war. Even if (or perhaps because) ideally, in Thailand, "with greater social status comes an increasing capacity to care for others," the residents took a dim view of politicians' morality.[5] They pragmatically differentiated between politicians who could and occasionally did help them and those who merely talked. Cultivating individual politicians seemed tactically wiser: the residents were few in number, but, in the capital city, small groups could make a difference in races such as the 2004 election for the Bangkok governorship, in which twenty-two candidates divided the electorate. So the residents ignored weaker politicians and let the more successful ones court them, knowing that even then the winning candidates would rarely advocate for the community. Performances of respect and hospitality notwithstanding, the Chao Pom knew from experience that they could not expect even as much help from their political patrons as the Zoniani could from theirs. In both cases, however, patronage belonged to older political structures more in tune with their archaizing aspirations; they could at least try to invoke a principle of moral reciprocity. Unfortunately, such ties also left them exposed to collateral damage whenever one of their protectors failed or ended up in disgrace on the national stage.

The state, to turn now to the third element in this complex story, has strong institutional means to assert its control over the discourse of cultural orthodoxy; it determines the selection of images and narratives that together constitute the official portrayal of national emergence and destiny. The state creates organs charged with the building and maintenance of national museums and the consolidation of key images and symbols. Those organs are also tasked with suppressing local claims to cultural purity as unacceptable effrontery when they directly challenge the cultural authority of the state. With the advent of tourism, a lucrative spin on nationalist concepts of heritage, the state has even more to lose from localist challenges and even more to gain by forcibly adumbrating local cultural irruptions to its central narrative. Today, as a result, its cultural institutions are fiercer than ever in their defense of official cultural orthodoxy.

The Nation-State and the Specter of Revolution

I now turn to these three components of the background to subversive archaism in more detail. The first of these, the capacity of local communities to ransack official historiography for potentially subversive ends, raises a central issue of state legitimacy. How does a nation that attributes its independence to rebellion deal with the persistence of rebellious attitudes and actions even after the achievement of national independence? How does the state respond when what is regarded as outrageous defiance acquires popular appeal and suggests dangerous parallels with historical tales of glorious resistance?[6]

The state's cultural machinery furnishes much of the historical material that subversive archaists imitate and turn on its head. Far from fleeing literacy, as Scott has claimed for anti-state populations in remote places, subversive archaists engage with it, and, by playing the official arbiters of cultural excellence at their own game, have occasionally managed to create significant degrees of embarrassment and irritation. Far from being averse to living near the center of power, for example, the Chao Pom, at least, resisted official attempts to expel them from it, while the Zoniani have gradually established themselves as a fearsome urban presence with strong capitalist urges and deep pride in the intellectual achievements of their sons and daughters who have achieved a university education.

Mischief-making masters of a carefully curated cultural civility, subversive archaists do not shun the official vision at all. Instead, they try to take it over, appropriating for their own ends its narratives of long-past revolutionary or military fervor and of clever diplomacy to deflect unwanted attention from colonial powers.[7] That is a clever move, because the image of patriotic resistance masks the core, the besetting paradox, of nationalism.[8]

All nation-states that have emerged from a war of national independence— and especially those that have done so with the direct connivance of colonial powers—face the possibility that a sudden crisis of legitimacy may erupt at any time. The untamed forces that challenged foreign rule and propelled the nation to freedom may take it on themselves to repeat that performance. This time, however, their criticism is directed against the supposedly independent nation-state's leaders and functionaries and directly challenges their right to rule. In Thailand, the tale of Rama V's clever negotiations with the British and French provides a model for diplomatic engagement with a bureaucracy seen as alien to the Thai spirit. In Greece, the guerrilla fighters who allegedly fought for national independence become, instead, an inspiration for rebellion against the state's own authority, which is seen as a continuation of foreign domination.

The Zoniani exemplify the latter strategy. They often invoke the schoolroom history of the so-called *kleftes* (the plural of *kleftis*, often rendered in English as *klefts*), the guerrilla heroes of the Greek national revolution, correctly noting that the word *kleftis* meant "thief" and implying that its use as a generic term for the nineteenth-century freedom fighters presumably originated in practices of the reciprocal raiding of flocks very similar to their own. Like the Zoniani today, the nineteenth-century guerrillas were organized in patrilineal clans.[9] So persuasive is this resemblance that a conservative newspaper dubbed the armed conflict between the Zoniani and the national police a "kleftic war" (*kleftopolemos*).[10]

That label was presumably an inadvertent slip into the villagers' self-view. Official discourse treats the klefts as quintessentially Greek, whereas hostile critics often try to question the Greekness of the Zoniani. The official discourse suggests total rupture with a "foreign" past in two particular ways: first, by recasting the term *kleftis* as a heroic category, turning into its opposite what had hitherto been its synonym, the term (*listis*) for brigand; and second, by anachronistically representing the pre-Independence phase of national history as a brutal "Turkocracy" rather than as an "Ottoman" system. In the latter regard, they ignored two crucial facts: that Greeks actually played an active role in the Ottoman bureaucracy; and that the term *Türk* was then used only as a derogatory term for country bumpkins. They also elide the role of Turkish speakers and other ethnolinguistic groups in what came to be retrospectively represented as a specifically Greek revolution, a move paralleled in the nationalistic revision of history in several neighboring countries.[11]

The social organization of the klefts on the eve of national independence was largely in terms of segmentary clan loyalties. At that time, despite the insistence of the Orthodox church on the equal significance of all forms of blood kinship, patrilineal relations provided a strong basis for local mobilization. Once the Balkan nation-states replaced the more diffuse organization of the Ottoman system, that aspect of the rebels' social world could not survive in the carefully managed accounts of the official historiography, while the realities of patrilineal clan organization underwent intense delegitimation under state law.[12] Not only were most forms of clan organization stamped out as conducive to banditry and as entailing inheritance practices that were unfair to (or demeaning of) women, but the historical record preserved only its faintest echoes, and those only in terms compatible with centralized bureaucratic control.[13] Entities larger than the nuclear family represented a grave risk for any state that claimed the moral authority of a family head. In Greece, a gradual shift from interpersonal violence to adjudication in courts of law served the state's goal of monopolizing the means of violence, as Thomas Gallant has cogently argued, but the more conservative traditionalists among the Zoniani have stood firm against this progressive erosion of their right to settle disputes through direct confrontation and have viewed recourse to law-courts as evidence of moral decline from the time when a villager's word was the only guarantee needed or accepted.[14]

Urban Greek sophisticates may see in the patrilineal clan a possible survival of the ancient Greek patrilineal clan (*genos*), but are equally likely to despise it as the basis of the decidedly retro phenomenon of vengeance killings.[15] Greek church and state—which in this respect have not progressed appreciably beyond Lewis Henry Morgan's evolutionism in their thinking—are similarly likely to treat patriliny as a folkloric relic of past barbarity. Some Greek orthodox Marxists argued that their society originated in a matriarchy later preserved only in the form of myth.[16] Others were determined to trace persistent elements of patrilineal reckoning to the ancient past.[17] These claims were largely Athenocentric, as indeed was the official rendition of ancient Greece more generally; the textual evidence came predominantly from Attic sources.[18]

In Thailand, patriliny is not an issue, especially in the rural north where men tend to vote according to the political complexion of their wives' villages.[19] In Pom Mahakan, perhaps under the influence of local anthropology students doing practice fieldwork on the site, one of the leaders posted a detailed genealogy of the remaining residents, but there was nothing to suggest an exclusive preference for the male line. Thais do not generally express preference for patrilineal kin, although, perhaps under Chinese influence, there is some recognition of status associated with specific surnames; this becomes more of an issue with the aristocracy and royalty, where surnames are clear status markers. The formal requirement for all citizens to use surnames arrived late, in 1913, as part of the Europeanizing of state record-keeping, replacing identification through the names of both parents or place of birth. Thais of Chinese origin often took—or were forced to take—especially elaborate names of Sanskrit or Pali derivation, which disguised their origins, even though they usually retained a collective memory of their patrilineal clan names. Individuals are usually mentioned by their first names (or a nickname), usually with a status prefix, rather than by surnames.[20]

In Crete, the clan remains an active—if besieged—relict of past social arrangements. For Thais, the equivalent of clan structure in this sense is the old mandala-based polity that subsisted up to the middle of the nineteenth century. Most Thais approach the old polity with formal expressions of deep reverence, but they view it as the antithesis of modernity and as incompatible with the Thai drive for "development" (*kanpatthana*) and "progress" (*kandamnoen*).[21] There is no contradiction between the reverence and the contempt that their attitude conjoins. Modernists often place tradition and antiquity on a pedestal of museological glory but, at the same time, excoriate living traditionalists for obstructing the nation's evolutionary forward march.

To their rebellious clients, civil servants often seem to perpetuate the values and actions of the former oppressors even though they are now supposed to serve as representatives and leaders of the resurgent nation itself. As has so often happened in postcolonial situations, where the fearsome outsider may reappear as the grotesque homegrown tyrant, the new elite appears to local communities as a reincarnation of the worst evils of the foreign colonizer or tyrannical despot, and, above all, as intolerant of what local people lovingly treasure as traditional values specific to their own localities.[22] In many well-known cases—"rebels" in the United States, guerrillas (Greek klefts and South Slavic hajduks) in the Balkans, "freedom fighters" everywhere—the officially heroized advance guards of the new nations are the model, sometimes explicit, at other times discreetly muted, for continuing resistance to government authority. Clan loyalties and the repudiation of official authority are antithetical to what in the nineteenth century became the new world order, the appropriately named family of nations.

Identifying with a heroic past of national resistance takes subversive archaism to the very heart of official historiography. Collective inversions of nationalist historiography such as those I have just described can be found in many countries. In both Serbia and Croatia, warring states emerging from the breakup of Yugoslavia, leaders on both sides invoked the image of the hajduk to justify what the international war crimes lawyers treated as atrocities.[23] In the United States, the term *rebel* gained positive implications for colonial Americans as they sought to throw off the British yoke, and this logic was reproduced in the Confederate states in a similar but ultimately failed attempt to reproduce the same inversion through secession from the federal United States. The nativist implications of these movements were directly analogous to those of the Greek and other Balkan revolutions. Continuing tensions that were left unresolved through the defeat of the Confederate forces continue to erupt today in right-wing and populist attempts to revive the Confederate legacy and its symbolism—attempts resisted by the federal bureaucracy (if not always by the politicians), not so much because federal leaders are necessarily themselves innocent of the racist sentiments that inspire such irruptions, as because the populists are reviving symbols of secession.[24]

The United States can at least point to its rejection of a foreign monarchy—doubly foreign if one considers that the House of Hanover was regarded by the British as German rather than British, and yet was imposed on North America by British rule. That history remains alive for many Americans: on the right, the emergence of the Tea Party movement, on the left the criticism that Donald Trump and the Republicans have tried to revive monarchy on American soil. The politicization of health precautions during the 2020 pandemic generated an especially toxic form of subversive archaism. Those who rejected the legal requirement to wear masks invoked the defense of personal freedom as the basis of national emergence; their insurrectionary rhetoric fused dangerously often with a racism that invoked slavery and segregation as virtues.

In Greece, a nation-state at least one of whose cultural founders, the philologist Adamantios Koraes, was an enthusiastic correspondent of Thomas Jefferson, the intrusive nature of the monarchy was no less obvious; but the monarchy itself, presented as a guarantee of independent statehood, proved more difficult to discard. Soon after the formal achievement of independence, the French and British governments engineered the appointment of a Bavarian prince as King Othon I. The monarch was not the "king of Greece"; he was "king of the Hellenes"—of a nation risen from the dead and proudly boasting of a national name of which, a bare century earlier, the newly constituted citizens' grandparents had little or no knowledge. The king's foreign origin—the Hellenized form of the Roman name Otho hardly disguised his identity as the Bavarian Otto—remained a persistent burden for the monarchy right up to its definitive abolition.

That decisive step in the democratization of Greece finally arrived in 1974 with the fall of military dictatorship and a popular vote by referendum to abolish the monarchy.[25] By then the monarchy, having done its work of providing a capstone figurehead for the recreation of the Hellenic ideal, could be jettisoned without damaging the body politic. Greece is arguably, acknowledged and persistent problems notwithstanding, one of the world's liveliest democracies today. By this point, too, it had become an article of faith throughout the land that the Greeks of today and the Hellenes of two millennia earlier were the same people, speaking the same language, and rejoicing in the same culture—a major shift from a century and a half earlier, when for many Greeks the designation of "Hellenes" was unfamiliar and even bizarre, and when non-Greek origins were far less of an embarrassment to public figures than they were to become over the course of the twentieth century.

The villagers of today's Zoniana do not reject the official historiography, with its emphasis on continuity with ancient Hellenic culture. On the contrary, they endorse it, fiercely defending its veracity—and, in words and actions, suggest that the bureaucrats do not understand it at all. In this sense, the literati have done their work all too well. Not only in Zoniana but throughout Crete and indeed much of Greece, relatively uneducated people cite etymological and other demonstrations of cultural continuity—especially place-names—with skill and passion, if not always historical precision. While Zoniani do not dispute the national narrative in this sense, however, they—and indeed many Cretans—actually go one better: speakers of dialects that still bear traces of an early regional version of classical Greek, they also claim prehistoric origins in a still earlier era named for the legendary king Minos.

Cretan cultural localism is fervent. Those who protest the strict conservation rules that now affect life in historically important zones have adopted the vocabulary and rhetoric of heritage in their battles with the state's conservation experts.[26] Yannis Hamilakis and Eleana Yalouri have examined this "loyal opposition" (to adopt a British parliamentary phrase) in a particularly dramatic moment. When some of the most prized Minoan artifacts displayed in the National Archaeological Museum in Iraklio were scheduled for display in Paris and New York, demonstrations broke out protesting this move as though the "national" of the museum's name made Crete, not Athens, the epicenter of the modern state.[27]

These demonstrations represented a form of subversive archaism. They challenged the legitimacy of the mainland capital, from which Crete had been semi-independent from its severance from fading Ottoman-Egyptian rule in 1898 until its incorporation into the Greek state in 1913. They implicitly but clearly rejected the primacy of what, from a Cretan perspective, had become the Johnny-come-lately glories of classical Athens.[28] That they *also* entailed a clear protest against the complicity of the Greek state in the continuing presence of American bases on Crete is significant: both issues underscored the continuing dependence of Greece on Western support. The intense national loyalty that drove the protest took a strongly localist form.

The demonstrators were not anti-Greek. For them, to be Cretan was to be more thoroughly Greek than the government. Their rhetoric invoked Minos and Daedalus, names from Crete's mythologized past. Their anger was directed at the bureaucracy, not at the nation itself; it also implicitly questioned the Athenocentrism of the state. The initial official reaction to the demonstrations seems to have been a mixture of stonewalling and perplexity, and perhaps also concern that Cretan pride could morph into a new outbreak of separatism. Separatist sentiment, however, has never been strong in Crete, and Cretans have played central roles in both national politics and the state bureaucracy. The demonstrators were instead displaying a superabundance of loyalty. That, not separatism, was the threat they posed to the central authorities. In the end, the prime minister gave orders to omit the Minoan artifacts from the materials being sent for exhibition abroad; the demonstrators' subversive archaism had achieved its immediate goal.

The state would not have dared to attack the crowd of demonstrators. Focused on the museum, an obvious symbol of national as well as regional identity, the demonstrations also represented a test of sorts for the democracy that had emerged from the wreckage of the military dictatorship. Compromise could be made to seem a victory for all parties (except, notably, for the execrable foreign powers that had dared to expect a loan of the country's most venerable antiquities). Subversive in its immediate tactics, this archaism was still complaisant in its long-term strategy. Its success at blocking the loan of the antiquities could also be viewed as a success for the nation as a whole.

That case is much harder to make when the hallmarks of traditionalism are those of the culturally intimate zone of illegality: vendettas, cannabis cultivation, animal rustling, domestic production and consumption of unlicensed alcoholic spirits, and the illegal firing of guns at weddings and baptisms. In that setting, which Zoniana exemplifies in the national imagination, claims to a venerable antiquity test the patience of the authorities in a very different way. They also challenge the comfortable assumptions of the increasingly powerful bourgeoisie and the deep-seated racism of significant elements of the forces of law and order. That is a situation in which ultimately it would have been far harder for state and local populace to avoid eventual collision—where, indeed, collision was in part the outcome of collusion, as when powerful politicians intervened selectively to protect miscreants who happened to be their clients. The intensity of the conflict in Zoniana is further exacerbated by the state's need to bury all surviving traces of the heroic banditry to which it attributes its own emergence as well as of its own deeply embarrassing involvement in local patronage.

A Different Form of Rebellion

The Greek and Thai states appeal to very different histories, but both lay claim to a sedimented and documented autochthony. Thailand, unlike Greece, does not claim to have been the civilizational source for an entire continent; on the contrary, Thai historiography bows toward Indic cultures, and especially the Sinhala of Sri Lanka, as the source of the national commitment to the Theravada version of Buddhism. National history is presented as the consequence of the exploits and achievements of monarchs, and the recent past is divided into periods that correspond to the reigns of the kings of the present (Chakri) dynasty. Whereas Greeks have known all along that their monarchs were foreign imports, Thais can reasonably claim theirs as indigenous. The powerful linkage between palace and nation has been used effectively to sustain the charisma of the institution and the power of the many regimes that have invoked it—albeit, as Irene Stengs has shown, in a radically transformed version of the Buddhist kingship that was also compatible with the European nation-state model and with Western models of rationality.[29] If for the Greeks the past is a glorious cultural achievement in art, philosophy, and literature, for Thais it is a progression of royal exploits leading to the establishment of the free ("never colonized") Siamese (and now Thai) state founded on supposedly scientific principles. Once again, we see how different visions of continuity—one popular, the other monarchist—conduce to a common cause, the legitimation of the nation-state.

The Greeks, with no history of owning a unified nation-state of their own, had to create one by carving out its territory piecemeal from an empire that had effectively absorbed them with the fall of Byzantium in 1453. The Siamese polity that preceded modern Thailand, while competing for space with Burmese, Khmer, and other foes, did not have to create an entirely new territory in this way. Its central core already had a recognizable form, although its territory underwent numerous fluctuations; it had a place among—and fought against—other, similarly conceived and organized polities, the antecedents of today's Burmese and Cambodian nation-states in particular. Internal revolutions, as we saw in the previous chapter, could be smoothed over in the name of a divinely ordered continuity of kingly succession, a process that still continues. Neighboring peoples—notably the Burmese and the Khmer—still supply the enemies necessary for a truly heroic narrative of kingly feats of leadership.

The Chao Pom adhered to the narrative of the continuous monarchy. They did so, not so much because they were afraid of being charged with disrespect for the throne, but because their historical association with various kings gave them access to state-sanctioned ways of talking about the architecture of their site. Each of the older houses, for example, was attributed to a particular reign (*rachakan*) of the Chakri dynasty, the third of these phases being the period in which the original settlement at Pom Mahakan was created by royal fiat as a home for palace bureaucrats.

The Chao Pom thus did not have a history of rebellion against a foreign occupier to which they could appeal in the national historiography. They did not, truth to tell, even seem particularly aware of the fact that the fortress that marked and gave a name to their community had been constructed to defend the Siamese kingdom from French aggression in 1782–86. They also could not directly criticize the heroized figure of Rama V Chulalongkorn (1868–1910), the great Westernizer, architect of Siam's crypto-colonial relationship with the Anglo-French colonial forces, and the object of veneration by the deeply Western-oriented middle class.[30] Had they done so, they would have seemed to abandon their own royalist leanings, particularly as, during the reigns of Rama IX and Rama X in which the events I am discussing occurred, these monarchs were increasingly seen as reincarnations of Rama V—a device that bound the middle class all the more strongly to the current occupants of the royal palace and may have partially discouraged critical appraisal of the monarchy as an institution.

The Chao Pom are visibly not of that same middle class. The men of the community wear panoplies of amulets and vivid tattoos to suggest the tough masculinity that middle-class Bangkokians associate with bandits (*nakleng*). Despite these appurtenances and their rumored underworld connections, however, they do not engage the local mafia (*phu mi itthiphon*, literally "people with influence") in their struggle with the city officials.[31] They mostly remain staunch supporters of the monarchy, but with a difference.

Their stance, unambiguously royalist in most respects, evoked an era prior to the reign of Rama V. While they were not averse to the conveniences of modernity—televisions abounded in the community, for example—they saw these as instruments for recuperating the trappings of an earlier age. They criticized the municipal bureaucrats—nominally *kha rachakan*, or servants of the monarchy—as inadequate to their noble task. They saw the modernist designs of the city's planning and public works departments as inimical not only to their cramped and ramshackle quarters and earthen pathways but also to the true spirit of old Siam, while their emphasis on internal diversity was more suggestive of the Siamese polity than of the intense ethnonationalism of the present regime and its immediate precursors.

As for the reigning dynasty, the Chao Pom temporized strategically. Thus, they endorsed honoring the queen with a park on the site even though this had been the main rationale for their expulsion. Instead of accepting the manicured lawn that the city officials had in mind, however, they created an elaborate flower garden to express their devotion in its place.[32] The bureaucrats, presumably aware that such a move was a direct challenge to their authority, immediately dumped truckloads of garbage on it, thereby retaking control of space and symbolism alike. Even the violence of that response failed to provoke the residents into any overtly antimonarchist response. The community rotating credit association, for example, continued to meet under a huge portrait of the queen, and the residents also found a way of presenting their cultural activities to a key member of the royal family during a museum event. Claims of fealty were not so easily squelched. As the crisis came to a head, and with a new king on the throne, some gave thought to the possibility of entreating a royal family member known to be sympathetic to their plight. One staunch academic supporter counseled against that idea. Such moves seemed doubly risky: too easily construed as disrespectful and therefore justifying even harsher punitive measures, they could also have made these archaizing residents mere peons of an increasingly unpopular monarchy that was actively seeking to reassert its centrality to the modern nation-state.

Patrons or Quislings?: The Hidden Hand of Colonialism

Not only an alternative vision of national culture but also deeply entrenched relations of patronage with powerful political and administrative actors sustained both communities' defiance. Those patrons, who often decried their clients' obduracy in their public utterances, nevertheless exacted political support and economic advantages in exchange for their interventions on behalf of clients caught acting in technically illegal ways. Such patron-client relations are necessarily hierarchical, and they reproduce the dependence of virtually any crypto-colonial or postcolonial state on the imperial powers. State authorities disguise that dependence with a rhetoric of nativism—and subversive archaists coopt the nativism of the state and its politicians in disguising their own dependence on their patrons' support.

The Thai nation-state trumpets its independence of the colonial powers rather than acknowledging the mid-nineteenth century as a time of increasing foreign interference, with the attendant and materially damaging humiliation of unequal trade treaties and territorial concessions to Britain and France.[33] Where the emergence of the modern Greek state is framed as the uprising of innately rebellious freedom fighters, that of the Thai state rests instead on allegations of Rama IV's and Rama V's success in warding off Western pressure by adopting Western statecraft and civilizational standards. Rama V may have been an absolute monarch to his subjects, but, to the colonial powers, he was a wily but ultimately manipulable conduit for their interests. Thai official historiography has never admitted Rama V's complicity in this humiliating relationship; nor has it acknowledged that he faced fierce opposition from his own aristocracy.[34] He successfully projected an image of independence from colonial control; under his guidance, Siam maintained in its dealings with the colonial powers the nominal parity of a sovereign state.[35] It was a formula that saved the face of monarch, land, and people.

"Face" (*na*) remains a central aspect of Thai everyday social relations; personal comportment (*marayat*) in speech and gesture and the complex game of "looking good" (*du di*) reproduce and reaffirm karmic hierarchy. National narratives must make sense in terms of ordinary behavior. Thus, in Thailand artful compromise at the highest level plays the role that Greeks attribute instead to endemic and bellicose resistance on the ground. Dominant self-stereotypes of belligerently rambunctious Greek egalitarians and smiling and accommodating hierarchically sensitive Thais both reflect and, in everyday self-presentation, embody the two nations' respective narratives of national redemption. Each stereotype also powerfully inflects the idiom of local resistance to government authority.

In both countries, the premise of crypto-colonial governance plays into the creative hands of the subversive archaists. For the Greeks, the foreign monarchy offered rich pickings for dissatisfied citizens convinced that they, not the bureaucrats, were the true representatives of the ebullient Hellenic spirit of democracy that had survived the "dark" years of Ottoman governance. Unlike the Thais, they could point to a fundamental flaw in the logic of their monarchy: if theirs was truly an independent state, why was its constitutional head a foreign monarch who had to change religion and learn a new language in order to cut an acceptably national figure?

In Thailand, direct criticism of the monarchy is ruthlessly suppressed.[36] Its assimilation of earlier eras, including the reign of Taksin, nevertheless exposes the present-day monarchist establishment to an appropriately indirect critique. Perhaps it was a vague awareness of such ambiguities that led the Chao Pom, implicitly but unmistakably, to invoke a pre-modern Siam now long submerged in the pageantry and rhetoric of the modern Thai state; this strategy allowed them to be loyal monarchists while still resisting the power of the state. The Siamese state enjoyed greater cultural independence from Western models and interference before than it did after the reigns of Rama IV and Rama V. Rama V is officially represented as an exceptionally wise ruler whose mystical charisma (*barami*) protected his people from colonial oppression. Communities like Pom Mahakan that invoked an earlier past, one that predated the massive Europeanization of everyday life, therefore ran the risk of offending against the current royalist-bourgeois ethics and aesthetics of official Thainess by implicitly highlighting the paradox of its substantially foreign derivation.[37]

The state and the local communities use readings of the past—selective, as are all historical accounts—to promote specific and sometimes divergent visions of present and future.[38] For Thai bureaucrats, like their Greek counterparts heirs to a foreign-inflected system of governance that was part of the price paid for formal sovereignty, foreign influence was something to be vehemently denied even as it was and is assiduously cultivated. Subversive archaism operates precisely by rejecting such denials and their attendant claims of authenticity. State authorities and local communities share an essentialist rhetoric. They differ, however, over which essentialism represents the true national spirit.

The leadership of Pom Mahakan, for example, made a point of preaching tolerance and generosity to minorities and arguing that their generous stance was the truly Thai attitude—this, in an increasingly nationalist Thailand that has experienced a notable upsurge in xenophobia and racism.[39] The Chao Pom could legitimately claim that their adherence to principles of cultural diversity was consonant with the founding values of the modern nation, a view shared with the more liberal and anti-authoritarian Thai leaders. They invoked cultural diversity as the basis of their own heterogeneous origins, thereby aligning themselves with the Siamese vision of a variegated empire (*anajak*) of tributary peoples that preceded the present-day ethnonationalist state.[40] Some hailed from the Lao-speaking northeastern region; two families were Muslims from an area near Bangkok; yet others came, at least in their own time, from other districts within the sprawling city. The community's embrace of diversity may in itself have seemed to pose an unacceptable challenge to the new urban order. But the Chao Pom could and did argue that they were loyal to the original values of the Siamese polity. They did not repudiate the idea of order as such. Faithful to the Thai nation, however, they did reject the state's homogenizing vision.

Zoniana, too, is in no sense an anarchist community, however insubordinate its members may sometimes be.[41] For long decades, villagers usually voted for establishment parties, their choices restricted by the dynamics of a well-entrenched system of patronage.[42] As the Zoniani began to escape the clutches of the pro-Western conservative politicians who had determined their access to resources, they shifted their electoral majority from a humiliating dependence on the political right wing to a freewheeling endorsement of predominantly but not exclusively leftist parties; the mainstream Greek political parties had by then begun to abandon the simplistic nationalism of earlier times. But the villagers did remain inextricably involved in the system itself.

Their complaints were reserved less for the democratic polity than for the state bureaucracy. Indeed, they often argued that they "had no state"—by which they meant that the bureaucrats were too corrupt or self-interested, and the available legal sanctions too weak, to ensure an equitable access to national resources. They never suggested that they themselves were anything other than loyal citizens; and, to the best of my knowledge, they have never advocated for Cretan separatism. During and after the tumultuous restoration of democracy in 1974, they freely criticized the Western powers, accusing them of treating Greece as a virtual colony. Avid readers of the freewheeling Greek newspapers of the new era, they had a clear understanding of the crypto-colonial dynamics still afflicting the newly democratic state and a cynical appreciation of the role their own political patrons played in its perpetuation. To speak of political corruption in this context is to affirm the multilayered reality of crypto-colonial subjugation.

What both communities share, then, is an awareness of the replacement of an older polity by a modernist nation-state of largely foreign inspiration. Each can appeal to heroic models from the earlier past, models that have achieved considerable currency in nationalist narratives in both countries. This strategy, if it is noticed at all, can only irritate bureaucrats as an obdurate fixation on an inconvenient history. It is a reading of the past that disturbs the collective, homogenized self-image that the national governments have labored long and hard to implant in the consciousness of their citizens.

National Culture, Local Refractions

We therefore now turn to the construction of that self-image. This, the third crucial factor in the background to subversive archaism, appears especially in the creation of state institutions charged with curating the state's version of national heritage. So-called national museums trace an evolutionary history from prehistoric emergence to the triumph of the nation-state. Such histories, exemplified by national museums in the Greek and Thai capitals, deploy archaeological finds and folkloric traces to trace a clear line from the point of national origin to the achievement of national redemption. Ironically, they reflect the evolutionism that reinforced the colonial project, largely through the emergent discipline of cultural anthropology on both sides of the Atlantic. Conversely, however, they represent the internal absorption of the logic of evolutionism with consequent inversions of its relationship with Western colonial domination. Instead of demonstrating that a particular people represented a throwback to primeval times, as imperial anthropology largely assumed, they announced a triumphant return, after long struggles, to the pinnacle they had always already represented.[43] Greece especially exemplifies this inversion of the colonial cultural myth, perhaps in part because of its uniquely ascribed role as the origin of Western civilization.

Appearing to minister to each nation's cultural needs and to celebrate its uniqueness and independence, in reality the cultural institutions of the state effectively perpetuate national subordination to foreign interests and reproduce the panoply of traditionalism that itself marks a country as not wholly modern and therefore needing foreign tutelage. They slot their nations into a global hierarchy of value, a postcolonial order sustained through cultural ranking. Subversive archaists, extreme traditionalists that they are, seize on these instruments and turn them against their bureaucratic operators.

In Greece, one key state institution stands out as the principal carrier of the ideological machinery for creating cultural origins. It is the Archaeological Service, founded in 1834 (two years after King Othon set sail for Greece) and charged explicitly in 1899 with "the Protection of the Antiquities and in general of the Cultural Patrimony" of the country.[44] Its active engagement in the creation of a material genealogy for Greek national culture was so central to the project of establishing a universally recognized national identity for the modern nation that it soon became recognized as essentially a state within a state. Its name still strikes fear into the hearts of any selfish citizens who might be prepared to sacrifice some minor local trace of antiquity to their desire for new construction and its profits, or simply for a decently modern home. Its insistent monumentalization of private houses deemed to be of historic interest remains a cause of considerable resentment.[45]

At any moment of national crisis, most recently in the conflict over the name of Macedonia, its archaeologists stepped up to the plate, often deploying considerable ingenuity in orchestrating archaeological scholarship for the national cause.[46] Significantly, too, it has not infrequently refused excavation permits to foreign archaeologists, in an act of defiance that belies the reality of the geopolitical hierarchy. This, too, was an effective disguise of a relationship of dependency, and a powerful riposte to the arrogance of foreign scholars, some of whom had, for example, demanded the destruction of an entire section of old Athens so that the American excavations of the ancient Agora could proceed.[47] Many of the foreigners, housed in the several "archaeological schools," not only participated in espionage and other unscholarly politics, but often displayed haughty contempt for local scholarship.[48] They also gave preference to the ancient over the modern Greek language, an attitude that only began to shift significantly after the restoration of democracy in 1974. That it has so shifted is an index of the gradual and uneven weakening of crypto-colonial hegemony.

In addition to archaeology, the Greek government has long supported other fields directed to demonstrating cultural continuity with the ancient past. Even before the creation of the Academy of Athens in 1926, government-supported folklore research sought to demonstrate that continuity. Continuity was understood as spiritual and cultural, but it often appeared to absorb then-fashionable theories of genetic inheritance, which conveniently converged with popular biogenetic models.[49] The common semantic ground of property (land and culture), properties (or character traits), and propriety (or civility)—the three terms are etymologically cognate in English—is thus expanded from the personal to the national, grounding the culturally and historically contingent emergence of national identity in the transcendence and permanence attributed to the works of nature.

The official Greek view of antiquity is uncomplicated. Woe betide any who seek to question the premise of unbroken continuity: their fate will assuredly be to join the rogues' gallery of "Fallmerayers." In confusing cultural with genetic continuity, however, Fallmerayer erred no more grievously than did his opponents.[50] In the nineteenth century, scholars viewed culture as an inheritance and few challenged the idea that it was genetic. This conflation has found new life in the metaphor, "It's in their DNA!"

The vision of uncomplicated continuity is anthropologically simplistic. It also makes little sense historically. There was no ancient Greek state as such, only quarrelsome city-states.[51] Moreover, beyond the broad lines of sharing what were to some extent mutually intelligible dialects and a broadly common religious tradition, these city-states differed enormously from each other in sociopolitical organization. While there is some unambiguous cultural continuity, it is often at a local level that could serve separatism as easily as nationalism. Certain songs from Rhodes, for example, known to folklorists as "swallow songs," have a close connection—closer than with related texts from other locations in the modern country—with a sixth-century BCE ritual text from the same island.[52]

To question the national continuity axiom even partially, however, is anathema to most Greeks. In Zoniana, as everywhere in Greece, such heresy is sternly rejected. After all, say the villagers, "our teachers" have shown us that it is nothing other than the fundamental truth. How dare one question the idea that ancient Greece had the "only" true civilization? How could we, as Greeks today, not be its rightful heirs?

That the villagers adhere to the official line on cultural history does not, however, mean that they accept all of its political implications. Since they distinguish clearly between state (*kratos*) and nation (*ethnos*), they do not find it problematic to view the state bureaucracy as a foreign body. It is precisely because they endorse the idea of a culture that long predates the state that they are able to criticize the state without departing from the official rendition of history. They will, for example, argue passionately for the ethnonational uniqueness of Macedonia as eternally Hellenic, and most reject any talk of compromise with Skopje over the national name. They are especially offended by any suggestion that they themselves are neither true Greeks nor, worse, true Cretans—worse, because, in the competitive context of fidelity to the national ideal, Crete can claim an especially venerable antiquity.

The Thai institutions of cultural nationalism had a slower genesis than the Greek. Greek intellectual leaders wanted to put their country at the symbolic apex of European culture, and did so with urgency as soon as they achieved independence; there was no time to lose, with the Ottomans making no secret of their desire to regain their lost territory and the Western powers vacillating as Russia also competed for regional dominance. The Thai situation differs, once again, in respect of the role of the monarchy. Where the Greek king essentially petitioned for inclusion in his own realm, the Thai monarchy set the criteria of cultural inclusion for the population as a whole.

It is thus not coincidental that the architecture of the National Museum in Bangkok recalls that of both the Grand Palace and some of the more grandiose temples. The Museum was founded during the reign of Rama V, in 1874, as part of an overall effort to create a robust Siamese kingdom capable of standing on its own feet both politically and culturally. In the next reign, that of Rama VI (Vajiravudh) (1910–25), the Fine Arts Department emerged from the palace's Office for Religious Affairs in 1912; it long remained heavily focused on the preservation of religious monuments. Rama VI's proactive assimilation of earlier monarchs to the Chakri moral lineage, moreover, and the gradual adoption of a European-style historiography and sense of temporality increasingly mandated attention to the monuments associated with the great events of the past.[53] Even under Rama V, however, Prince Damrong Rajanubhab, as minister of the interior (1892–95), had promoted archaeological research throughout the kingdom. This use of archaeology to emphasize historical linkages between the provinces and capital followed, unsurprisingly, a design already well-established in the neighboring colonial possessions.[54] It was unconcerned with ordinary lifeways; much of its focus remains heavily committed to the preservation of royal monuments. Under Rama VI, it received further impetus from the growing impact of European (especially German and Italian) nationalism. If Greece had to show itself historically and philosophically anterior to Europe at large, Thailand had merely to demonstrate the kingdom's moral and cultural equivalence with the European states. Thai conservation practices, less focused on preserving original material remains than on perpetuating sacredness through architectural enhancement, architecturally embodied the virtuous kingship while nourishing the discourse of an integral national culture.[55]

The Fine Arts Department and other conservation offices thus remain primarily agents of this royally centered view of history. While there have been changes in recent years, the current political situation does not encourage a more grassroots approach to heritage conservation. The continuity of the Thai nation-state remains tied to the person of the monarch. Thai citizens who wish to make a case for their cultural specificity must do so as loyal subjects of the throne; ethnic minorities—the Khmer speakers of Surin Province are an important example—frame their heritage as a local variant on a loyal, royal Thainess.[56] Thailand, like Greece, has built its identity around claims of continuity; but these are claims tied to institutional practices and a sociomoral hierarchy rather than to vernacular practices.

Local Refractions of Nationalist Scholarship

In Greece, a seeming mark of the success of the nationalists' propagation of neoclassicism is the extent to which the premise of classical origins is parroted throughout the land, no matter how lacking in formal education a speaker may be. The Zoniani play the Greek philological game with a zeal that would have impressed the eighteenth-century German philologists; they connect the village with the name of Zeus by connecting a now-defunct local exclamation, *ni za*, with the classical *ma ton Dia* (by Zeus!).[57] They also claim a preclassical pedigree. One young man who married into the village and played a radical part in the management of the village's sole hostelry explained, when rooms named after family members had to be renamed after a family split, that the use of names like "Minos," the legendary preclassical Cretan king, was a necessary resuscitation of their collective history—which also happened to mask the embarrassment of family dissension.

Such recourse to the language of the learned is common throughout the island. Villagers of Alikambos, an inland community further to the west, assured me in 1967 that the name of their village was derived from classical Greek *als*, "salt," and thus meant "salt-flat," although the much more probable derivation is as "the field of Ali"—in other words, of a Muslim ("Turk"). Indeed, philological acrobatics are not confined to countries like Greece and Italy, although in both countries classical roots offer especially dramatic and frequent examples. As Melissa Wanjiru and Kosuke Matsubara have shown for the Kenyan slum area of Kibera, place-naming can be an effective form of contesting colonial, post-colonial, and crypto-colonial cartography, by invoking both local specificities (in Crete these were the basis of popular topography until the early twentieth century) and world events.[58] In places where there is already a widely recognized tradition of philologizing, local people can sometimes utilize this device as a form of resistance to official interpretation. In this sense Greeks, and Cretans in particular, can turn their burden of neoclassicist historiography on its head by using respectable etymological arguments to contest official understandings of the land, its ownership, and its history.

The Zoniani, moreover, have their own learned advocates. Locally born (and now retired) schoolteacher Dimitris Parasiris insists that the local dialect preserves elements of the Greek associated with the prehistoric Linear B writing system, elements that have disappeared elsewhere on the island. His research has been partly financed by the venerable Academy of Athens; he has thus engaged one of the state's most venerable cultural instruments in research that potentially contests the state's Athenocentric perspective.[59] In a country where nationalist discourse endows the academic disciplines of philology and archaeology with something approaching sanctity, etymological connections with the distant past are a symbolically powerful enhancement of a community's status.

History and Hierarchy: Contrasts and Convergences

Subversive archaists thus actively borrow from the ideology of the state. What were the bureaucratic arrangements that created the models they were subsequently going to turn back against the formal state? In Greece, the pattern is clear and well documented. Its roots there lay in West European models of cultural management, with the added complication that Greece was the one place to which Europeans in general were willing to attribute a collective European spiritual point of origin. In that context, the work of folklorists, archaeologists, and philologists—some of whose scholarly interests overlapped considerably—acquired central importance, and was first institutionalized in the creation of the Archaeological Service and later in that of the Academy of Athens Folklore Archive. In reality, however, these institutional arrangements simply provided a formal and financial recognition of the central role the cultural disciplines had already played in the state's nation-building efforts. The enormous investment placed by the Greek state in the exploration of folklore—*laoghrafia*, the study of "the people" (*laos*)—is a testament to the centrality of a continuous Hellenic bloodline to the national imaginary. Hierarchy operated in the sense that learned scholars felt themselves entitled to edit the lore of the "ordinary folk," but they never ceased to assume that the core of Greekness lay in the folk masses or that they themselves were members of that historically privileged population. Editing folk texts was as much the outcome of that membership as it was of their supposedly superior learning.

In Thailand, the dynamic was very different, since Thainess is assumed to radiate out, in diminishing intensity, from the person of the king—a logic that, at least in its formal properties, does seem to reproduce the core cosmological principle of the premodernization polity. The exploration of Thai culture certainly assumed demographic continuity, but its pursuit has mostly been in the hands of royal and aristocratic personalities until comparatively recently, and their influence is still strong. Their predominance is reflected in the evolution of the various institutions charged with discovering and recording the national past. The Thai Department of Fine Arts does not have quite the state-within-a-state status that the Archaeological Service enjoys in Greece. It was nevertheless the institution out of which Thailand's Ministry of Culture grew; the ministry then gobbled up the department, which continues to operate as an influential arbiter of conservation practices. There were moments during my fieldwork when it became abundantly clear that some of the department's individual employees were well-disposed to the residents of archaeological sites who wished to remain in situ and to become guardians of the national heritage displayed there. Nevertheless, its role remains one of safeguarding orthodoxy and preserving the monuments that support the royalist canon of Thai historiography.

Officially, at least, the department has rarely shown the slightest interest in preserving "vernacular" architecture—a term that itself, unintentionally for the most part, reinforces the deeply embedded distinction in Thai political culture between a royalist power clique (*ammat*) and the powerless *phrai*. The term *phrai*, which is often simplistically translated as "commoners," implies something more demeaning: total dependence on noble or wealthy patronage.[60] The Chao Pom often invoked this historical conflict as they did legal battle with the haughty Bangkok bureaucrats, implying that the latter acted as though they had rights over the residents' very lives.[61]

The authorities' attitude is embodied in the urban landscape. Gazing across old Bangkok from, for example, the Temple of the Golden Mount, one sees a dense forest of temples and palaces; the humble dwellings of the poor, already all but invisible, are fast disappearing. *Phrai* by definition do not possess "righteousness" (*khwam chawp tham*, literally the love of *dharma* and here carrying connotations of legitimacy as ultimately derived from dharma). Dharma is the prerogative of kings; mortals too far removed from royal status are considered insufficiently Thai and therefore virtually incapable of possessing dharma.[62]

Thai ritual hierarchy thus converges, thanks to the aggressive Westernization policies pursued by Rama V and his successors, with the imperatives of a foreign-derived conception of modernity and class. There is no place here for the unsanitary, ghost-ridden, and dilapidated wooden houses of the past. Even the old homes of wealthy aristocrats are rarely protected from the wrecking ball. Only in a few areas, where the Crown Property Bureau hopes to recreate an impression of bygone times (albeit prettified in a thoroughly modern way), do we find ordinary homes and workplaces undergoing serious, historically attentive restoration. Significantly, the most prominent examples, in the form of Chinese-style shophouses, are in a heavily tourist-oriented zone flanking the Grand Palace.

The erasure of the vernacular is a consequence of a karmic hierarchy that, for obvious political reasons, few expect to see reversed, although subversive archaists—as at Pom Mahakan—do fight to preserve old houses as part of their assumption of a historical and traditional mantle of culture.[63] Their willingness to serve as guardians of the historic site in exchange for the right to live there does not contradict the principle of karmic predestination. To the contrary, it confirms it by offering to accept a humble janitorial role in exchange for minimal protection for the community's basic needs.

The assumption of this karmic mantle by the Chao Pom did implicitly challenge the crass consumerism that they associated with the bourgeoisie and the bureaucracy, but it also allowed the residents to avoid questioning—and indeed required them to endorse—the pre-eminence of the *thammarat* and of the hierarchy in which he is the cornerstone holding the entire social edifice together. Throughout their long struggle to stay on the site, the Chao Pom never saw any contradiction between their fervent royalism and their utter disdain for the city bureaucracy, or between their passionate devotion to preserving the old houses in the name of the nation and their militant opposition to those state and municipal civil servants—nominally, let us recall, servants of the kingdom—who were so intent on destroying both the houses and the community in the name of modernization.[64]

Some of the carefully crafted old houses that were demolished could have been claimed as a significant part of the royal as well as the national patrimony. Situated in a community created by kingly dispensation to house bureaucrats in the nineteenth century, they recalled a time and a political system that fit the residents' narratives far better than they did that of the modern bureaucratic nation-state that supplanted that era and its political structure. They belonged to a polity of another kind and another time, and their destruction represents the violent erasure of political arrangements that are now held to be incompatible with the workings of a modernist bureaucracy.[65] Where the Zoniani have become expert etymologists, the Chao Pom learned the language of architectural scholarship. It was a less successful strategy for two interrelated reasons: because architectural historians do not have the long-standing purchase on national cultural debates that philologists do in Greece, and because vernacular architecture had less hold on the Thai national imagination than the idea of ancient origins had on the Greek.

The appeals to preserve the oldest houses were backed by prominent Thai architects and other scholars, but their efforts fell afoul of the karmic hierarchy that still undergirds Thai social relations. The authorities were tactically astute, appearing at first to temporize and to offer the possibility of a compromise that would leave at least some of the older houses incorporated into the projected park. In the end, however, the houses were all knocked down. This official act of destruction, in the absence of any provable hypothesis to the contrary, strongly suggests that the destruction was intended to silence all traces of an alternative history.

It was the residents' devotion to a historic site, on the other hand, that attracted the support of individual members of both the Crown Property Bureau and the Fine Arts Department. Those entities are powerful arbiters of what is considered worthy of preservation, but ultimately they are subject to the requirements of the palace and the central government. Individual sympathies, even on the part of its own staffers, have no relevance for this larger structure of inequality. For the same reason, functionaries of the city administration who expressed some support for the Pom Mahakan community were always those who had no power. Moreover, the city administration could not afford to let it seem as though individual sympathies at any level could interfere with its execution of the law; the loss of administrative face and the charge of failure to discharge its duties would have been too dangerous. As for the Fine Arts Department, its jurisdiction, as became abundantly clear, was no more extendable to vernacular wooden architecture than was the remit of the Greek Archaeological Service to either the remains of non-Hellenic phases of national history or the architectural efforts of today's poor that did not fit the neoclassical aesthetic.[66] In both countries, the administration of conservation was dictated by a nationalistically defined class hierarchy and the values of its highest ranks. In Greece, the official position and its popular endorsement were rooted in the symbolism of genetics and blood; in Thailand, in the logic of karma. But the effect has been very similar: an appeal to the inevitability of national independence and statehood.[67] Greek blood symbolism and Thai karma alike, moreover, also confirm as eternal and irrevocable the real-time social hierarchy of societies that—each in its own distinctive way—also lay claim to egalitarian principles.[68]

Rhetorics of Belonging and Distance

To understand the extent to which nation-states tolerate internal disobedience and insubordination, we must examine how they use the metaphor of the collective self as a family or some other kin-group. At the same time, conversely, certain forms of kinship allegiance threaten the legitimacy and authority of the bureaucratic state. Muddied definitions of "family" permit a decidedly slippery semantics of kinship, allowing both the nation-state and its subversive archaists to pay lip service to a common ancestry. And while the image of the nation as one happy family, sharing the common substance of blood, suggests intimacy and belonging, it is coupled in official rhetoric with condemnations of rebellious communities as traitorous offspring, already held at arm's length and deserving of expulsion, excision, and extinction.

The symbolic distancing of these communities as remote or inaccessible is at once spatial and moral: it places entire groups of people beyond the pale, creating a structure of official self-exoneration for officially sanctioned assaults on their lifestyle. Caldeira, writing of São Paulo, frames marginalization as an elite response to the threat posed by democratization and social liberation, and points to the erection of well-nigh impenetrable physical walls as both the material instrument and the symbolic expression of this new structural violence. The related process of "spatial cleansing" removes people from historic sites and monuments.[1]

In Buenos Aires, again, as Emanuela Guano demonstrates, urban enclaving and a discourse of civilization-versus-barbarism shore up the middle classes' fragile self-image against the social, cultural, and economic gains made by the poor, a dynamic that certainly also applies to Bangkok.[2] Exclusion is thus not exclusively physical. It is also discursive, as when the removal of a community from a historic site such as Pom Mahakan also erases it from history. It may also take the form of declaring the residents' location a no-man's-land, a conflict zone, or simply as impenetrable. The creation of such no-go zones occurs in city and countryside alike. It fuels self-fulfilling libels that presage violent action.

Ultimately these contests, like kinship, are about who has the right to define belonging. Kinship affirms a variable degree of membership; marginalization denies it altogether. The rhetoric of belonging, however, is also often double-sided, permitting one side to claim as the basis of cultural membership what the other side—the state—prefers to regard as intolerable insolence. The tomb robbers described by Greenland, for example, are both lawbreakers and yet, at the same time, exponents of an ideology of physical rootedness in their native soil that allows them to look down on the desk-bound bureaucrats. In this sense, the tombaroli are true subversive archaists, able to sneer at the bureaucrats in their own officially approved language of romantic archaeology and philology. In so doing, they enjoy a fair measure of popular support, especially as many Italians have in their possession what the state considers to be illicitly owned minor antiquities.[3]

In their struggles with the state, the tombaroli rely for protection on their membership of local communities and their tightly knit kinship solidarities. Elsewhere, deeply rooted local and kin-based allegiances both contest and actively infiltrate state power. This is the arena of patron-client relations. Through a shared rhetoric of obligation, honor, and hospitality, the traditionalism of the state clashes with the actual traditions of local communities. As Anton Blok has noted, the state tries to arrogate to itself the entire panoply of virtue associated with such notions.[4] The mediating patrons, however, create the semantic and moral confusion that treats illegality as business-as-usual.[5] At stake is a relationship between the encompassing family of the nation-state on the one hand and more or less corporate kin groups on the other.

Kinship, Patronage, and the Spatiality of Power

Nationalist kinship metaphors usually appear in generalized terms that elide the specificities of local kinship structures. This, too, contributes to the semantic fog—a protective fog that, like the mountain mist so beloved of Cretan shepherds out on a raid, hides a routinized set of practices officially viewed as chicanery. The word *ikoyenia*, compounded from the words signifying "house" and "clan," usually denotes the nuclear family. In Crete, however, it is sometimes used as a synonym for *clan*, providing, in its intimations of harmless domesticity, an unthreatening semantic mask for the enormous political clout that a clan can sometimes muster in defiance of law and the official norms of good citizenship.

The usual basic kinship model for the nation-state is that of the nuclear family, which is a conveniently simple structure. But when social actors speak of "family," what do they actually mean? In the most explicit cases, such as that of Turkey, the land is the mother and the state is the father of a docile and unified populace.[6] Anything larger than the nuclear household (one couple plus offspring) potentially competes with the state for citizens' loyalty. The nuclear family is easy to discipline and to fit within the larger frame of the nation; clans and extended families, by contrast, signal trouble. As for fictive kin—godparents, for example—they are often precisely the people who become the political patrons of the poor, conniving with them to subvert both the fiscal power of the state and its capacity to provide fair and efficient care for all its citizens.

Even nuclear families can focalize loyalty in ways that short-circuit bureaucratic ideals of fair play. For the transhumant Sarakatsan shepherds of the Greek province of Epirus, for example, merchants acted as go-betweens, linking them to politicians who could secure them special favors.[7] These politicians showed scant interest in dealing directly with the shepherds, presumably because the largest Sarakatsan corporate social unit was the nuclear household. The returns on direct involvement would have been too small. It was easier to insert an additional layer—the wool, meat, and cheese merchants—between the urbane politicians and the rude shepherds.

The fact that favor-peddling operated more diffusely than in Crete did nevertheless mean that the access of these poor northern Greek shepherds to basic resources depended on players who sought both to maintain the authority of the nation-state and, by undermining it through their ramified patronage networks, to profit from it. Powerless to oppose the politicians' strategies, but bitterly aware of the obligations they thereby incurred, the poor could blame their plight on the politicians' overweening power, which they thereby confirmed and strengthened. The politicians avoided dealing directly with the rabble, while the merchants scrambled to extract whatever advantage they could from mediation. With the votes of the merchants as well as of their clients securely locked in, the politicians seemed—collectively if not always individually—invincible.

The Zoniani operated from stronger ground, at least until recently. With some especially large clans ramified across the island, they and the residents of neighboring communities in the Milopotamos district long enjoyed the direct patronage of predominantly pro-Western, conservative politicians. Those patrons not only looked the other way when their constituents were caught stealing but also, perhaps demonstrating an intentional disregard for the formalities of the law, allowed them to fire off salvos of welcome with their mostly illegally owned guns during the patrons' triumphal visits to the Milopotamos villages. Celebratory gunshots (*balothies*) have come to symbolize the paradox of local identity in the modern age. They signal to outsiders that the people of Milopotamos enjoy a protected status as traditionalists, that they represent the Greeks' fierce love of independence, and that they can expect to get away with a wide range of illegalities because these acts are both symbolic of that independence and protected by their patrons. That these actions also condemn the villagers to live under the shadow of a reputation for banditry has, for the politicians, proved an added benefit: it reminds the villagers, amid all their vaunted independence, of their continuing dependence on their patrons.

This system has been further protected by two systemic misrepresentations. The first is that patronage was, more or less by definition, a "Turkish"—or, more accurately, Ottoman—institution. That assumption is belied by its extraordinary persistence during the years of more or less constant Western tutelage of the Greek state. Clearly, while accusing the Greeks of corruption, Western actors were benefiting from its continuation and perhaps even exacerbating its centrality to Greek social life. Stories about "corruption" are often told by precisely those who have the most active interest in perpetuating allegedly corrupt practices. The European Union, for example, has long treated Greece as a client state, despite all the rhetoric of full partnership. Instead of giving Greece credit for the remarkably robust survival of its democratic institutions during times of economic crisis and international humiliation, the European Union leadership, and especially its German component, has castigated Greece for its alleged proclivity for corruption, overlooking the fact that the most shocking bribery scandal of recent years was engineered by a major German company that had also conducted similar illegalities in Japan and elsewhere.[8]

Accusations of corruption reveal the social significance of familistic metaphors. Nation-states officially oppose corruption because it damages the national family and especially because it undermines the authority of the metaphorical family head, who is usually a paternal figure. In China, for example, the neologism *guojia* linked the territorial land (*guo*) to the hearth-home (*jia*) and the patrilineage (also *jia*), justifying, especially under socialism, the rapid growth of the nation-state's precedence over any other kind of loyalty. That structure was locked in by the paternal image of Mao Zedong, although, as Hans Steinmüller has pointed out, paternalistic names that look affectionate also allow some play to irony and mockery; we may suspect some pragmatic official connivance in the cultural intimacy revealed by such subtly expressed disrespect.[9] In Turkey, the paternalism of Ottoman rule, already expressed through familistic metaphors, underwent, first, a transformation that made the land and the state the mother and father of all citizens, and then harmonized this static structural metaphor with dynamic changes taking place in modern Turkish family life.[10]

The Clan and the Hearth: Social Aggregations against the State

When Greece became a nation-state, much of the Balkan peninsula was still inhabited by groups exhibiting more or less intense allegiance to patrilineal identities. Especially in the mountainous areas of Albania, Montenegro, Serbia, mainland Greece, and Crete, rebellious rural men, organized in clans, could eventually trouble national authorities as much as they had their Ottoman rulers. In Greece today, however, the state's preference for bilateral kinship and the nuclear family has prevailed as the dominant model; the patrilineal clans of Crete's mountain villages stand out as exceptional. Their situation is thus markedly different from that of the Soqotrans in Yemen, for example, or the vying political and sheikhly factions of the Jordanian and Saudi nation-states. The Cretan villagers' preference for the clan as a semi-corporate unit pits them against the ideological principles of a nation-state anxious to defend and reinforce its European identity and inclined to regard clan loyalty as a foreign phenomenon. Local politicians, however, still profit from the way in which Cretan clan organization funnels voting power into concentrated nodes. In this respect, the relation of the Zoniani to the state's preferred understanding of kinship is more like that of Chinese citizens, whose preference for dealing with officials sharing the same surname would be viewed in public discourse as corruption but is widely understood to be the ordinary, culturally intimate way of getting things done.[11]

In Greece, such practices are gradually eroding, and today clan identity does not always afford real protection. As the police can easily identify a Zonianos by his surname, they can also turn that emblem of pride into a means of humiliation. The clan becomes a symbol of what differentiates the Zoniani and their neighbors from other Greeks. Subversive of state decorum and of democratic process, it is also the framework within which the villagers articulate their ideas of personal and collective dignity. As the old patronage system gradually collapses, the clan morphs into a liability, a sign of retrograde politics that sullies the ideal order of the modern state.

An identifiable Zoniana surname—one of the same surnames that generated such fear in the cities—was sufficient cause for arbitrary inspections: "With the slightest cause, they [the police] would take you in" and even trample villagers' bodies with their heavy boots. "They would say, 'Just say something so we can "play" you! Just talk!'" The state thus acknowledges the clan as an important, if undesirable, social structure. Using it to humiliate individuals might seem intended to undermine its local legitimacy. In reality, however, such actions reinforce local pride and unify whole communities in opposition to an unsympathetic state.

The speaker I have just quoted was more fortunate than most. Stopped at a checkpoint with tire-piercing metal spikes placed across the road, he was forced to pull over "by three cops, real gorillas!" They asked where he was from. "Zoniana!" "Get down!" Holding him at gunpoint, they threw the clothing items he was transporting onto the road. Then they discovered "a little waistband knife" that was over the legally permitted size. But one of the armed police officers made a gesture to him to indicate that all would be well if he behaved. This gesture suggested a willingness to collude, but also served as a reminder that, although his surname was not that of a clan the police regarded as particularly dangerous, the fact that he was a Zonianos would still mean that they could show they were doing their duty merely by harassing him. "But they went on and on!" The Zonianos explained that he was out late because he worked at a hotel, and that this was his time for going off work: "No matter how many times you search me, you won't find a thing!" In the end, they let him go.

The segmentary clan is thus both an adaptive advantage and a liability for the Zoniani. The authorities are forced to deal with it as a social reality, and police excess sometimes also backfires because the villagers are very well aware, as this last incident shows, of their legal rights. A surname is a marker of clan identity; it is not, however great the suspicion, a guarantee of culpability in the eyes of the law. It remains a symbolic and social strategic resource in the hands of skilled local actors, in part because it still enjoys a robust existence.

In Thailand, the earlier polity known as *moeang* has a more evanescent character, with consequently different implications for solidarity against the bureaucratic state.[12] A set of concentric entities, often conceived as a cosmological arrangement or mandala reproduced in earthly form, it represented a hierarchical structure with, at its center, the generative presence of royal power. That power, as Scott so nicely puts it, "fad[ed] gradually to zero at the outer circumference."[13] Some sort of moeang is found throughout the Tai language family and perhaps beyond; the house (*bahn*) is treated as a microcosmic version of the same structure, and indeed *bahn* can also mean "village."[14] During the reign of Rama V, this flexible concentricity gave way to a centralized authority in which the moeang was now a physical capital city, its authority over the national territory a still-contested but powerful force, its internal structure determined more by infrastructural needs than by the symbolic force of cosmology. The outer edge became the border of a sharply demarcated nation-state, and every effort was invested in reversing the old system to make royal power as evident on the frontier as at the center.[15] The fearsome and semidivine figure at the center of the mandala had now become the benign, all-knowing father of his people, a personalization that became especially powerful in the recently concluded age of King Bhumibol (Rama IX). The ritual framing of kingship nevertheless retained most of the older paraphernalia and aura of sacrality.[16]

There seems to be little popular awareness today of the idea of the mandala as the basis of all social space. For example, I never encountered any explicit recognition in Bangkok that the mandala informed residents' domestic spaces in the way that John Gray has identified among the Kholagaun Chhetri of Nepal.[17] Gray's analysis, however, is useful here in that it demonstrates how cosmological assumptions underlie spatial organization even when their physical manifestations have been erased. Indeed, as in the Thai case, these unspoken assumptions legitimize internal structural inequalities. Even in socialist Laos, as Grant Evans has suggested, traces of the old moeang hierarchy may explain the arrangement of statues of national leaders.[18]

Conversely, monuments that suggest hierarchy in mandala form may, in a country where authoritarianism and egalitarianism are fused in ways that are puzzling to outsiders, also conceal other interpretations. It is worth noting that several of the architects whose design for the new parliament building in Bangkok have a notably leftist past; their reiteration of the mandala form throughout the enormous and very solid-looking building—ironically trumpeted as an expression of the Buddhist insistence on the impermanence of all things—both announces and at the same time questions the durability of hierarchy. The mandala shape appears everywhere, even in planters placed at the bottom of the light-wells. Here too, then, the pre-modernization moeang emanates, with the vaporous vagueness of a discreet ghost, from somewhere within the building's ostentatious solidity, itself a paradox inasmuch as it is said to represent the inevitable impermanence of the material. So perhaps the moeang has not vanished even in official circles. Its chimerical balancing between hierarchy and democracy, however, offers no assurances about the future trajectory of the nation and its polity.[19]

If the Chao Pom had indeed, however unconsciously, been breathing new life into this ancient model, they could not push past the ambiguity of its name. A moeang can simply be a city in the ordinary English-language sense, and the Chao Pom unarguably lived in the physical city. Moreover, they did not conserve the older polity's most hierarchical aspects. They reimagined it as a democratic space, albeit one in which, for example, hierarchy might appear symbolically at community meetings in the form of seating arrangements, with the young women seated lower and with their shoes respectfully removed and their "mermaid" posture expressing deference to their elders; older people sat or stood at the outer edge, the men's heads placed noticeably higher than the women's, while the community leaders took turns at standing in front and dominating the proceedings with their speeches and instructions. By now, any palpable resemblance to a mandala had vanished; the spatial organization placed the weakest members of the community in the center. Height had replaced concentricity as the primary spatial expression of authority. But authority, in the form of a ritualized sense of hierarchy, had faded not a whit; it had learned instead to cooperate with more openly egalitarian ideals.

Within this modern moeang, the domestic unit was the key to the assimilation of the nation-state to older concepts of community. The nuclear family—"those who gather around the hearth" (*khrawp khrua*)—subsists to this day as a model for national solidarity. It can also, however, serve as a site of resistance to the bureaucratic state.[20] Such solidary familism was an important element in the resilience of Pom Mahakan as a community, which regarded itself as a family in; as in a home (*bahn*), the residents (*chao bahn*, literally "people of the village *or* home") would foregather for feasts to honor political visitors and merit-bearing monks, contributing food according to their skills and resources.[21] Such large-scale performances of familism may even have contributed to official hostility; the quasi-corporate solidarity of any kinship structure demographically larger than a nuclear household inevitably underscored the community's ever more tangible identity (*tua ton*) and thereby made it a more vulnerable target.[22]

Kinship structures represent both a resource and a threat for the bureaucratic state. They are a resource because they can, as in the metaphor of the king as father, be used to energize affect and allegiance. But they are also a threat because they offer an alternative to state governance, one that offers greater psychosocial and material comfort. They are also an internal threat because opportunistic politicians and bureaucrats, operating as patrons of such entities, can exploit them against the interests of the citizenry as a whole. When kinship groups exceed the nuclear household—as with both the Cretan patrilineal clan and the Thai communal *khrawp khrua*—they furnish the organizational and conceptual basis for stubborn self-differentiation from the state. Whereas in Crete the segmentary patrilineal clan provides solidarity that can on occasion be used to mobilize large groups against state authority, Thais like the Chao Pom can strategically expand their kinship resources—those of the nuclear family connected with others by often nothing more substantive than neighborliness—only by the imaginative expansion of the nuclear family into the *khrawp khrua* of the entire community. Collective feasting materializes that metonymical family as a community of fictive siblings (*phi-nawng*), a microcosmic part of that larger kindred whose father-figure is the king.[23]

Familiarity and Distance: The Remoteness of Kinship Systems

Belonging and remoteness, the twin terms of this chapter, may initially appear to be strange bedfellows. Is belonging, with kinship as its main source, not the very antithesis of remoteness? In reality, there is no contradiction here. It is into places the nation-state treats as remote or unapproachable that the politicians and bureaucrats who together constitute the established order have inserted their capillary sensors, picking up those gossipy hints of scandal and misdemeanor that tell them which citizens are most in need of protection from the state's legal and punitive arm. Moreover, they seek not only individual clients (as with the Sarakatsani) but—especially—groups large enough to make an electoral or financial difference. Societies like Zoniana with its clans, or even Pom Mahakan with its collective self-perception as a single "family," offer real opportunities for the consolidation of electoral power.

Patrons often find rich pickings in places regarded by the state as no-go zones. Appearing in public as defenders of collective order, they reinforce the local solidarity of kinship and quasi-kinship groups against the formal interests of the state. Far better that such things take place in supposedly remote locations: out of sight is out of mind, at least as far as specific relationships of complicity are concerned.[24] That strategy avoids dragging an embarrassing reliance on supposedly outmoded forms of kin loyalty into public view—and into the view of a legal system forced to be censorious once the breach becomes visible.

Geographical remoteness may offer advantages to state and community alike. Soqotra offers a striking illustration. Soqotra clearly shares with Zoniana the aura of extreme remoteness coupled with an emphasis on patrilineal clan membership. As with Zoniana, too, the ideological image of remoteness is not entirely consistent with the complex connections Soqotrans have with the region and beyond. But there is an important difference. For the state, remoteness has not so far been used as an excuse for military incursions into Soqotra. On the contrary, it has proved useful to both the Yemeni state and the Soqotrans themselves. For its ecological riches, Soqotra is often compared with the Galapagos Islands and has become a tourist attraction.

This circumstance encouraged a very different kind of invasion from that experienced by Zoniana: a neoliberal enterprise system clad in the appealing rhetoric of environmentalism sought to exploit the touristic and other material advantages of biodiversity. Ecology is a very place-specific feature. Attempts by the Chao Pom to appeal to the unique flora of their micro-niche, by contrast, had absolutely no impact at all on their eventual fate. After the final destruction of Pom Mahakan, the authorities placed botanical labels on trees the Chao Pom had regarded as sacred, transforming them from religious into environmental objects; but this, obviously, not only failed to serve the now-evicted residents' needs, but with deliberate obtuseness erased their place-specific understanding of the significance of the trees. The desire of the Zoniani to exploit a local cave for tourism similarly cut no ice with the authorities when it came to dealing with the villagers' alleged involvement in illegal activities; the development of the cave was also delayed by a long ownership dispute with another village. In Soqotra, however, the expansion of tourist facilities has virtually eliminated the already improbable threat of military occupation by the national government.

The Soqotrans, in short, may be less of a threat to their national government precisely because they are both a minority population and, unlike Zoniana and Pom Mahakan, genuinely remote. They have adopted an environmentalist and heritage-oriented rhetoric that does not claim expertise about the encompassing nation as a whole; on the contrary, they have embraced both marginality and remoteness, and what makes them distinctive is a resource both for them and for the state. These circumstances have largely kept them out of trouble.

By contrast, neither the Zoniani nor the Chao Pom want to be thought of as marginal. They are proud of their respective identities as members of their national majorities. Despite official attempts to question their origins, they have the authority of majority status on their side. When they claim expertise on matters of heritage, they are directly challenging the authority of the state. When they can call on visiting experts, they also significantly widen their base. I was often interviewed by journalists about the situation in Pom Mahakan, where some of my writings were prominently displayed in and near the communal meeting area. In Zoniana, my writings were seen as a recognition of the villagers' social values and thus as a counterweight to journalistic sensationalism. Such efforts may help to reinforce local dignity to some extent. But they rarely influence official views. Bureaucrats usually ignore inconvenient knowledge, whether local or academic, as irrelevant to the prescriptions of law and as only selectively relevant to questions of national heritage and identity.

Collusion and (Dis)illusion

In dealing with the state, Zoniani know very well how to talk the talk. No less than the rhetorically gifted leaders of Pom Mahakan, and with the added advantage of a local dialect into which they can contrastively retreat for collective privacy, the Zoniani have an impressive command of the language of electoral democracy and of due process. They take no credit for the absence of a police station in their midst, but claim that it suits the police just fine to treat the village territory as "inaccessible, untrodden" (*avato*). The usual village view is that the police have generated a self-fulfilling and pessimistic prophecy, ensuring that nothing—including a collective reputation for lawlessness created by the police and their compliant media allies—will ever change.

There is some basis for their cynicism. Even before the events of 2007, some cannabis cultivators were diverting to their fields the water allocated for vineyard irrigation; the village president of that time refused to cooperate with the offenders but—in a move that illustrates the way village solidarity operates— also refused to report them to the authorities. As he explained, he could not bring himself to be a *stambitis* (traitor), using the term for collaborators during the German occupation during World War II, even if that meant deserting the vine cultivators who were genuinely suffering during a time of drought.[25] Village solidarity trumps all other considerations—even when, as in this instance, it cost the president his position in the elections that followed soon thereafter.

There were also suspicions that some people from a neighboring village had made advantageous arrangements with particular police officers so that the latter would discover cannabis only on the Zoniana side of the village boundary. Such claims of preferential treatment are not uncommon. The officer in charge of the original raid was accused—by some of his own subordinates, among others—of having sent advance warning to the village. He had apparently hoped thereby to avoid potentially fatal violence by giving specific villagers the chance to clear their houses of incriminating materials, but the hotheads spoiled his plan; after the raid went so disastrously wrong, he was put on trial for collusion.

The main trial of the alleged village criminals had already opened up the suspicion that someone in authority had tipped off the villagers. A commentator in *To Vima*, a widely respected Athens weekly, observed, "The leadership of the Ministry of Public Order has often announced extraordinary measures against the 'warlords of Milopotamos,' but these efforts have remained a dead letter. At the same time it has been suggested that there exist 'underground' connections between high-ranking police officers and the hashish cultivators of the area, as well as connections between the 'big guys' of Athens and the same circles" of cannabis growers.[26]

These details show how easily subversive archaism can feed on a substrate of active collusion between local community and state. Ostensibly the trial was an exercise in the rule of law. Villagers, however, saw it as an attempt to intimidate them collectively. One savvy Zonianos, himself the object of an extensive police inquiry that eventually gave the prosecutors only enough material for a very light sentence (for which other villagers also had a suitably cynical explanation), explained the situation as a rhetorical strategy: the police like to pile story upon story in the hope that the sheer weight of seemingly incriminating evidence will seal their case. The court record is replete with scenes of heavily armed villains transporting quantities of illegal drugs or waving (and firing) Kalashnikovs as they carried out audacious holdups or desperately tried to deflect the pursuit of heroic police officers.

Although the police leadership was unsurprisingly exonerated, the evidence suggesting that a high-ranking police official must have warned the culprits of the impending house-to-house search remained credible. Police witnesses at the trial claimed as much as they blamed their former chief for the violent village reaction that followed. One elderly villager—and certainly no friend of the cannabis growers—bluntly declaimed, "He [the police chief] created the whole mess [*aftos ta dhimiouryisen ola*]!" And he added, "[This was all] so they wouldn't have to set foot in the off-limits [*avato*] village," sarcastically using the usual term for the village's alleged inaccessibility. Another villager assured me that the police chief must have been taking bribes (*etroye*, literally "he was eating").[27] The trial documents hint at ramified additional collusion between the more lawless villagers and the police, and perhaps beyond them to some major politicians.

The stench of opportunistic patronage has never evaporated. Many Zoniani suspect that the sudden decision to crack down on Zoniana reflected ties between the powerful clans of a rival village on the one hand and ministerial power representing what was emerging as the stronger faction within the governing party on the other. That suspicion was reinforced in turn by the rumor that an ambush had been laid for the police in a house in the rival village but that the police—ever eager to avoid tangling with the tougher and politically protected village men of that community—were easily persuaded by the politically well-connected mayor to desist from investigating.

Consider, for example, this passage from the trial record in which a police officer is giving evidence:

As I understood it, Mr. [Andonis] Vitorakis [the police chief] was not involved in the operation that day. In charge of the operation were Messrs. Petousis and Savvakis. Mr. Savvakis was acting on the orders of the General Headquarters for Crete, that is, Mr. Vitorakis, heading in the direction of Rethimno. Mr. Savvakis stayed back at the Murderer's Bridge [a toponym]. As far as I am aware he had never taken part in such operations. We assumed that we would be given some cover, but there was none. . . . As we went along we learned that we were going to search for drugs in the house of Mikhalis Klinis. They didn't tell us that at the house where we were going there would be some danger. They told us that there would be reinforcements for us. At the time we were going to the village—that is, around 10 p.m.—the people would be at work. Since there was a reaction on the part of the villagers, there must have been a leak. I don't know how and with whom the leak would have originated. I don't know if Mr. Vitorakis had orders from the Headquarters in Athens. We came to the conclusion that it was a planned ambush and that they were waiting for us. The officers had made no provision for protecting us in this specific operation. When the first shots came, I got the impression that they were not shooting in the air. The first shots came from the left-hand side of the road as we were going up. After one hit the windshield, we stopped in the middle of the road for about five seconds. The marksman must have been 150–200 meters away. I don't know the effective range of their weapons. If someone had wanted to kill us, he could have done it in those seconds when we had stopped. I have no way of knowing, and to this day have not found out, whether the Zervos brothers were among those who were shooting.[28]

In a few words, a disgruntled police officer, angry about the danger to which he had been exposed (and in the course of which he did in fact sustain a bullet wound), manages to suggest that the commanding officer either had no idea what he was doing or was engaged in some unspecified collusion with the villagers, and that the senior officers were prepared to sacrifice the lives of their subordinates. Also notable is the witness's view that the Zoniani had never intended to kill anyone.

One media report that appeared four years after the original confrontation, while not sympathetic to the armed men from the village, shows that others shared at least some of these suspicions. The writer calculated that the ambush could not have involved more than ten villagers, whereas forty-five police officers had arrived en masse. All the officers were wearing bulletproof vests, but they did not expect any armed resistance "as there had been some personal contact and understanding between the suspect and a high-ranking officer of the Greek police." When they saw the number of police officers, however, they thought that "the Police had sent more than the expected forces for a simple house search . . . and would proceed to a wider operation." And so, frightened at the prospect, they took up their Kalashnikovs.[29] The fusion of a segmented community, reacting to an external invasion, was underway.

This writer also suggested that for the police, after the first clash and the fatal wounding of one of their number, the time of "inaccessibility" was over. The villagers, however, have a very different impression. They could hardly avoid noticing that, once the lockdown period was over, the police once again seemed largely indifferent to the villagers' activities. "Now the police don't come here. And once again they look the other way. [They say,] 'Whatever happened, happened!'" as one local observer remarked. His comment, along with the closing of the nearest police station and the increasing rarity of police visits to the village, suggests that he and his fellow villagers would always expect such tacit collusion, either because the police are afraid to tangle with the villagers or because they are already engaged with them in a nexus of complex and largely illegal mutual obligations. Such conspiracy theories may initially seem entertaining, but they represent the intrusive, contaminating, and heavy-handed state presence with which poor and marginalized people must often contend.

To the villagers, the police chief's eventual acquittal was a foregone conclusion, and consistent with what they saw as an orchestrated entrapment that might one day justify further hostile state action. Although the villagers had been warned of the impending raid, the ambush clearly took the police by surprise. Less honest officers had much to lose: the subsequent punitive raid ordered by the minister of the interior must have wrecked whatever lucrative relationships they enjoyed with villagers. The trial and its outcome confirmed the villagers' conviction that the entire sequence of events was as scripted as the stream of media abuse. The police, by generating and promoting a negative stereotype, appear to have set the stage for the creation of a public consensus that would allow them both to avoid confrontation with the Zoniani most of the time and yet also to conduct brave sallies into the mythologized eyrie whenever the villagers got too cheeky.

Patronage and Power

The interdependence of sophisticated national politicians and small rural communities reinforces class differences disguised by the rhetoric of friendship and hospitality. Such linkages are rampant, and people know that highly placed politicians often depend on them; those whose job is to maintain law and order reach pragmatic and often technically illegal arrangements with local actors. The politician who arranges to suborn witnesses to help clients who steal sheep or cultivate cannabis in Zoniana has an analog in Pom Mahakan, where one community leader was able to earn some money by sleeping in a police cell so that the crooked businessman who should have been there could get out during the night-time and pursue his financial affairs under cover of darkness. To the community leader, the one-ninth of the bribe the businessman had paid the police officer in charge was sufficient to support his family, facing destitution because his political activities occupied all of his waking moments.[30]

We can widen the range of observation by considering the case of Kibera and other Nairobi slums, where local officials collected rental fees for housing that was considered both unsafe and illegal.[31] When eviction was threatened, ostensibly to clear areas around rail tracks and power lines, it emerged not only that police had often collected rental fees from the residents, but that receipts for other such payments were issued by Kenya Railways itself. The residents were clearly victims of a power shuffle within the bureaucracy: "People have been increasingly occupying space near the rail line and under power lines for decades and they have occupied these places with the full knowledge and sanction of the Government," the report points out. The sudden decision to evict exposes pragmatic arrangements based on existing but now weakened (or no longer useful) structures of patronage.[32]

One of the settlements (Raila Village) was named for a powerful Luo politician, Raila Odinga, but inhabited by members of a tribe (the Kisii), not his own, whose support he evidently hoped to maintain in this way.[33] Odinga, a former prime minister of Kenya, has in opposition consistently called for an end to corruption.[34] Odinga's rhetoric is the public expression of a pragmatic politics that represents favoritism as beneficence—but that presumably will not protect clients from violence when the balance of power shifts in new directions.

Governments, NGOs, and the evictees themselves all invoke some version of the principle of the rule of law and the protection of the common good.[35] The same holds true for police actions against gun-running, prostitution, and drug production and procurement. In this context, as in both Pom Mahakan and Zoniana, patronage carries specific dangers. The residents know too much. Their presumed protectors' political survival must compete with the residents' interests; the fall of these politicians, conversely, implicates their clients. But while the relationship continues, assertions of undying friendship and mutual esteem are dramatized as conspicuous mutual affability.

Creating Remoteness

In physical reality, the village is not remote at all. The voyeuristic thrill-seekers arrive there in comfortable modern transportation. Zoniana is connected by road to both Iraklio and Rethimno, two of Crete's three major coastal cities, and today also enjoys fast access to the mountain pasturage through a series of narrow but usable roads snaking up to key locations high above the village and well into the cloud-covered areas above the tree line. It also enjoys frequent reminders of its international connections, through visits and phone calls from kin and friends.

Most villagers own smartphones. Long gone are the days of the monopoly exercised by one powerful villager, coffeehouse proprietor and manager of the only telephone in Zoniana, whose stentorian commands would occasionally boom through the entire village over the loudspeaker system, the formal words imbued with the moral authority of his uncompromisingly local diction: "So-and-so is requested to come to the Telephone!" (Apparently this request usually meant that the person called was actually being invited to a game of cards by the Telephonist, as he was called; very few people other than the visiting anthropologist received calls from anywhere in those days, and external communication was generally infrequent and usually by letter.) Today phone calls are no longer a matter for inspection by the entire village, and foreign connections are commonplace.

During a 2018 sojourn, for example, I was suddenly hailed by a voice out of a cruising car, speaking in a theatrically exaggerated foreign accent and asking whether I spoke English. This turned out to be a Greek Australian whose close friend in Zoniana had originally put us in touch. A year earlier he had welcomed us to his restaurant in Essendon, Victoria; he had positioned a blackboard on the sidewalk outside, proclaiming "MEAT THE SYMBOL OF MANHOOD" over my name. This man—whose wife coincidentally hails from the village on Rhodes where I did my original doctoral field research—had now returned to his native village, not far from Zoniana, for a summer visit.

A few days later, I also narrowly missed a visit by the former rector of the University of Crete, a distinguished ophthalmologist who had saved my eyesight with his original laser treatment some nine years earlier; his presence was perhaps not so surprising as he was the leading light of the University of the Mountains, an organization intended to promote greater communication between the mountain villages and academia.[36] But even his visit showed how Zoniana was connected to a much wider world. Before the 1960s and the junta's road-building activity, Zoniana was arguably remote, or at least difficult to reach. Today it is no longer remote in any literal sense.

It remains remote, however, in Edwin Ardener's conceptual sense: ideologically and in the perception of outsiders, especially (in this case) of politicians and bureaucrats. Ardener insisted that remoteness was not a matter of being on a physical periphery in relation to some core population, arguing instead that "in so far as a remote area is (as it always is) part of a much wider definitional space (shall we say the dominant State) it will be perceived, itself, in toto, as a singularity in that space."[37] The absence of roads can be cited as evidence of remoteness long after roads have actually been built. Greenland describes the Italian administrative expression *prive di strade* (lacking roads) as "a term that translates literally into 'deprived of roads,' but can also be invoked to excuse state inaction [against the tombaroli] on the pretext of impenetrability."[38] Charges of remoteness suit officials averse to direct confrontation or, as in Zoniana, preparing public opinion for the dramatic operations ahead.

The territory of Zoniana, many decades since the first major roads provided access by bus, truck, and car, is still officially considered "untrodden." It has long suited the authorities to capitalize on this version of remoteness. The term *untrodden* (*avato*) does not exclusively mean rural and mountainous places. Exarcheia, a district of central Athens that many middle-class citizens profess to regard as totally unsafe, is a densely populated area whose only claim to being untrodden is moral panic, created and fanned by police and media alike, about its allegedly dangerous denizens. I have walked through the area, dined in its elegant and inventive eateries, and visited my Greek publisher there, always without the slightest sense of menace. The charge of danger is no more convincing than the warnings I received about visiting Pom Mahakan. They reflect, at best, a willful ignorance that, at worst, becomes a pretext for official brutality. They represent fear of what Ghassan Hage helpfully calls "a possible counterwill that needs to be dealt with in the process of nation building."[39] They show, moreover, that, contrary to nationalist claims, nation building remains an ongoing project. That project not only elides inconvenient populations such as those described by Hage, Guano, and Caldeira; it also entails spatially eradicating the culturally intimate evidence of rebelliousness (in Zoniana) and cultural diversity (in Pom Mahakan)—in other words, of what historically, but now embarrassingly, enabled the creation of the unified nation-state itself.

That a well-armed police force could not take over the entire Zoniana territory at any time of its choosing is absurd, as is the idea that law and order could not be maintained in Exarcheia. Claims of remoteness and impenetrability serve a political purpose. They are performative devices, statements designed to play on an already nervous public's anxieties by creating distance even (as in

FIGURE 3.1. Giving Nazism the Boot: Exarcheia, Athens. Photograph by author.

Athens and Bangkok) under conditions of literal proximity, and to prepare the way for securitization. But whereas graffiti that richly adorn Exarcheia explicitly proclaim antinationalist and antifascist sentiments (fig. 3.1), the people of Zoniana and Pom Mahakan, while they sometimes condemn racism and intolerance, do not fit the antinationalist label at all.

These supposedly remote places disturb the modernist polity. They hint at alternative ways of organizing social and political life. The Zoniani insist, for example, on respect for their own laws as well as for those of the state, but their increasing mobility and entailment in urban networks make it increasingly nonsensical to view the village as inaccessible. The Chao Pom were not remotely located in any literal sense; they lived in the very core of the old dynastic capital. Illegalized as squatters, however, they could plausibly be treated as outsiders, remote from the values of middle-class Thais, in a country where the rural underclass and rural minorities are tellingly, and contemptuously, called "people [from settlements] on the outside" (*khon ban nawk*).[40] Inaccessibility is not a physical reality. It is a characterization wished upon dissenting communities by hostile bureaucracies and it represents an extreme form of intentional political marginalization.

4. COSMOLOGIES OF THE SOCIAL

Cosmological Polities

The assumption that religion shapes cities is widespread. Reframing it, how-ever, as a proposition that *cosmology* shapes *polities* broadens the scope of the analysis, removes the bias of urban and official definitions of religion, and al-lows us, transgressively, to treat subversive archaists in the same framework as the nation-state. The emergence of new nation-states often does owe a great deal to the enthusiastic support of majority religious establishments, but noth-ing in the concept of polity necessitates either acceptance or rejection of reli-gious identity; in many, they are inextricably fused.[1] Framing this discussion in terms of cosmology, moreover, avoids distracting arguments about whether communism and other state ideologies are religions.

Cosmology certainly infuses the ways in which even the most resolutely secularist nation-states symbolize and materialize their identity. The Ankara mausoleum of that Turkish arch-secularist, Mustafa Kemal Atatürk, offers a dramatic illustration. Bruce Kapferer, among others, has argued that national-ism produces rituals that resemble religious rites in significant ways, and David Kertzer has demonstrated that Italian communists appropriated the structure of Catholic feasts as an effective way of making inroads into the electoral strengths of the then-dominant Christian Democrat party.[2] Within the cul-turally intimate spaces of the dominant cosmology, moreover, unexpected pragmatic adjustments to social reality are possible. As Paolo Heywood's work now shows, LGBT citizens, leftist and religious alike, have found a culturally comfortable means of accommodation—a "double-[faced] morality" (*doppia morale*)—with the pressures that persistent church attitudes would otherwise create for LGBT parishioners.[3] This accommodation, too, is part of a cosmology that transcends the boundaries of both church and state; it evinces a polity that is thoroughly inclusive and, indeed, civil.

Nation-states may reuse elements of earlier religious practices much as architects incorporate older decorative fragments in official buildings. Because such fragments may not be recognizably religious in an ecclesiastical sense, treating them instead as an area of cosmological negotiation between the state and local populations is more productive. Earlier strata of religious and symbolic practice re-emerge in surprising contexts. In Vietnam, as Shawn Malarney has shown, the socialist regime has found it expedient to restore the hitherto prohibited "superstition" of ancestor worship, since it provides an excellent model for discipline and obeisance to the father figure of the state.[4] In China, the rehabilitation of Confucius may have been similarly motivated.[5]

These practices do not mean that state and citizens interpret what is performed in the same way. Sometimes the state simply ignores potentially subversive implications, treating discreet tolerance as a lesser risk than confrontation. Phill Wilcox, for example, describes the apparent paradox of royalist worship—secretive ritual offerings to a statue of the last crowned Lao king, Sisavang Vong—in the heart of Luang Prabang in socialist Laos. Perhaps the Lao state tolerates this unexpected veneration of royalty as, instead, an act of respect for national cultural heritage. Wilcox suggests that such veneration is especially possible in Luang Prabang, where international recognition of the architectural heritage has generated patriotic pride.[6]

As such unexpected tolerance shows, ideologies are poor predictors of both official and citizen responses. Apparent continuities with the past often mask attitudinal and ideological change. As Kapferer shows, religions that purport to promote peace and love can be locally re-interpreted as validating acts of extreme violence, whether as Crusades, jihad, or the murderous attacks on Muslims and Hindus led by Buddhist monks in Sri Lanka and Myanmar.

While such violence is often nationalistic, religious fundamentalists sometimes actively oppose nationalist movements. Such was the role of the senior Greek Orthodox clergy in the emergence of the post-Ottoman Greek state. While rural priests and monastics, most of them natives of their village communities, sided with the insurgents, the ecclesiastical leadership in Istanbul feared the consequences of revolution for themselves—rightly, as it soon turned out— and their successors were no less apprehensive of the significance of the newly born state's enthusiasm for pagan antiquity.[7] The Neo-Orthodox critiques of the established national Orthodox Church of Greece as too bureaucratic, Cartesian, and Western spring in part from a related distrust of state institutions.[8] Possible parallels may lie in the opposition of certain Ultra-Orthodox Jewish groups to the establishment of the Israeli state, and in the emergence of religious caliphates seeking to erase national identities in the name of Islam.

Cosmologies of the Nation-State: Greece

The cosmological shaping of urban space is apparent in the old city of Bangkok, where modern planning has overlain, but not destroyed, traces of an older moeang structure that is well-documented in rural communities.[9] Zoniana, despite its spatial and conceptual distance from Greek ideas of urbanity, also exhibits cosmological features in two particularly important respects. One is that those even temporarily in a higher location have moral superiority—even though, or perhaps because, it implies political weakness through distance from the centers of power. The other is the role of segmentation, which organizes the spiritual as well as the social domain.

The clash between state religion and local practices takes us to one of the core areas from which subversive archaism draws its substance. While each of the communities described in this book largely professes allegiance to the dominant religion of its nation-state, both, in instructively different ways, draw on older cosmologies to challenge the hegemony of the state. In both countries, critics have leveled claims at the dominant establishment for what are derided as modernist, bureaucratic, or even "protestant" patterns of religious practice—in Greece by the Neo-Orthodox movement, in Thailand by reformist monastic orders such as the Dhammakaya.[10] In contrast, neither of the local communities discussed here explicitly set itself against officially recognized religion. Monks from a nearby temple ministered to the merit-making and funerary needs of Pom Mahakan, while in Zoniana the current, locally born priest is the son and grandson of his two immediate predecessors. In both places, however, archaizing practices, linked to kinship and other local social forms rather than to church or state, provided a cosmological framing for acts of political defiance.

Let us start with Greece, where ecclesiastical opposition to nationalist neoclassicism was a true birthing pain. Greek leaders looked for validation in Western European eyes to a cultural tradition that the church had spent two millennia trying to extirpate. Nationalist folklorists and historians who sought pagan survivals that would legitimate the new Greek nation-state faced a hostile clergy, who have continued to watch for possible recrudescences of paganism. Their purism erupted in 2011 in mass demonstrations against what some devout churchgoers believed would be the use of the number 666, with its (for them) diabolical implications, on official biometric identity cards.[11] Scholars searching for the ancient roots of the modern state, which often funded their efforts, have found themselves at odds with the leaders of their professed "national" religion, although they also made valiant attempts to overcome the difficulty by demonstrating that Christian saints had absorbed the names and functions of the ancient deities. Some also argued that ancient Greek philosophy was an anticipation of Christian theology that might otherwise not have so successfully flourished on Greek soil.[12]

A consistent trail leads from the higher clergy's hostility toward nationalist folklorists' excavation of ancient religion in rural folk practices to their indignation at being labeled a "Jewish religion" by pagan revivalists among the leaders of the neo-Nazi Golden Dawn political party.[13] Some of the Golden Dawn leaders have advocated reintroducing the worship of the twelve Olympians in place of Christianity—an act of subversive archaism resembling the German Nazis' revival of ancient religious rituals as folkloric revisions of Christian festivities.[14] Golden Dawn's abrupt decline and elimination from the national parliament in the 2019 elections suggest that their views were not popular, but their complex and ambivalent relationship with Orthodoxy does reveal, albeit in exaggerated form, the continuing tension at the core of the national cultural project.[15]

The Zoniani exploit church *and* state discourse while expressing hostility toward both; this apparent contradictoriness lies at the tactical heart of subversive archaism. They often poke fun at the church's alleged venality, for example, while treating a range of local practices (such as cures for the evil eye and ritual laments for the dead) as evidence of the antiquity of their lived piety and polity. Such contradictions make fertile ground in which to grow an archaism separate from, and in certain respects contrary to, the official antiquarianism of the state.

Segmentation as Cosmology

The villagers' casual conversations reveal a view of the universe that is refracted through the local system of patrilineal clans, reordering the official religiosity of church and state around activities that both church and state oppose. Elsewhere in Mediterranean Europe, one encounters only slight traces of patriliny.[16] But in Zoniana, segmentary and patrilineal lines of fission and fusion frame all social relations, from local interactions to dealings with the state and its bureaucracy. As with the Nuer famously studied by E. E. Evans-Pritchard, the Zoniani's use of a segmentary social idiom goes far beyond the temporal relation with the state; it addresses the divine itself.[17]

When Zoniani swear at one another, their idiom reproduces the segmentary logic of their social relations. An angry villager will, in one expression, "screw your Virgin Mary." Moreover, the holy image thus refracted can be any saint. In the logic of segmentation, our enemies' saints cannot possibly be *our* saints; it is therefore acceptable to treat them with disrespect. Zoniani were generally able to discuss this phenomenon quite directly, whereas other Greek villagers, asked why they seemed to differentiate their own divine figures from those of others, dismissed the entire mode of blasphemy as "just a bad habit."[18] Blasphemy is definitely *not* something that more conventionally law-abiding villagers want to discuss with outsiders.

In Zoniana, by contrast, antagonisms split quickly along patrilineal clan lines, a social idiom that is opposed to both church and state models of kinship. Village devotions are deeply bound up with practices, such as animal theft, forbidden by secular and religious law alike. The use of holy icons and remote churches to establish the guilt or innocence of suspected animal-thieves, and the respect for St. George as the patron saint of animal thieves, are examples of this intimate relationship between the social and the religious in contravention of state and ecclesiastical legalism. The Zoniani would understand fully Durkheim's famous claim that religion was nothing other than society's objectification and worship of itself, or Evans-Pritchard's analysis—grounded in a critical adaptation of Durkheim's perspective—of the way in which the Nuer concept of spirit was "refracted" both through the segmentary structure of Nuer society and through the multiple manifestations of nature amid which the Nuer lived.[19]

Both the greater reverence shown for some icons of a given saint than for others and the more casual idiom of blasphemy fit the segmentary view of the Zoniana social universe. In the village one can even, in occasional moments of real anger, hear the name of God similarly refracted, while localist politicians may occasionally invoke "the God of Crete"—who is certainly not Zeus, despite the villagers' claims of historical connection with the worship of that deity in antiquity.[20]

In societies with strong clan structures, segmentation is the principle that organizes all knowledge. Indeed, as Shryock has shown for the sheikhly politicians of Jordan, truth itself is refracted through the multiplex divisions of the clan system.[21] The same has been said about the concept of heritage in nearby Yemen.[22] And for Greeks the term *istories*, literally "histories," means "quarrels," because the stuff of which noteworthy events are made passes through, and is organized by, the divisions and fractures of the social world.[23] In all these cases, reality is refracted through social relations.

A similar logic informs the polities known as moeang in Southeast Asia. Here, indeed, a conceptual convergence subsists between the clan segmentation of Crete and the diffuse political structure of the moeang. As Michael Di Giovine has pointed out in his discussion of Italian vernacular devotions, local churches and shrines represent both shared piety and local specificity. Like the traditional moeang, and in a pattern that has even been traced in Asia to broader geopolitical relations today (as he tellingly argues using Tambiah's "galactic polity" metaphor), shrines of the Italian saint Padre Pio exhibit very similar characteristics. Satellite shrines radiate out from the powerful center in a pattern of "overlapping systems of sanctuaries organized around core power centers and more peripheral, satellite shrines that orbit them" but that show correspondingly greater independence of form and meaning.[24] Shrines in the vicinity of Zoniana, in the same segmentary logic, are dedicated to divine personae refracted through intensely local interests at the periphery of church and state authority. While there are obvious differences between European Christianity and the Hindu-Buddhist traditions of Southeast Asia, the parallel is striking, as is the persistence of such models within ethnonational states in both regions—states, significantly, that have every reason to suppress all traces of such a potentially fissile perspective.

Here we see cosmology at its most totalizing, an encompassing vision of the social and the divine in a single frame. For the Zoniani as for the Chao Pom, all knowledge is social. The Chao Pom, like other Thais, call each other *phinawng* (older-younger siblings), thereby encapsulating an age hierarchy within the expression of familial egalitarianism.[25] In Zoniana, social knowledge is equally relativistic, expressed through the segmentary distinction between insiders (*edhiči mas*) and outsiders (*kseni*, ancient *xenoi*). In Crete these terms specifically imply relative distance in the clan system; villagers view all social relations through that prism.[26] Their geographical remoteness, partial though it is, has allowed the Zoniani to maintain their clan identities, which, in their eyes, have preserved their moral and cultural purity. The outside is a generalized otherness, beyond their clan system. And to a state and an older academic establishment accustomed to viewing indigeneity as a guarantee of superiority over foreign scholarship, the villagers could, like the Italian tombaroli, insist that their knowledge was more authentic than that of city-bound officials and academics: it was born of chthonic experience.

The retired teacher who has invested so much effort in proving the deep antiquity of the Zoniana dialect, for example, himself a scion of the largest clan, produced a beautifully drawn genealogical tree-diagram of his clan that would not have disgraced Evans-Pritchard.[27] In thus linking his philological skills with the archaic structure of the community, he bestrode a tectonic conceptual chasm: on the one side he had mastered the official state historiography with its claims to classical antiquity, while on the other he exemplified a male-centered view of the social universe that departs in most respects from the official, ecclesiastically endorsed, Western European model of kinship.

The persistence of a patrilineal clan structure is not an explicit element of Zoniana's subversive archaism; place-names, local dialect forms, and the association of their district with the pre-classical worship of Zeus are sufficient evidence of the village's ancient roots. The cosmological significance of patrilinearity is more diffuse: it is a framing of the entire universe in segmentary terms that allow Zoniani to intimate that theirs is the only real historical truth, that their antiquity is somehow better than that of the bureaucratic state.[28]

Their clan structure has also served a more practical goal, as Zoniani sought, first, to buy up lowland pastures they could reuse to build restaurants and hotels, and then to establish themselves in the major cities of the island, especially Iraklio. The state authorities appear to have implicitly recognized this effective expansion of an originally very localized kinship system when, at the same time that they raided the village, they also sent other equally heavily armed colleagues to lock down and search the Ghazi section of Iraklio. Ghazi, a bustling suburban neighborhood, is a second (or now even primary) home to many Zoniani. Zoniani are everywhere; and wherever they go, like the Man lineage of Hong Kong studied by James L. Watson, they have prospered and expanded their interests without losing their sense of collective identity.[29]

The reason for their success is clear. It lies in the capacity for virtually infinite expansion that the structure of unilineal clans provides. Walking through the streets of Iraklio, a knowledgeable visitor quickly sees numerous unmistakably Zoniana surnames on shops and offices. In what is both a reversal and a validation of the attitude of the police to Zoniana surnames in the village, in the city these proudly displayed surnames provide sure protection against threats of extortion and burglary; they inspire fear even in underworld toughs. Even as patriliny looks increasingly outmoded, its trace in the surname acquires new force.

Like Watson's Chinese migrants, the Zoniani have been able to deploy the solidarity that accompanies a unilineal clan structure to good effect—not as globally as their Chinese counterparts, at least thus far, but with a similar sense of utilizing kinship as a resource while rejecting—indeed, transcending— the territorial limits of the village. They have certainly not disappeared; they have, however, regrouped. Meanwhile, in the village itself, some of them appear to be delighted that the police action at least provided the motivation to clean up their act and learn to behave ostensibly like good citizens—to demonstrate a civility that is recognizable as such by the state.

Social Realizations of the Cosmological: Hospitality and Solidarity

The segmentary cosmology informs two other dimensions of life in Zoniana that are germane to my argument. These are, first, the significance of hospitality; and second, the relation between the deeply agonistic stance of Zoniana masculinity and the emergence of social solidarity during the Greek economic crisis of 2009 and after.

Hospitality is fundamental to village civility. Lauded in official folklore and history as an ancient virtue, it exemplifies archaism as a potential weapon of subversion.[30] It is also a useful political tool, suggesting a quintessentially ancient tradition in which Zoniani excel even in comparison to other Cretans. But it also signals to knowing insiders who each host's particular patrons are.

Hospitality is ambiguous; generosity and displays of affection reciprocally require guests to submit to their hosts' rules of conduct.[31] Thus, a Zoniana shepherd might play visiting officers at their own game, by pressing them to eat meat that is the only material evidence of his involvement in animal theft, then openly laugh about what he has just made them do; local propriety prevents the officers both from refusing the offer of food and from reacting punitively when they realize what has happened. This ambiguity reproduces the larger structure of mutuality that binds community and state together in tense, often conflictual interaction.[32] While a widespread bit of neoclassical ideology sees Greek hospitality as the heritage of Ksenios Zefs (Xenios Zeus), the ancient god of strangers and guests, hospitality is more usefully read as itself an agonistic activity that today, as Evthymios Papataxiarchis has demonstrated, infuses the logic of solidarity in many ways.[33] In this dual role, it is all of a piece with the villagers' creative capacity for being good Greeks and rebellious citizens at the same time—in a word, subversive archaists.

Segmentation, while opposed to the logic of the bureaucratic state, is demonstrably also the basis of values—notably hospitality and solidarity—that the state ostensibly endorses. Hospitality has been the theme of the tourism industry virtually since its inception; solidarity with the recipients of state charity is lauded. But in a segmentary frame, both values take on a very different complexion. The hospitality extended to outsiders can actually be a means of socially controlling them; applied to migrants, that implication has important legal and ethical consequences.[34] Solidarity with those outsiders, or with other Greeks in specific situations, is far from incompatible with the dynamics of agonistic relations, but instead represents the inclusive ("fusion") side of segmentary politics. While solidarity might seem to be an endorsement of state-directed attempts to repress or divert internal factionalism and keep the peace, it often appears as an anti-state movement, once again revealing the segmentary proclivities that keep erupting despite the state's official maintenance of a unitary surface.

The meaning of hospitality is similarly bifurcated. On the one hand, it symbolizes the nation's ability to define its borders and collective culture; the nation accepts its guests on condition that they acknowledge its cultural unity. On the other hand, hospitality is a means of reversing an interpersonal power imbalance defined by the pseudo-genealogical distance of national identity. In this logic, my British and American connections made me the target of aggressive one-upmanship in Zoniana. My hosts declared, "You have nothing here"—that is, I had no possessions in the village—and therefore, in accepting their generosity, I also conceded their moral advantage.[35] Another villager warned that if I ever departed from community norms he would not be able to continue our friendship. Such warnings do not negate the reality of the affection I was shown; they simply clarify the social context in which such affection is admissible, showing thereby the potentially powerful guest's dependence on acceptance by the host.[36] Similarly, the rapid swelling of solidarity with migrants in Greece, especially during a period when the neo-Nazi Golden Dawn movement was agitating against them, follows the segmentary logic of hospitality.[37]

In this segmentary worldview, the logic of solidarity is that of unity achieved in the face of overwhelming exterior hostility.[38] The German (and more generally European Union) bullying that exacerbated Greece's economic crisis from 2009 on triggered solidarity both among previously quarreling factions and toward the newly incorporated outsiders, the migrants foisted on Greece and other Mediterranean states by the Dublin III Regulation.[39] The sudden effusions of solidarity were a response to debt brought about, many Greeks claimed, by ruthless usurers (*tokoghlifi*) who, knowing full well that Greece could not meet the fiscal obligations of huge loans, nonetheless happily entrapped the country in a downward spiral. That indebtedness would benefit German and other West European exporters and bankers, allow these foreigners to strip Greece of its sources of clean energy, and subject the Greeks themselves to a decade of hunger, misery, and humiliation. A 2015 protest banner reading "No to local and foreign usurers" (*okhi se dopious ke ksenous tokoghlifous*) acknowledged two levels of segmentation when attacking the greed of bankers (fig. 4.1).[40] Internally, among the swelling numbers of the precarious, civility

FIGURE 4.1. Athens Speaks: Out with Local and Foreign Usurers!
Photograph by author.

intensified in the face of what was perceived as foreign-orchestrated oppression, in which Greek bankers figured as quislings. This civility demanded hostility toward the financial elite; but it concomitantly took the form of mutual support among the population at large.

Katerina Rozakou incisively notes that the first appearances of Greek voluntarism appeared to contradict the standard anthropological image of Greek society as the site of agonistic male factionalism (so well represented by Zoniana!).[41] Solidarity reveals the segmentary worldview that emerges when state failure entails submitting to foreign bullying: with and against migrants, with and against government agencies, and so on.[42] Solidarity is a conditional arrangement. In rethinking and reshaping the polity, solidarity activists are resuscitating a submerged but durable segmentary social order.

Segmentation in Zoniana is, unsurprisingly, clearest in the management of patrilineal ties. Villagers are as proud of their reconciliation ritual (*sasmos*, a revealing metaphor meaning "pulling straight [like a string]") as they are embarrassed by the persistence of the violence that necessitates it.[43] Hospitality, solidarity, and blasphemous swearing are three outward expressions of the conceptual framework in which Zoniani relate to the nation: a segmentary understanding of the universe, realized, in everyday village life, in social relations that resist the homogenizing hand of the bureaucratic state. Patrilineality becomes, in this context, a collective good to be defended against the extraneous hostility of the state.

Segmentary processes especially characterize political relations among patrilineal clans in Zoniana. But segmentation in Greece, indeed in Europe, is a much larger process, one that is not necessarily tied to particular kinship idioms.[44] Even when it is so entailed, as in Zoniana, it has implications that extend far beyond kinship. Although segmentary clan structures may threaten the very foundations of the bureaucratic state, segmentation subsists, independently of any such kinship structure, within so-called pyramidal European nation-states.[45] The European ideal is itself powerfully segmentary, as the European Union demonstrates at the bureaucratic level.

Segmentation is thus not a sign of alterity.[46] To the contrary, it is arguably common to all humanity. Evans-Pritchard's attempt to create a discrimination between segmentary and pyramidal societies *within an assertion that all societies have politics* was an attempt, by a British colonial critic of British colonial rule, to reconcile the assumption that Westerners uniquely enjoyed the formal structures of government with the recognition that the natives, too, had politics. This highly conditional acknowledgment is in itself a recognizably segmentary way of looking at the world, no matter how much Evans-Pritchard thought that segmentation was about "them" rather than the colonial, or Western, "us." As Alan Rumsey has noted, it means that the theoretical significance of Evans-Pritchard's formulation "exceeds itself"—and, I would now add, simultaneously shows him to have been inextricably caught up *inside* a social reality to which he evidently thought himself extraneous.[47]

The problem for Europeans is that the ideological construction of their collective identity erases all the subsidiary levels at which it could fragment.[48] Such is the work of the nation-state, with its tendency to increase the element of ethnonationalism as the easiest way to stabilize that unity at the expense of internal differences. Bureaucrats do not have to deal with such wrenching paradoxes. Their task is simple: to eliminate all palpable traces of segmentation, which they know by such pejorative names as "separatism," "tribalism" (as we saw in the case of Soqotra), and "mutiny."

The Zoniana term for "patriline," *yenia*, is etymologically cognate with its classical equivalent (*genos*). Patrilineal kinship, which had been displaced by the kindred-based system favored by the Christian churches for many centuries, enjoyed something of a European revival in the eighteenth and nineteenth centuries as powerful local dynasties sought to consolidate property, but national governments had little tolerance for such local accretions of power and most modern nation-states pay little attention to patrilineal solidarity.[49] Where it does appear, as on Crete, the national authorities view it with a jaundiced eye, wondering when it will fuel new acts of insubordination. For the Zoniani, who do not dwell on the possible classical origins of their social structure, it is simply their traditional social order and as such is part of what constitutes their generic sense of superiority *as Greeks*. It thus also underwrites a segmentary view of the universe that allows them to be loyal Greeks and insubordinate citizens, devout believers and proficient blasphemers, at one and the same time. This perspective is the social framework of their particular brand of subversive archaism and the cosmology that legitimates their pride and allows them to question, openly and in daily conversation, the legitimacy of church and state alike.

Political Cosmology I: From the Siamese Moeang to the Thai Nation-State

In Southeast Asia, the European model of the nation-state is mostly a late arrival. But whereas elsewhere in the region it was the continuation of colonial rule, in Thailand, from around the mid-nineteenth century, it displaced the older concept of a territorially flexible polity, organized on earth in the form of the cosmological design of the mandala, in which kings wielded a highly conditional form of power under constant threat of invasion from without and usurpation from within. That structure had classically segmentary properties, as Sunait Chutintaranond has argued for the Siamese city of Ayutthaya that preceded Bangkok as the national capital; the existence of parallel mandala-like moeang, at multiple levels of segmentation, was a constant source of instability.[50] When Rama I moved the capital to Bangkok, he reproduced there the formal layout of Ayutthaya; the wall with its fourteen fortresses, including Pom Mahakan, is the clearest physical expression of this modular patterning. But with modernization, especially under Rama V, such evidence of an older, segmentary political order had to be suppressed as thoroughly as clan loyalties were silenced in much of Greece. There could now be only one moeang: the nation-state. The historic rupture was systematically erased from official memory, although it is clear that—again as in Greece—the older, segmentary structure still conditions citizens' understanding of the political order.

The mandala is to Siamese traditionalists what clan segmentation is to Cretan society: a cosmological perspective embodied in the Realpolitik of a past polity but inflecting action under the new order. In old Bangkok, the spectral presence of the pre–Rama V polity, the archaic royal moeang, implicitly legitimates the local community as one possible refraction of itself.

Representing the community as a family plays on that model. It sets it up, not against the king-father, but within the royal aura and against the bureaucracy. Thus an apparent accommodation to official ideology allows a fair amount of play to civil disobedience. Arjun Appadurai recommends that we treat the nation-state as a cosmological construct. By the same token, we may view these familistic structures as embodying alternative cosmologies. That helps to explain why such tiny communities—Appadurai's "small numbers"— threaten the totalizing way in which the ethnonational state encapsulates its constituent parts. The ethnonational state abhors internal exceptions, even, or perhaps especially, when those exceptions conjure up earlier historical phases of its own emergence.[51]

The Chao Pom's invocation of the moeang contradicts the state by positing an alternative antiquity, social organization, and moral order. In contrast to the ethnonational state, this polity was broadly inclusive in both ethnic identity and kinship models, territorially elastic (Stanley J. Tambiah described the historical moeang as "pulsating"), and clearly divided between those who were thought to be predestined for leadership (*phu nam*) and those who humbly defined themselves as followers (*phu tam*)—the latter a self-categorization no Zonianos would even contemplate.[52] The status of *phu nam* is an ascription of karmic charisma analogous to, but at a much lower level than, the dharma and barami of the king. As such, it delicately evokes the conditional power of the king in the old moeang structure. As Patrick Jory usefully notes, charisma could be "as useful to figures in authority *as it could be subversive*" at such lowly levels.[53]

The Pom Mahakan president struggled in vain to persuade his followers of his desire to step down from his role, arguing that "power was not something we have seized" (*amnat mai chai sing thi rao yoed*), and called for "democracy" (*prachathipatai*) within the community. But he admitted that others feared or were embarrassed to oppose him; part of his authority came from a general recognition of his powerful personality and his willingness to pitch in and set a good example. In arguing for a reciprocity of respect, he also showed that it did not preclude the hierarchy of leaders and followers, since all had roles suited to their individual characters. The residents were thus adamant that the president could not escape the consequences of his authoritarian character. Without actually calling his position predestined, they did their best to make it so. His constant, visible efforts sealed his fate as he strove, in his words, to "fit with a new generation that has a new way of thinking," but that was evidently still willing, even anxious, to concede to him the traditional—and dangerous—mantle of leadership.

That one disgruntled elder and his family fought the president for years did not change the inevitability of his role; the Siamese kings had contended with their own aristocratic rebels. The ruler in the moeang might passionately promote democratic participation, but he was both respected and resented—often by the same people—for his assumption of leadership made acceptable by this sense of ascription and confirmed by his energetic hard work. Although the residents continued to hold elections even after the Bangkok administration withdrew recognition from them as a community, those who won were almost always the same recognizable leadership figures: the president, treasurer, and one hardworking elder were never defeated. One sole embittered loser attempted to rally disgruntled members around him and secretly parlayed with the authorities. He eventually died of natural causes without managing to rally more than a handful of supporters among his own family and immediate neighbors. His widow stayed on site to the end, commemorating him in the name of their fireworks shop, and was eventually reconciled to cooperation with the leadership. After the final demolition, she left the signboard of their shop in the mud and garbage at the gateway where, disagreeing with the president, he had, more than a decade earlier, passionately argued for maintaining defensive barriers to prevent city officials from entering. On the signboard, like a last cry for recognition, his honorific title of *lung* (father's brother), attached to his personal nickname, recalled an earlier, happier time when he had led the residents in exuberant ritual drumming and spoken eloquently at community meetings.

The other leaders, unlike him, saw no reason to break the law by barricading the entryway into the site. Having broken with them, the dissident tried to present himself to the authorities as a defender of legality, but his sudden conversion made no impression on the authorities. Most other residents rallied around a leadership about which they often grumbled even as they gratefully accepted its durability. After the dissident's death, his wife and daughter were gradually reconciled to the leadership as they realized that the city authorities had been attempting to incite factionalism in the community. The bureaucrats' goal was to make the last remaining residents leave—"not," as his daughter put it, "to move elsewhere, but just to get out." Like many others, she and her mother had no obvious place to go, and no alternative housing was provided. In the end, they, too, suffered the fate of the remaining residents, cast out into the chaotic city to fend for themselves.

Like the Zoniani who used the electoral system to advance the cause of various patrilineal factions, the Chao Pom, advised by an array of activists, had adopted a democratic organizational style, but one that projected rather than restricted the president's power.[54] With his histrionic talents and fearless confrontation of government officials, the president—although frequently criticized for his hectoring style—was considered the only resident truly capable of speaking truth to power. He commanded an impressive level of formal political rhetoric; this rhetoric often flavored our conversations, apparently because he could never bring himself wholeheartedly to abandon his leadership role. He had the added advantage of being from one of the very few families of more than a century's residence at the site; his grandfather, a respected artisan, had fashioned traditional musical instruments. Indigeneity, in the moeang system, is an integral component of leadership; here, too, the local structure reflects the larger monarchical polity. Moreover, even when others obeyed his exhortations to express their disagreements with him, they were thereby, ironically, obeying his orders. By thus reaffirming their role as loyal if argumentative followers, they participated in the collective performance of democracy projected—often through stentorian loudspeaker announcements and equally loud amplifications of the actual proceedings—at the city of Bangkok beyond the thick wall of the old moeang.

Three or four months before the end of the struggle, the community went silent. Soldiers had taken over from the bureaucrats and told the remaining residents, "If you don't surrender and move out of this place, you are enemies of the military."[55] The president himself admitted to living in a state of suspicious caution and fear, not only for himself but also for his family members. Earlier negotiations had effectively been negotiations about negotiations; the authorities had skillfully prevaricated by appearing to consider the arguments for saving each of the older houses while deflecting each attempt with vague assurances of further conversation. Many residents simply gave up in despair, realizing that the discussions would yield no concessions.

By September 2017, only a rump remained. The president could do no more for the community itself, but still tried to save eleven houses of historic interest, a project in which he had the support of the Association of Siamese Architects. These houses included one that had a Chinese-style cupboard with a long, multiple-sectioned door that folded several times over, and another that stood on high stilts allowing for the breeze flowing along the nearby canal to refresh tired bodies relaxing under the closed rooms. The Association had entered the fray relatively late, and clearly has regretted not being able to do more; its website continues to lament the loss of the Pom Mahakan architectural ensemble, perhaps more remarkable for its completeness as a building complex than for any truly outstanding feature distinguishing particular houses.[56] Six months later, and despite the Association's active interest and negotiation with the city authorities, all the houses disappeared in the furious finality of demolition.[57] Whether truly as an act of revenge or simply because the city bureaucrats were themselves constrained by fear of higher authority, they apparently had never entertained any serious intention of leaving a trace of the community in place.

Where once there had been a living community, the authorities posted a few signs (now in Chinese as well as English and Thai), similar to tourist markers planted all over the city where old communities had been forced out. These paraded nostalgia for a few innocent-sounding elements of tradition—an alley of birdcage sellers, another of charcoal vendors—but completely obliterated the memory of the people who had performed these roles. A new, bureaucratic idiom of unintentional, humorless commemoration blocked from recall any trace of the insubordinate traditionalism of the Chao Pom now scattered among the slums and high-rises of the voracious city. The only lingering memory was that of a few unsympathetic neighbors, glad, they claimed, to see the troubling community forever obliterated.

Political Cosmology II: Patrilineality and Patronage

Both Pom Mahakan and, in Greece, Zoniana suffered from the ill fortune that befell their respective political patrons. In Thailand, the Democrat Party, a royalist-conservative party, had provided much of the political patronage that the Chao Pom were able to enjoy. But it was meager support. Pom Mahakan managed to stay visible in part through arranging visits by notables from the party.[58] But these visits represented an increasingly problematic tutelage. The Democrat Party had been tainted, perhaps irrevocably, by its association with the Yellow Shirt monarchists despite attempts to downplay the connection, and was weakened by corruption scandals, possibly engineered by members of other parties or by disgruntled civil servants within the city administration. One of these scandals engulfed the one senior official, former Bangkok governor and party stalwart Apirak Kosayidhin, who formally endorsed a plan that would have saved the Pom Mahakan community. The party's attempt to build a socially responsive reputation was also undermined by events. Party leader Abhisit Vejjajiva's personal reputation was stained by his order to fire on Red Shirt protesters in 2010—an event that helped to precipitate the military coup of 2014.

The Chao Pom prided themselves on knowing the difference between politicians who were merely seeking votes and those who were genuinely sympathetic and could provide access through their own intraparty connections. Denials by community leaders to the contrary, however, many outsiders suspected that they were allowing themselves to be manipulated for tactical advantages that would ultimately serve only the politicians' interests.

Pragmatism and disappointment eventually converged. The residents' royalism became increasingly muted as they became aware of the palace's interest in clearing an ever larger area as a monument to the dynasty's glory. That expansion included the wholesale removal of the popular Dusit Zoo and the forced eviction of numerous riverside communities; the chill soon spread to Pom Mahakan as well. Portraits of the old king and queen had already begun to disappear from the residents' demonstrations, although a large painting of Queen Sirikit was always set up over the community's rotating credit fund activities. During the later street revolts, community leaders were able to negotiate an agreement with the Red Shirts to shelter Pom Mahakan from their operations—a sure sign that the common experience of poverty was stronger than ideological commitments to palace and party. Indeed, the community shared with the Red Shirts the plaint that they were treated as *phrai*, dependent commoners.

In both Pom Mahakan and Zoniana, patronage proved an unreliable source of protection. Whereas in Zoniana powerful men sought political alliances that would protect their families, sub-clans, and clans, an approach that left the village as a whole vulnerable to the patronage enjoyed by more powerful neighboring villages, the Chao Pom typically negotiated personal and family interests with police officers and other street-level officials. With politicians and senior bureaucrats, they would only deal collectively, refusing to appoint representatives and insisting that the entire community should participate.[59] The bureaucrats could be forced to receive them, if only to avoid visible conflict and authoritarianism, but the residents' political patrons could not force the bureaucrats to do more than that. Even the well-disposed Bangkok governor, Apirak Kosayodhin, was no match for the wily city officials in their determination to evict. Once the military were in charge of the country, despite performances of democratic process, there was no space left for effective negotiation at all.

In Zoniana, with the restoration of democracy from 1974 on, the villagers turned the party-political basis of local elections into a classic confrontation between clans and between subsets of these clans, in true segmentary fashion.[60]

The more powerful the clan, the more effective were its ties to senior members of the ruling political elite, mostly members of the New Democracy conservative party. What had originally seemed to be a system that protected sheep thieves from jail terms in exchange for guaranteed bloc votes apparently turned into a more serious protection racket, and it is not clear that such connections have entirely lapsed.

The complex of confrontation and collusion between the Zoniani and the Greek state has had a long gestation. During the pre–World War II period of military-backed government, many Zoniani had fallen afoul of the central authorities, mostly for acts of animal theft. With their powerful patrons immobilized by a centralized dictatorship, the villagers found themselves facing the wrath of the state directly, and sheep thieves received heavy sentences of prison or exile to distant provinces. But the conservatism of the regime meant, as it did again during the equally repressive dictatorships of 1967–74, that the politicians who had profited from their patronage of the powerful local patrilineal clans would eventually reappear in their old guise as protectors and bosses, dealing in favors much as they had done before.

In late 1974, a few bare months after the fall of Greece's military regime and the decisive return to democracy, politicians were back at work, assiduously baptizing as many powerful shepherds' babies as they could, and at remarkably high speed. No actual figures are available, and the local practice of informally but wholeheartedly involving multiple sponsors at baptisms would make any such figures extremely unreliable (and probably too low, at that). But local comment had it that Konstandinos Mitsotakis, later prime minister and at that time head of a local political party (the Neoliberals) with almost exclusively Cretan membership, baptized thousands of children in an impressively short time.[61] Although this claim is probably an exaggeration, its frequent reiteration suggests agreement among local people that the numbers were significant.[62]

Such remarkable displays of local clout, backed up by appearing at events at which the illegal firing of gunshots (*balothies*) celebrated his local supporters' electoral power, set Mitsotakis on a rapid rise to national power and ultimately, after taking his Neoliberals into the New Democracy party and making a successful bid for the latter party's leadership, into the prime minister's chair. The shepherds had clearly helped propel their man into the top job. The deputy Neoliberal party leader was one of the two national parliamentary representatives for the district that included Zoniana, and he and Mitsotakis made a formidable pair. They operated in two seemingly irreconcilable directions: on the one hand, as traditionalists (often clad in ostentatiously local garb) when spreading their influence and largesse in the villages; on the other, as modernist, business-friendly liberals in Athens. Their Janus-faced performance perpetuated a tough alliance between business interests and modernist governance behind a mask of amiable traditionalism.

Not for them the rhetorical protestations of one of the New Democracy stalwarts from the neighboring village of Anoya, who, with the full majesty of ministerial office, demanded in parliament the ruthless suppression of animal theft on Crete even while he was allegedly arranging to pay for the negation of some of the thieves' trials by bribing witnesses to retract their testimony. A Zoniana shepherd commented on a scene he claimed to have witnessed in the district capital in the late 1970s, "What a joke it was . . . a government minister, now, with the shepherds. With the thieves!"[63] The Neoliberals' strategy, which was later to set them and their successors up in a still ongoing, largely covert struggle for power against the Anoyan strongman and his patrilineal kin within the ranks of the New Democracy party, was to soft-pedal the rhetoric and hide behind their carefully cultivated reputation as amiable pragmatists. They knew that a more laissez-faire stamp was essential to the maintenance of their standing in both the moralistic chambers of parliament and the cynical circles of highland Crete.

The Anoyan adopted a blunter strategy. He relied on that same local cynicism as well as extensive local kinship ties with other politicians and animal thieves to remind his constituents just where their loyalties had better lie. The Neoliberals' softer line may have been decisive in Mitsotakis's bid to lead the New Democracy party. The Anoyan came to a less happy end. Thanks to an angry highlander prepared to break the usual code of silence, he was tried on charges of interfering with witnesses in the trial of a local cannabis producer—essentially doing for his client what he had done for so many animal thieves and anticipating the shift in the focus of illegal activity from sheep to drugs—and died, perhaps from acute embarrassment, while awaiting the outcome of his appeal against a one-year jail sentence.

The Greek idiom of patronage is usually blamed on that reliable bogey, the Ottoman Empire. In fact, however, the inequalities locked in by patron-client relations have a long history that in Western Europe dates back at least to the days of feudal seigneury.[64] As with manners and morals and more generally the fashioning of a Greek national culture, Western European countries played a significant role in giving patronage its twentieth-century form. That relationship is both causal and formal; patron-client relations at the local level reproduce the larger relations between the more powerful Western nations and the Greek nation-state, and reflect the dynamics and pragmatics of crypto-colonialism.[65]

The patron-politicians usually hailed from parties favored by the Western powers, which nevertheless regularly criticized Greece for the endemic "corruption" that in reality they were effectively encouraging. An unexpectedly germane illustration was a high-profile corruption scandal, one of several that have erupted since the 1974 restoration of democracy in Greece.[66] Between 1999 and 2006, Siemens, a huge German conglomerate, bribed politicians as well as some employees of the national Greek telephone company to secure the purchase of security and communications equipment. Several of those charged were preemptively jailed; the trial began in 2017 and ended two years later and fourteen years after the explosive news of the scandal first erupted with prison sentences meted out to twenty-two of those accused.

The Siemens affair was not only a national scandal. It also, surprisingly if somewhat indirectly and selectively, involved Zoniani sentenced at the trial that followed the 2007 clash with the police. These villagers found themselves in the Korydallos central jail in Athens together with some of the former employees of Siemens's Greek subsidiary. The hapless businessmen—people who were "like you," one of the villagers remarked caustically to me, incapable (in other words) of knowing how to behave and especially how to defend themselves in prison—were viewed by most of the other prisoners as traitors who had sold out the nation for personal profit, and were therefore seen as fair targets for the delicate attentions of the tougher jailbirds. In short, they were constantly being beaten up. The Zoniani, however, took exception to this, feeling that their values were insulted by such unmanly bullying, and appointed themselves bodyguards to the Siemens suspects.

Whether it was a cause or an effect of this chain of events, they found themselves being given legal advice by a prominent society lawyer who had himself been accused of involvement in the Siemens affair.[67] One of the most sophisticated of the Zoniana group, a man who was accused of masterminding a plot that he swore had never happened, got onto the phone to this lawyer, now an elderly and distinguished figure in Athens society, hoping (unsuccessfully, as it turned out) to set up a meeting with me. Addressing him by his first name and in the warmest of tones, he assured him of his willingness to do anything he needed. Precisely what was being bargained here was unclear to me, but it did seem that the conversation revealed a relationship that was not entirely one-sided. Requesting a similar favor of another legal expert, now a parliamentary deputy and member of the same clan as the former minister, he adopted the same rhetoric of familiarity and equality. My interlocutor was clearly no ordinary client seeking the protection of his patrons, but a man asking for minor help for a friend in the context of a much larger and mutually beneficial exchange of favors.

At the very least, what these details demonstrate is the deep capillary intrusion of village interests in the highest levels of law and governance. I would for the moment go no further than that; Greece already has a plentiful supply of conspiracy theories.[68] But it is easy to see why, when officials laugh off the idea that the Zoniani have their tentacles into the structures of state governance, their laughter is uneasy and defensive. There is a long history of electoral entanglements between Greek national politics and Cretan clan dynamics.

Noisy Politics: Gunshots and Fireworks

These patron-client relations have also protected the acquisition and retention of an impressive array of heavy weapons—one of the features that the antiterrorism police raids were ostensibly intended to end. Their failure to do so is still the subject of ironic comment in the village; one man claimed that the authorities had found only about 10 percent of what was concealed in and near the village and that most of what they had confiscated was old and out of date. Men in Zoniana make a point of showing off their familiarity with guns. I have already mentioned guns' role in political welcomes; men also go to weddings and baptisms armed with (usually) small arms that they use to signal their joy on such special occasions, but also as symbols of their aggressive masculinity. Larger weapons such as old machine guns left over from World War II were formerly used to start dowry processions, but this practice has been discontinued as part of the larger campaign of public decorum that followed immediately on the 2007 confrontation. Indeed, for several years gunshots (*balothies*) were banned altogether. Gradually, however, they crept back, perhaps as a cautious means of testing whether the authorities were really paying attention. (In this regard, at least, they were not.)

Because gunshots are a sign of joy, they are still disapproved when a recent funeral overshadows happier events such as weddings or baptisms. On one such occasion, the father of the groom, when welcoming the huge crowd he had invited as a demonstration of his standing as a powerful and wealthy shepherd, asked that gunshots be avoided out of respect for the family of a widely respected villager buried just a day earlier.[69] His wishes were respected at first, but suddenly in the middle of the night, after many of us had retired to bed, we were startled by a fusillade—which villagers shrugged off as merely what happens when, as is usual at the gargantuan wedding feasts so beloved by the villagers, men get drunk.

Gunshots raised a double issue. On the one hand there was the sense of decorum that made them inappropriate in the immediate aftermath of a funeral. One man complained that the rapid succession of weddings and funerals taking place in a recent summer made people indifferent to the sadness of their fellow villagers, but it seems that some degree of compression—weddings and funerals following each other in close succession—was unavoidable inasmuch as the demographics meant that the proportion of funerals to weddings was increasing. Despite such constraints, there seemed to be widespread agreement that gunshots should be avoided when others were in mourning; the village is still sufficiently tightly knit for such a request to be thought reasonable.

On the other hand, there was also the question of how far these proud men were prepared to act in ways that might be interpreted as a surrender to the demands of the state, and in particular to the state's known hostility to the bearing of arms—a key component of Zoniana masculinity. Some of the village elders were adamant that from now on the villagers should desist from actions that put people's lives and the village's reputation at risk. But it is clear that others differed and were not prepared to give up a practice that could be justified—as so much else—in the name of tradition. Now, however, since gunshots could not be loosed off in the presence of politicians (who would have been nationally embarrassed by it in a way that the elder Mitsotakis had not confronted), they had become much more unambiguously a mark of irreconcilable difference between the state and the village.

The changing role and status of balothies nevertheless also suggest that the gap between state and village is becoming even less explicit than before. In earlier years, the father of the man who hosted the wedding just mentioned had told a policeman he considered importunate, "We have two laws here," punning on the homonymy between the words for "shoulder" and "law" in the local dialect (*nomos*).[70] In this remark, he was demanding respect for local norms, something he could expect from a police officer well versed in the unwritten laws of the mountain communities and anxious to avoid unnecessary conflict and its potential for ending with bloodshed.

While many Zoniani today nurture similar assumptions about local sovereignty, they are much less likely to articulate them in so many words. Confrontation has not destroyed the imagined polity of the Zoniani, as the persistence of the clan structure indicates, but it has muted the formerly more explicit rejection of state authority. The change is more about style than substance. It may perhaps best be understood in the context of changes in the idiom of masculinity. When I was doing my original fieldwork in Zoniana, men would eat only meat in public and regarded salads and vegetables as unacceptable for true men, their consumption a mark of the femininity associated with failure or code violation in a would-be sheep thief. Today powerful men in the village may admit to a distaste for the carnivorous excesses of the past, and some even boast of the quality of their green produce as a new way of expressing masculine pride. In the same way, in the micro-political arena, they may also parade their masculinity by showing a mastery of the language of compromise, a stance that would have been unthinkable even twenty years earlier.

Their newfound mastery of a more diplomatic mode of engagement does *not* mean that they accept the political implications of compromise as such; most of them have little or no interest in becoming slavish followers of the law. Their social mastery is a mastery of strategy and ruse, as it has always been, and that means—for those who still view the state with distrust, or who pragmatically view negotiating with its officials as an unfortunate but unavoidable necessity—also being able to lull the bureaucrats into at least a semblance of acquiescence. Moreover, along with the other changes in the idiom of local masculinity comes a new understanding of the workings of capitalism. Whereas at the time of my original fieldwork men saw opening a coffeehouse as an important investment in which the display of self-regard (*eghoismos*) that it entailed was also the force that drove entrepreneurs to ever greater success, now there is a new model to which self-regard can be assimilated: that of responsibilization, the neoliberal dismissal of dependence on an unreliable state system in favor of aggressive entrepreneurial activity and the concomitant assumption that the weak, as in the traditional village code, had only their own moral failings to blame for their pitiful state.[71]

In seeking to reduce the bureaucrats' interest in their affairs, the Zoniani may have succeeded to some degree. The village is visibly surviving. There is little obvious official oversight of the village now, although it is not clear whether this is because the authorities have relaxed their vigilance or because, to the contrary, they are still intent on building up the conveniently self-fulfilling prophecy that represents Zoniana as that wild and untrodden zone of legend. Boys of ten or twelve ably drive pickup trucks at high speed through the village and on the surrounding roads without the slightest interference from the police; a prominent village official has run a makeshift restaurant without a permit; and guns and knives are once again appearing as necessary accessories to male dress, although for the most part more discreetly than in years gone by (fig. 4.2).

Most villagers—those who advocate for official styles of civility as well as those who hanker for the aggressive masculinity of the past—agree that the

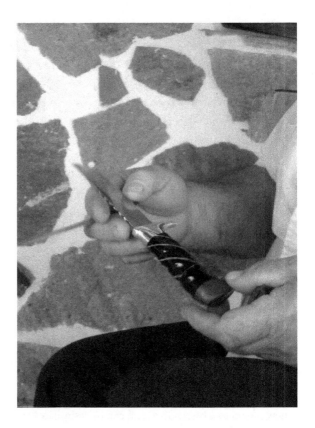

FIGURE 4.2. Testing a Knife: Zoniana. Photograph by author.

ambush that led to the police officer's eventual death was a dreadful, stupid mistake. But the reason for which so many Zoniani take that position speaks less to a sudden attack of collective conscience than to two more plausible factors: their long-standing view that such wild behavior, which was not approved by the village collectively, is destructive and morally wrong; and the untoward official attention, now fading, that it brought the entire village. A few more deliberate souls even celebrate the moral cleansing that the aftermath of the ambush brought on the village as a whole, while others, more opportunistically, note that the state began to invest more in infrastructure as a way of strengthening those civic attitudes and the individuals who represented them.

In Pom Mahakan, there were no guns. When the residents wanted noise, they would ignite fireworks, often while also projecting loud music through the community's broken-down public address system. The fireworks were often set off on the curbside next to the community's fireworks shop. Where some Zoniani delighted in testing the limits of legality with their gunfire, demonstrating the politicians' complicity and daring all comers to challenge their protected status, the Chao Pom had no such room for provocation. While rumors abounded that the fireworks were illegal, the fact that they were sold from a curbside location right outside the community's main gate suggests otherwise. Unlike the Zoniana gunshots, the fireworks—which were just as noisy but a good deal less dangerous—were not, as far as I could ascertain, illegal, or even manufactured in the community; at the worst, firing them off from the public curbside could have been construed as a basis for official intervention.[72] By this point, however, the question of legality was immaterial. The residents' reputation as lawbreakers was already widely touted as justification for the impending eviction.

This contrast reveals another, perhaps more significant difference. Where the Zoniani were willing to confront state officials head-on, knowing that powerful politicians were widely believed to be complicit in some of their illegal activities, the Chao Pom, cognizant of their weak support network, instead typically engaged officials in a game of much shorter-lived expectations. In that contest, exaggerated politeness underscored the officials' arrogance but denied them, as far as possible, any pretext for hostile action. To some bureaucrats the Chao Pom spoke with elaborate courtesy and honorific pronouns; to other officials, they affected a fragile mutual intimacy through the perfunctory performance of good manners—a *wai* made too rapidly, a respectful kinship term (*phi*, "elder sibling") prefixed to a nickname. These affectations of courtesy and intimacy made for subtle theater, but also made it clear that the Chao Pom had reached the limits of their power to influence outcomes. They had, in a sense that hits home in Thai more deeply than in English, been brought low.

Topographies of Status and Morality

The symbolism of height provides an additional arena of comparison between Zoniana and Pom Mahakan. The Cretan villagers' understanding of the moral topography is explicitly laid out in their rules of etiquette, especially those concerning ways of greeting. They follow highly formalized rules for greeting in the coffeehouse, on the steep paths that connect them with the summer pastures, and on the roads leading down to the cities and plains.[73] The physically lower person must always be the first to acknowledge the higher with a solemn expression of respect. It is the implications of this simple rule—that the mountains are morally superior to the plains and cities corrupted by an excess of power—that the state bureaucracy has never shown any interest in learning. It is the same subtle symbolic inversion of brute inequality that we find in the internal logic of hospitality, whereby a powerful guest is at the host's moral mercy. This assumption of the moral high ground informs both the solidarity internal to the community and the solidarity extended to those hapless migrants the state has marginalized and illegalized in the same way that it has marginalized and illegalized the polity of "untrodden" Zoniana.

While there is no ambiguity about these rules in the village, they exist only in vestigial form, if at all, among urban Greeks. That difference, for the Zoniani, is itself a sign of their moral superiority and greater civility in relation to the rest of the population and, especially, to the bureaucrats. In Pom Mahakan, by contrast, the residents reproduced a modality of etiquette (*marayat*) that was instantly recognizable to any Thai. The symbol of Bangkok itself is the image of the god Rama atop an elephant—the god incarnated in all the kings of the ruling (Bangkok) dynasty, riding on the royal animal, and surveying his subjects from a great height and distance.

In Thai public life, the appearance of a royal personage often requires a sudden rearrangement of bodies, as no commoner may be seen physically located anywhere above the head of a member of the royal family. The expression of status through height, thus exemplified, is reproduced in countless everyday contexts. Community leaders in Pom Mahakan were especially careful to follow these principles. In greeting a highly respected elder, especially one who had worked for the palace, the community president would *wai* his greeting so that his clasped palms would obscure his face. When he wanted to show how conditional his respect was toward city police performing the hated bureaucrats' orders, he would still raise his palms to a respectful level, but would rush the gesture so that it would be understood as perfunctory.

The residents certainly understood this play with relative height as political symbolism. The layout of community meetings clearly embodied that understanding, as community members easily and un-self-consciously slipped into postures appropriate to their relative social positions.[74] The preoccupation with height is not an invention of the modern Thai state; it is fundamental to the ritual practices of rural villages in northern Thailand, for example, and is probably common to all polities of moeang type, but it continues to pervade everyday comportment and interaction today and is reinforced by a common awareness of royal protocol.[75]

I end the present chapter with these images of height as the expression of moral status to make a larger point. At first sight, there is a radical difference between the two communities. Zoniana is an aggressively egalitarian but competitive society; status springs from individual prowess, social and physical. The Chao Pom, by contrast, remained at least nominally devoted to the palace, and maintained the hierarchical idioms of respect that are expressed through the symbolism of height and that connect the humblest communities to the royal realm. Their code of conduct marks the moral community that conjoins all Thais—royalty and commoners, elder siblings and younger siblings—in a single, acutely status-differentiated realm.

There is nonetheless an important area of convergence between the symbolism of height in the two communities. In Thai and Greek, as in English, being "below" is demeaning. Greeks famously resent being "employees," *ipallili*, a word that literally denotes being "under others." Zoniana and Pom Mahakan both perform codes of etiquette that both accept that spatial symbolism and deploy it for their own tactical ends. The difference is that, in Zoniana, greater height confers *moral* superiority while acknowledging *political* weakness. Thai symbolism is more one-dimensional. The Chao Pom, enmeshed in city life and in the symbolic system that placed royalty at the apex of society, repeatedly enacted their subjugation in their daily interactions with officialdom. While the Zoniani have been able to recoup their losses to some extent, their already impressive domination of city and plains a material comfort at the time of their collective humiliation, the Chao Pom had no external sources of wealth, were caught in the logic of their adherence to the rules of marayat, and consequently were eventually unable—brief flashes of creative impudence notwithstanding—to assert their moral right to collective survival. Razing their homes to the ground was the final abasement, the final palpable proof that neither public support nor covert patronage could save them from their karmic destiny. They had now, quite literally, been razed to the physically and symbolically lowest level of human existence.

The State in Context

A central assumption of much political theory, and especially of approaches characterized as "methodological nationalism," is that the nation-state is the primary unit of territorial and cultural organization.[1] From this perspective, there is only one basic kind of polity; all nation-states are variants on that grand schema. The success of the colonial powers in imposing a broadly common vision of governance extended far beyond the parts of the globe that they controlled directly. Virtually no country today lacks the main lineaments of this exported nation-state model.

Subversive archaism suggests that the state is not the only acceptable or most venerable form of polity. But what is a polity? If it is not (always) a formal bureaucratic organization but sometimes instead a shared way of life or an evanescent moment of mutual understanding, it may be more useful to begin not by looking at formal structures of governance but by investigating the forms of urbanity and civility that it encompasses.

Three terms that appear to be etymologically related—*polity*, *politics*, and *police*—comprise a scale of increasing formalization and regimentation. Etymology is often used for legitimating power and cultural authority, as both the Greek state and the Zoniani use it, but it can also be used conversely, as a challenge to the assumptions that underlie that power.[2] In that sense, etymology is like civility, with its two faces as, respectively, generosity in the face of difference, and an all-encompassing, repressive, and rule-governed politeness. The modalities of civility, as Sharika Thiranagama has astutely noted, "can conflict with each other, given that civility can be either hierarchically produced or governed by an egalitarian drive toward public forms of dignity and equality."[3]

When we write of *civility* and *etymology*, we are using words of Latin and Greek derivation, respectively. These etymological connections, like the classical orders of architecture in colonial universities and administrative buildings, function as signs of unquestionable authority. They echo long after the demise of the colonial *imperium*. The classical architectural orders continue to decorate the buildings of the wealthy and influential, including their imposing shopping malls, from Bangkok to Singapore and Shanghai. In the same way, words like *civility* and *civilization* preserve the normative ring of Latin just as do the Greek-derived *politics* and the adjective *politic*—a terms that combine politeness or civility with awareness of the consequences of a tactless or inappropriate action.[4] The city (especially the *capital city*) serves as the model and primary point of reference for ideas of civility and civilization (which are often conflated with each other and with the dual meaning of *urbanity*).[5]

This normativity so long attributed by colonial leaders to ancient Greek and Latin can and must be questioned. The easiest and most subversive way to do this is by appealing to the modern languages. Since the Western powers for so long treated the modern Greek nation as a debased version of an antique original, and since Western Europeans have often decried in modern Italy the decline of ancient Roman discipline, examining the fate of these terms in their modern incarnations allows us to rescue alternative interpretations to those imposed on the global hierarchy of cultural value by the most powerful countries of the age of empires.

Again, this duality fits the ambiguity of civility. One can insist on a code of manners that constantly reinstalls an aristocratic or upper-bourgeois aesthetic as the incontestable sole criterion of acceptable comportment; or one can instead work with the Italian notion of being *civili* in the sense of generosity to those others who do not necessarily fit the canon. In Italy, a country where the authority of the state has traditionally been weak, a mischievous awareness of the fragility and contingency of legal arrangements prioritizes social solidarity over formal obedience. Being *civili* means living tolerantly and politely with difference; it means getting on with a disparate range of neighbors, sometimes, should that be necessary, in defiance of the law.[6] It is about embracing the multiplicity of cultural forms that urban life offers; it encompasses the possibility of conflict and difference, but within a shared commitment to muddle through to some form of acceptable accommodation.[7] Even the treasured concept of *civiltà*, which can only weakly be translated as "civilization" and seems very far removed from the repressive Thai adjective *siwilai* that is also derived from the same root via English, favors the model of the more democratic medieval polity over that of imperial Rome, the latter tainted to this day by the memory of Mussolini's militaristic self-projection as a reincarnation of the Caesars.

Slipping from Latin to Italian thus resocializes concepts such as "civilization" and "civility." Given the major role that classical education played in the colonial project, this is a significantly insubordinate move; it challenges the arrogant self-assurance of the colonial cultural project—of what the French call, significantly, *la mission civilisatrice*.[8] What works for the Latin languages, moreover, works even more dramatically for Greek. The condescending or even contemptuous attitude that many foreign scholars in Athens formerly entertained toward the modern language has waned almost exactly in tandem with the increasing and noteworthy role of Greek archaeologists in deconstructing the effects of neoclassicism on modern Greece's national identity politics—a remarkable reversal for a discipline that along with folklore initially provided the bedrock scholarship that legitimized the emergence of the new nation-state and its civilizational aspirations.[9] While a repressive version of being "civilized" (*politismeni*) has long held sway in the rhetoric of the Greek bourgeoisie and the state bureaucracy, there are now new civilities and solidarities that question the old order, especially when they are wielded by citizens who do not see in the state the incarnation and guardian of national virtue that it claims to be.

What Is a Polity?

Both theologians and anthropologists, in their very different ways and for significantly different ends, have used the concept of polity to denote a system of governance that is significantly more generic than the idea of the state and is informed by an ethic of shared understandings of the universe. It as much cosmological as political. Beyond this rather vague formulation, anthropologists have not often seen the term as needing theoretical elaboration.[10]

The origins of the term *polity* are straightforward. It is derived from Greek *politia* (classical *politeia*). In the standard literary Greek of today, *politia* has a treble meaning: as a political system; as a city in its dual role as the symbolic center of power and as the fount of human refinement; and as a mode of social existence—what we would more informally call a "way of life."[11] It is useful here to recall that the original title of the Kazantzakis novel on which the film *Zorba the Greek* was based is *The Life and* Politia *of Alexis Zorbas*. Zorba, the endearingly rambunctious antihero, inhabits a universe animated by emotion, feeling, and pleasure, and comfortably disregards the formalism of intellectuals and bureaucrats. His is a polity that allows for individual inventiveness, cunning, ingenious adaptation, and utter contempt for the narrow life of "pen-pushers" (*kalamaradhes*). It is the living antithesis of official pedantry.

Zorba's polity is the space of freedom from ponderous self-importance, made visually and musically explicit in Michael Cacoyannis's film rendition. "Dance? Did you say . . . *dance*? Come on my boy!" And to the plangent twang of the bouzoukia ringing out Mikis Theodorakis's music there on the deserted beach, Zorba pulls the now-willing young author's body away from the deceptive traps encircling his mind, away from the conventions of state and school, into the accelerating pulse of the dance—a discipline no less ordered and no less intelligent than the formal structures of law and logic, but one that liberates the soul instead of caging it.

In this sense, the idea of the polity resonates especially well with the story of Pom Mahakan, where the preservation of a way of life (*witthichiwit*) was the community's most forceful and most public claim to legitimacy in the eyes of the larger Thai public. In this sense, the polity is an ethical space: it is the consensual community reached by people acting with full awareness of constructing a distinctive social environment. Like the Zoniani, the Chao Pom made moral and existential claims for their polity. Their polity served as a reminder that what today seem like aberrations from the reality of an ethnonationalist modernity—including an ability to absorb people of varied ethnic and regional identity—once constituted the norm associated with kingly power.

The polity presented by the Chao Pom is one that Italians would recognize as *civile*. That does not mean that we would find all such ways of life morally acceptable. How, for example, should one react to the (English-language) graffito in Rome that pronounced "Fascism a Way of Life" (fig. 5.1)? Fascism, like neoliberalism, has always presented itself as an ethical system, and, as such, must also be credited with a vision of the ideal polity, albeit one that is violent and exclusionary—the very opposite of what we see in Pom Mahakan. Even leaving aside the state, not all polities are truly civil. But the concept of polity does have plenty of space for civility as an attitude of generosity and openness.

Such openness defies the exclusivism of the ethnonational state. It also exemplifies and celebrates an amiable mixture of complicity and disobedience; it prioritizes social relations, patronage included, over the letter of the law. Colleagues at a Chinese university I visited some years ago assured me that the anticorruption ban on official banquets for more than five persons would not be observed for more than a couple of months after promulgation. They were right, as it turned out, for reasons that Hans Steinmüller's *Communities of Complicity* would subsequently also confirm: everyone understands both the necessity of

FIGURE 5.1. A Revenant Fascist Polity? Photograph by author.

announcing such laws and the state's pragmatic complicity in allowing their force to evaporate.[12]

One common meaning of *politia* in Greek is that of the formal bureaucratic state. Translating the term as "state," however, does not convey its implications. Solemnly dignified with a capital initial letter, it has a strongly admonitory flavor, suggesting that the institution or group of political actors thus named is not doing its job properly and is now being called to account. In other words, even by its own standards this formal Polity falls short. Here are two topical examples. In the first, published in a center-left newspaper under the eye-catching heading "Holy Broadside from the Monks of Mount Athos," we read that the monks, from their sequestered eyrie, condemned "the Polity" for agreeing to allow the incorporation of the name of Macedonia into the official title of the neighboring Balkan state.[13] That action had clearly offended the monks, who supported the nationalistic position that Macedonia could only be an exclusively Greek name. In the second example, a leftist newspaper straightfacedly reported the conservative New Democracy party's limp reaction to the vandalizing of the Thessaloniki Holocaust memorial: "the Politia must be even stricter in confronting such phenomena."[14] Theoretically, the Polity in these finger-wagging statements is the state itself. The implication, however, is that its egregious failure to represent the will of the people is the fault of its bureaucrats, collectively known as the state (*kratos*). The kratos, in other words, is the inefficient, corrupt, and unworthy managerial staff of the Polity.

The kratos comprises the formal structure of governance and the bureaucrats who carry out that task, and this entity is just one of many possible polities that co-exist. Anthropologists of Greece have long noted the disdain most Greeks express for the kratos, which they see as a foreign-imposed straitjacket on the *ethnos*; it is a very different polity from that imagined by Cretan highlanders.[15] Ironically calling the kratos "Politia" reminds us that, for all their moralizing about wickedness in Zoniana, the journalists are also Greek; and, as Greeks, they are no more enamored of the state than are the villagers. They, too, and as professional observers, have noted its moral failures, which is presumably why they sometimes seem to delight in official discomfiture—as when they point a derisive finger at allegations of police ineptness in Zoniana.

The semantic richness of the Greek term indexes many possible varieties of polity. These may include individualistic ones like Zorba's, the imagined ideal Polity invoked by the journalists just quoted, and long-lasting ideas reflecting older and partially forgotten ways of life and surfacing only when the state's inadequacies become apparent. My present use of "polity" includes all of these, as well as the sense of *politia* as the city as a seat of power and the lifestyle associated with government. This last usage is common in Zoniana, whereas in standard Greek speech the more neutral term *poli(s)* more neutrally indexes an urban place. A polity is always social before it is physical, but its physical context is understood as the material basis for its incarnation as a way of life.

Alternative Polities

The disobedient lifestyles of places like Pom Mahakan and Zoniana are no less aptly described as polities than are the administrative structures controlled by the ruling classes. But they follow different rules and social principles. Many aspects of Zoniana life, for example, would strike outsiders as exotic, even bizarre. It is thus, unsurprisingly, on these—reciprocal animal theft, blood feuds, and cannabis cultivation—that the more sensationalizing journalists seize as grist to the mill of calumny.

Are these features really so extraneous to the universe of Western normalcy? Such features do in fact lurk not so far back in the history of the most formal nation-states. Not only was patrilineal descent an important organizing principle for many of the medieval and early modern European aristocracies, and again in the nineteenth century, but people were executed for stealing animals in incidents that remain in popular memory—a sign that they were no more condemned locally than they are in Zoniana today. From the hanging of one of my wife's distant English ancestors for stealing a sheep—an incident that surely enhanced our status in Zoniana!—to a Swiss acquaintance's recall of the execution of one of his ancestors for a similar offense in medieval times, there are hints that such things were commonplace all over Europe in a less bureaucratically controlled era. Perhaps an awareness of that much earlier stage in the state's campaign for social hegemony lingers not far beyond consciousness even today.[16]

While these memories may linger as romantic folklore, their persistence in contemporary society is not something any nation-state wants to see treated as heritage. They are not part of that authorized discourse. The persistence of reciprocal theft and revenge killings nonetheless remains an important part of the popular inheritance of values in some places and for some people. From time to time these values' recrudescence as polity—as a "way of life" now suppressed as primitive lawlessness—inflames the glowing embers of subversive archaism. The militias of the western mountain areas of the United States are the ideological heirs of the Hatfields and McCoys. Despite its ideological purism, moreover, state law sometimes exhibits traces of similar attitudes. The misleadingly named legal category of victims' rights allows relatives to view the execution of a kinsperson's murderer; it does not restore the life of the actual victim but acknowledges those kinsfolk as an extension of the victim's personhood. In other countries, customary law may explicitly take primacy, as when the patrilineal kin of a murder victim in Saudi Arabia decide the murderer's fate. In short, there are aspects of official law that preserve, and may reignite, the moral defense of reciprocal violence that the law in other situations condemns as illicit revenge.

Viewing communities that do not conform to a national code as polities in their own right may not be so difficult, once we separate the concept of polity from the more restrictive one of state. A further and perhaps more intractable difficulty with the idea of the polity is that some polities exist only in moments of intense encounter. The consensual and contingent sense of the polity as a way of life varies in tangibility; its hide-and-seek quality, so useful in the face of bureaucratic intransigence, is hardly likely to endear it to humorless officials.

Gregory Feldman uses the word *polity* in precisely this sense when he examines the community of undercover agents tracking and at times engaging with illegalized migrants in Europe. He argues that these agents and migrants together "constitute a polity, however fleeting, based on their own worldly viewpoints."[17] His reading of polity comes close to Étienne Balibar's reading of civility as a moment of mutual understanding in which people collaborate to institutionalize their resistance to violence, regardless of whether the violence originates with organized crime or springs from the power of the state.[18] Unlike states, some polities may lack formal bureaucratic structures and written legal codes, but they offer a space for the pursuit of common interests and the exploration of differing views by people forced, however briefly, into proximity. The recognition of a social arrangement as a polity does presuppose, at least in theory, some degree of active engagement in the production of civility. In a polity, people seek common cause, whether or not they succeed in achieving that goal. Dictators, for all their talk of order, eviscerate the state of all but rhetorical traces of polity.

In contrast to Balibar's attempt to work toward a general definition of civility, Feldman adopts a focus that is thoroughly ethnographic. In this, and in his important recognition that polities do not require institutional arrangements, he comes closer to the model proposed by Shigeharu Tanabe for the emergence of communities—or a sense of *communitas* in Victor Turner's usage—among marginalized groups in Thailand. Tanabe's argument has high relevance for the Pom Mahakan case.[19] Both Tanabe and Feldman focus on the recognition of a *potentiality*, of a sense of polity that appears inchoate but inspires loyalty and provides a context for action. Such recognition entails an opportunistic engagement that does not necessarily affect the long-term persistence of structural violence but instead creates a civility tailored to specific, real-life interactions—some of them between officials and the heterogeneous population under their charge.[20]

The transient nature of the polity in this sense—of a potentiality not always realized in practice—partially explains why it has been so hard to grasp. The polity does not always have an easily apprehended structure; in these more fleeting forms, it seems intangible. Yet Feldman's identification of the polity in such evanescent moments is crucial for understanding the human capacity for openness. This is a polity that too easily fades from view when confronted by the rigid structure, Weber's famous iron cage, that is the price we pay for the conveniences of modernity. Yet it never entirely dissipates. Zorba is always lurking somewhere in Pericles's shadow.[21]

Feldman's insight thus encourages us to view these small communities of subversive archaists as polities. For much of the time, they simply present themselves as segments of a larger national society. Their emergence as polities partakes of the evanescence that Feldman describes. Official intransigence often eventually forces them to acknowledge what binds them together as a moral community. Their moments of greatest danger arise when they become tangible as alternatives to the state. When the Chao Pom recognized the humanity of the soldiers and officials who were tormenting them, they were refusing the logic of the governing polity; their compassion for their implacable foes, and especially for the poor workers who were obliged to carry out the demolition, made them seem perilously *different*. In this, too, they had become too tangible, too easily reified as something with a tangible identity (*tua ton*) beyond the state's control or even comprehension.[22]

Much the same can be said about the situation on Crete. Except at times of high crisis, the encounters between Zoniani and uniformed enforcers of state power tend to restrained politeness leavened, perhaps, by a touch of malicious humor on the part of the villagers—as, for example, when they treated a police patrol to a sumptuous meal and then told them they had eaten all the evidence of the animal theft they were supposed to be investigating.[23] Since there was now no evidence, the police had no legal recourse to do anything other than gracefully accept their tactical defeat. In such moments, the villagers' polity, much like the Soqotrans' hospitality to Yemeni state bureaucrats, encapsulates the state's representatives. But their mischievous humor also exposes the fault lines between the state's and the villagers' respective ideas of polity; bureaucracies do not generally exhibit much humor at all.

It was also occasionally possible to discern fleeting moments of collusion between the two sides. The villagers' polity expanded, in such moments, to encapsulate officials they already knew and with whom they could share a degree of sympathetic amusement or practical complicity. Much as the Chao Pom leaders might address a jovial but clearly ill-intentioned Bangkok city official with an affectionate-sounding nickname, preceded by a respectful but familiar term of address, Zoniani would address police officers and politicians by their given names, thereby assuming a familiarity that sometimes created moments of apparent empathy. Such expansions of non-state polities to incorporate state officials are frequent—but they are forever fragile and may even be a form of entrapment. Actual collusion, especially patronage, must be kept discreet.

Civility and Racism: When the State Becomes Impolitic and Uncivil

Heath Cabot has emphasized the more sinister side of the *police-polity* connection, suggesting that the Greek police commit acts of constitutionally unsanctioned violence, and do so with impunity. The Zoniani would endorse that view even as they cite occasional instances of police compassion or helpfulness.

In particular, the villagers were furious that a police officer had allegedly warned some of them about the search that triggered the fatal ambush. Even if the officers' goal was to ensure that they would find no weapons or drugs and therefore avoid a great deal of trouble, the villagers regarded such maneuvers as self-interested, not as altruistic. In general, villagers viewed the police as hostile, devious, and dishonest. I heard detailed accounts of extortion by police officers who would dig up cannabis on the Zoniana side of the village border but not on the other side: "they didn't see it, because they didn't want to. [The Zonianos] wouldn't pay them off." Later, as the trade took hold, said this same informant, one police officer was caught warning his friends in the village that a raid was imminent—a precursor of what happened in 2007. "They [the police authorities] discovered what he'd done afterwards. They 'roasted' [punished] him; he left" the force. But that did not increase the villagers' respect for a police force in which such illegality should never have occurred at all. On another occasion this same villager was hauled off five times to the provincial capital, Rethimno, for interrogation about a field where some cannabis plants had clearly been removed in anticipation of a raid. Asked over and over whose plants they had been, he finally exploded: "You, who warned them so they could remove the planting, why do you ask *me*? The one who warned them, you know him!" At that point, realizing their own peril, they finally let him go.

Another Zonianos insisted that the first cannabis had been brought to the village by a police officer, who then tried to entrap two Zoniani into joining him in trading it. One of his intended dupes suspected a trap and excused himself saying that he had to go and vaccinate his sheep. Already uneasy at this turn of events, the other villager saw a police car where none should have been and realized that his suspicious colleague had been right. He managed to dispose of the cannabis so that when the police stopped him "they searched him and didn't find anything on him, so they let him go free." Then, later on, "he ran into the policeman who'd pretended to be his friend" and accused the man of setting him up "so you could bolster your position [in the force]." This, remarked my interlocutor, is how "the law forced the citizen [*politis*] into outlawry [*evale ton politi stin paranomia*]." The speaker points up the irony of a self-defeating state that sends the villager back into his own, technically lawless polity—the place that the media mockingly called, as another villager recalled, "the independent state of Zoniana."[24] The villagers find themselves entrapped in a self-fulfilling prophecy, made all the more ineluctable by enhanced visibility at the national level. The stage for confrontation is set.

Greece's rural police force has evolved from what was officially a gendarmerie (*khorofilaki*, literally guardianship of place) to a specifically urban-based entity (*astinomia*, the body that regulates the city). The city has now officially taken control of the entire country: the *politia* as urban center has occupied the *politia* as the space of civil life. Urbanity, or civility, has become an uncivil weapon. This shift in the status of the police has accompanied (and perhaps explains) the gradual loss of a respectful and knowing mutuality between police officers and villagers and the emergence of a more literal interpretation of the duties and rights of the police—an interpretation that leaves no space for the villagers' traditionalism. I once addressed a police academy whose commanders were of the old school, but whose cadets were focused only on eradicating what they saw as the criminality of the mountain villages; the officers preferred negotiation, but the cadets saw any concession to tradition as demeaning and, almost impertinently snubbing their officers' more temperate approach, demanded immediate and violent repression.

Cabot's recognition of the police-polity connection also allows for the occasional flashback to the idea of polity. Amid all the (often convincing) accusations of far-right sympathies and arrogant behavior on the part of many police officers, there are brief moments of transcendence by the occasional police officer who, like Rozakou's complicit immigration official, and indeed like the bureaucrat who helps to generate Feldman's evanescent moment of true polity, works from a position of personal empathy with those over whom he has been granted power. On the one hand, as Cabot points out, these more well-disposed police officers are implicated in smoothing the surveillance work of the state; their presence may not be as benign in effect as it appears on the surface.[25] On the other hand, it always raises the possibility of that fleeting, evanescent sense of polity—of empathy and decency—that is *not* exclusively dedicated to surveillance and control.

Ambiguous cases of this kind certainly appeared in both Pom Mahakan and Zoniana. In Pom Mahakan, interactions with the city police were often cordial, even jocular, and some residents maintained a friendly mien even when talking to their most implacable foes in the city bureaucracy. Until the endgame, the police had always tended to compromise with the residents, which is also why, as I was told, the residents were not afraid of the police. They were, however, afraid of the army; and events were to prove their worst fears right.

In Zoniana, acts of individual empathy and compassion still point to a truly civil form of polity that sometimes emerges in relations between citizens and police. When a disgruntled villager complained that during the lockdown officers had ripped up the plastic tubing he had installed as a makeshift irrigation system, justifying their malicious act on the grounds that such a system could only have been used for cultivating cannabis (it was not), one of the more senior officers intervened and made the rogue police officers replace the tubing—a physically demanding task. Such moments have often been observed in the brief encounters between police and migrants suspected of illegal entry into Greece as well. It is precisely here that Feldman sees that fleeting sense of polity. That polity corresponds to a social decency that has little or nothing to do with the letter of the law.

Conversely, however, the calumnies heaped on these communities by state bureaucrats are decidedly uncivil. They also reveal the hierarchy of identities on which both the residents and the bureaucrats based their moral claims. Police murmurings that the Zoniani are not merely criminals but also "not real Cretans" (with doubly racist aspersions cast on their supposedly "Gypsy" ancestry) match Thai bureaucratic accusations that Pom Mahakan is full of drug addicts and prostitutes and in any case "not a real Thai community" (because it does not fit the bureaucratic model of a community growing from a single kin-group and engaged in a single profession).[26] In emphasizing their identity as Thais ("we are Thai people"), the Chao Pom claimed participation in national sovereignty and thus also in a generic right to inhabit the land, pushing back against the official tendency to equate Thainess with a middle-class sensibility and to treat ethnic minorities as well as the urban poor as karmically undeserving of full inclusion.[27] As Giuseppe Bolotta says of poor urban Thais in general, and especially those with ethnic minority status, the ruling classes regard such people as *insufficiently* Thai.[28] In this view, the purest distillation of Thainess (*khwam pen thai*) appears in the upper-class manners and mores promulgated under the Phibun regime and reinvigorated today by its current successors; ironically, as we shall see, this cultural complex seems to owe more to European than to indigenous models. It thus often provokes a negative reaction among working-class Thais even when they seem to be paying lip service to it. The Chao Pom, although insistent that they were true Thais, also acknowledged that some of them were of northeastern (Isan) origin (and would therefore be viewed by the elite as more Lao than Thai).[29] In their cultural activities, the Chao Pom both performed Thainess and parodied and inverted the state's claim to be its sole arbiter.

The unofficially expressed racism of people in official positions has a deep history in both Greece and Thailand, where it was especially intense during the Cold War. Greek royalist authorities treated all alleged communists as "Bulgarians," even forcing them to Slavicize their surnames to justify their eventual expulsion from Greek territory. In Thailand during the student uprising of 1976, the military claimed that the student protesters were Vietnamese (and therefore communists), attempting thereby to justify the murderous attack that followed.

In the case of subversive archaism, such ethnicized labeling is especially significant because it counters the residents' claims to represent a truer form of national identity. Calling the Zoniani "Gypsies" and the Chao Pom a ragtag band of people of mixed origins was perhaps the most wounding insinuation among the verbal attacks that preceded the violence.[30] These accusations, which conform to the pattern Heatherington in her ethnography of Orgosolo calls "cultural racisms," provoke a counter-essentialism of communal solidarity and accentuate the appeal of subversive archaism.[31] On the other side of the Thai-Lao border, Phill Wilcox has shown that members of the Hmong minority in Laos use their apparent acquiescence in the government's assimilationist policies to promote their openly acknowledged desires for a better education—and, thereby, their private dream of a separate Hmong political entity with the Hmong language as its official tongue. Assimilationism does not win hearts and minds; at best, it can command expressions of fealty. But it also offers cover for other alternatives, especially among those who prefer, for the moment, to avoid rocking the national boat.[32]

The bureaucratic racism underlying the full range of exclusivist and assimilationist policies means that even members of the ethnic majority, faced with attacks on their cultural purity, may feel constrained to assert intense ethnic allegiance. This is what has happened in both Pom Mahakan and Zoniana. In neither place has it led the communities to adopt the racism of the state, perhaps because they themselves feel victimized by it.

To put these attitudes in a larger and contemporary context, we should note that both Greece and Thailand are facing significant influxes of foreign migrants—in Greece, from Africa and the Middle East; in Thailand, from Myanmar and Cambodia. The resulting crises have intensified the racialization of, and hostility toward, foreigners of obviously different appearance and low economic status. Police officers routinely assume that any unknown assailant or thief must belong to one of these despised groups and could not possibly be local, even if many ordinary people reject the incivility of such state-sanctioned (or unofficially official) assumptions and engage in acts of solidarity with the persecuted outsiders.[33] It is remarkable that in neither of the two communities have I ever heard the kind of racist discourse that fascists direct at those who do not fit their ethnonationalist vision.[34]

The challenge to identity, however, is not the main issue for these local communities, despite their frequent invocation of nationality as the basis of the rights they accuse the state of disregarding. They would probably not bother to assert nationalist values without the external provocation of the state, but in fact they both represent extremes of this kind of rhetoric—in Zoniana with their invocations of millennia of national history, in Pom Mahakan with declarations of total fealty to land, monarch, and religion. These are assertions of collective dignity in the face of hostile bureaucracies. Dignity is the coinage of civility, and adequate housing is widely understood to be an important requirement for its achievement. The state, with its threats of eviction and demolition and of prison and exile, constitutes the most serious threat to civility from the local perspective.[35]

In earlier times, as we have seen, both Zoniana and Pom Mahakan enjoyed more civil relationships, in this socially accommodating sense of civility, with their respective police forces. In Pom Mahakan, collaborative relations between residents and police eroded in response to the increasing militarization of the Thai nation-state and the breakdown of old patronage networks. The police themselves—often suspected of pro-Thaksin sympathies—were increasingly subjected to military surveillance, which cast a long shadow over their involvement with local communities.[36] Similarly, police respect for the tough men of Zoniana seems to have faded with the increasing bureaucratization of the force and with its growing penetration by ultra-rightist ideas.[37] At the very moment in which the police were damning the Zoniani as beyond the pale of civilized behavior, they were themselves engaging in acts of spite that looked remarkably like petty distortions of the Cretan code of vengeance they had sworn to suppress.

Advantages of Minority Status?

The incivility of the authorities is an attitude of exclusion, a conceptual frontier that corresponds to the characterization of the local territory as remote and untrodden. Again, just as some members of the police (and of the public) cast aspersions on the Greekness of the Zoniani, the Bangkok authorities have tried to attack the genuineness of the Chao Pom's Thainess. These racist attacks, intentionally or otherwise, reciprocated the communities' negative opinion of the bureaucrats as foreign-dominated betrayers of national virtue.

In this context, it is revealing that the city government would allegedly have been more generous to Pom Mahakan had the community been composed of a specific minority.[38] A bureaucrat compared Pom Mahakan with Ban Khrua, a Cham Muslim community established by royal charter under Rama I. That royal charter was probably Ban Khrua's main guarantee of security, but Ban

Khrua also posed no challenge to bureaucratic identity management since its claims were precisely about *not* being ethnically Thai. In the same way, during a period when Muslim communities throughout China were increasingly pressured to abandon their religious traditions, local Chinese relocation authorities favored a Muslim (Hui) community, thought to be at risk of becoming restive, over a majority (Han) community.[39] Minority status does at least mean that communities so designated are not competing with the central authorities over the definition and content of national culture.

Persecuting a minority requires little effort in terms of public relations with the majority population, but is understood to entail risks ranging from internal terrorism to external interference—risks that can be conjured up in a rhetoric that demands national solidarity in the face of any real insubordination. This, for example, has been the Chinese policy in Xinjiang, but also, conversely, explains the Chinese authorities' relative restraint in dealing with the much less disaffected Muslim Hui of Xi'an. In the latter case, the authorities clearly hoped to avoid confrontation. Their policy appears to vacillate, opportunistically perhaps, between violent repression and judicious compromise.

By contrast, persecuting people who claim quintessential majority identity requires a complex campaign of preemptive justification. Such a campaign must accuse the community of betrayal, illegality, and ethnic impurity.[40] In the increasingly nationalistic Thai state, the logic of diversity that underlay the Siamese polity has largely yielded to more monochromatic ideals of citizenship; Pom Mahakan's invocation of diversity was ignored as merely unmannerly.[41] The residents' multiple geographical origins, in which the older doctrine might have recognized a microcosm of the entire Thai polity, became a liability and a mark of something *lacking* in their Thainess.

Minorities are a generic problem for ethnonationalist regimes.[42] But they do not threaten the *cultural* legitimacy of the state. If they are small enough to be contained or even favored, they provide useful propaganda material inasmuch as they seem to attest to the regime's tolerance and generosity, as in the case, already mentioned, of the Khmer speakers of Thailand's Surin province.[43] Even if they rebel, their actions do not challenge the state's claim to represent the national culture; they simply feed existing prejudices that provide an easy pretext for repression. The only archaism possible for them is that of claiming aboriginality, which sets them apart from the historically intrusive majority; indigeneity, as Ronald Niezen has argued, rests on political arrangements that generally work against seriously undermining the authority of the bureaucratic state.[44] By contrast, communities that belong to the ethnic majority but do not passively accept the official version of tradition constitute a potentially far more radical, if perhaps less expected, cultural and political challenge to state authority.

Civility and Polity: Coexistence in Sacred Space

Zoniana or Pom Makakan could hardly, except in moments of journalistic excess, be called states. We can, however, recognize them as polities, thereby juxtaposing them with the nation-state, along with many other structures of governance. This move utilizes two axes: a historically vertical one in which the state is compared with antecedents such as the mandala-shaped *moeang* and the segmentary patrilineal clan; and a socially horizontal one, in which it is compared with concentric entities of various scales of magnitude, including local communities.[45]

The historical antecedents resemble what Thomas Gibson calls "symbolic complexes . . . each of which has a relative autonomy from the others and an independent genealogical origin."[46] In Pom Mahakan and Zoniana, however, these complexes represent a unified and immediacy-driven distillation of real historical experiences rather than a plethora of ideological constructions. They do not engage in a shoving match with other complexes of a similar nature but push up against the relatively rigid order of the bureaucratic nation-state. They may persist over very long periods of time, allowing for creative play at the level of everyday life and narrative. Acknowledging such reversion to older structures is not a rejection of history. It is, rather, recognition of an active and conscious conservatism and of the resuscitation of polities erased from present-day awareness by modernizing, developmentalist ideologies.

The state's rejection of local communities' reversion to older cultural norms springs from a narrow understanding of what a polity should be. Accordingly, it is important to resist the allure of what we might call "methodological statism": the assumption that the state—which historically is just one of many documented possibilities—offers the only viable model of a true polity.[47] An example of this flaw is the Eurocentric celebration of the ancient *polis* as the root of civility, a myth that obscures the modernist nation-state's descent into ethnonationalism. While, as Caldeira points out, it is an assumption with which modern liberal thought invests the spaces of cities, it no longer holds for fragmented cities uncivilly redesigned to protect privilege and reject public displays of difference.[48] It also ignores older polities, some of which were never part of the European liberal world. The concept of polity means something larger and perhaps more diffuse than the materiality of the city; it is far more general, transcultural, and transhistorical than the modern, ethnically defined nation-state.

The Southeast Asian moeang is often translated simply as "city," but "polity" would capture its implications far better and would allow us to trace its transformation from a cosmological space characterized by elaborate hierarchy under a monarch into a megacity like Bangkok. Hierarchy does not disappear in that transformation; it retains many of its former accoutrements as powerful actors seek to exploit the symbolic power of an ancient heritage. Bangkok, to continue with that example, did not stand alone, although it progressively extended its power over the many other moeang in its vicinity. Traces of erstwhile local autonomy nevertheless persist as potential challenges to the capital's suzerainty. Thus, for Chiang Mai, the center of the former northern Thai Lanna ("million fields") kingdom, the moeang is *the* city, but also the social expanse over which it holds sway; its dialect is known as "the speech (*kham*) of the moeang"—a language defined by the regional center but incorporating a considerable spread beyond its confines. Bangkok, in aspiring to be a modern capital, tried to reject the moeang model both at home and in the provinces. Subversive archaists resist that erasure.

More critical attention to the historical root of the term *polity* alerts us to the limitations of terms like *city* and *state*. Thinking of the modern Greek usages, rather than solely the ancient *polis*, suggests a revelatory transgression of conventional wisdom. Greeks today refer to Athens as a *poli(s)*, a city, but to Istanbul as *i poli* (*the* city), thereby invoking a theocratic, imperial, Greek-speaking Byzantium rather than the semidemocratic society of classical Athens. *Politismos*, culture or civilization, is what emanates from that center but spreads in progressively weakening ripples to the furthest extent of its effective control. Such traces of a premodernist past warn us not to conflate persistent local forms of polity with either the modern city or the nation-state, and remind us that a modernist reading of the ancient Greek term may not shed much light on present-day urban practice.

Some of the models evoked by the subversive archaists are of at least partly religious inspiration. This is certainly true of the classic form of the ethnic Tai moeang, which conflates the idea of a city with that of a moral community. Richard O'Connor has argued that the separation of the religious from the political is a Eurocentric misrepresentation. What he says for the moeang also holds true for the classical *polis*, where the Agora was a place of commerce, worship, and debate, all at the same time, and often in ways that defied disentanglement. That *polis*, as O'Connor so genially reminds us, was a moral community and a cosmological concept as well as a physical space and a civilizational center. At least in these general terms, it thus resembled the moeang.[49]

Janet Chernela uses the term *moral community* to delineate the identity of groups that do not willingly commit violence internally, a category that includes transient identities. This approach relativizes the idea of the moral community in a way that is also consistent with the refraction of the divine through the shifting divisions of society.[50] It places the moeang and the segmentary clan in a common framework; both are physically shifting entities that, at any given moment, define the limits of acceptable violence and the range of ethically imperative solidarity. It also describes the harmony that the moeang, at any level of social aggregation or demographic size, is supposed to assure its denizens—a harmony that waxes and wanes, or "pulsates" in Tambiah's expressive metaphor, with the extent of the moeang leaders' authority. It works equally well for the Zoniani, with their multiple levels of segmentation; the moral community expands and contracts according to circumstances, and this is reflected both in the constant shifting of alliances within the community and in the villagers' pragmatic treatment of the divine in moments of blasphemous anger. The Zoniani think of their whole village—and even of their nation—as a moral community, while at other moments restricting that sense of allegiance to a much narrower, patrilineally demarcated group.[51]

This pulsating image of moral community fully captures, albeit in a more structured context, Feldman's evanescent vision of polity.[52] Polity subsists in fragile agreements or social contracts to avoid violence and to act with mutual respect; it is suffused with a respectful moral authority that may be unconnected to any formal institution. Where physical place materializes social membership, spaces and buildings may exude and represent that social piety. Elements of an inchoate, diffuse religiosity, moreover, have wafted down to our own times from antiquity. Many ancient Greek temples were converted into churches; the new Christian leadership understood the importance of preserving "placeness" as a basis for capturing local piety for the larger ecclesiastical cause.

Such persistent piety may even become totally detached from anything that looks like formal religion at all. Eleana Yalouri, for example, argues that the Acropolis of Athens, even without its specifically formal religious associations, retains an ultimately irreducible aura of the sacred for present-day Athenians; immanent sacredness has long outlived its official form.[53] Setha Low has shown that the Central and South American plaza represented an analogous focalization of the polity. Like the complex around the central pillar (*lak*) of the moeang, the plaza was the innermost of a set of concentric spaces that together represented differentiated distance from a power at once temporal and spiritual.[54] Its reappearance as the core of the capitalist shopping mall and city center, while brashly secular in modern industrial terms, may nevertheless also contain traces of that earlier cosmological ordering of the universe now transmuted into a ritualistic celebration of wealth.

The placing of religious shrines in front of Thai malls suggests precisely such a sanctification of commerce. Like the Madonna images on ordinary houses in Italian towns, the shrines are explicitly religious gestures.[55] Also like those images, however, they mark a relationship between place and piety that may at times seem more social and economic than religious, and that may "pulsate" in configurations that recall both the moeang and the segmentary clan. Clerics may struggle to expropriate such expressions of local piety for established religious institutions or to eliminate them altogether, but their robust survival points above all to their social significance and their capacity to accommodate constantly shifting levels of allegiance and belonging.[56]

Older layers of piety thus nourish local archaism and alternative civilities. Calling this phenomenon cosmological rather than religious helps to explain its persistence in an age of frequently self-declared secularism with its attendant rejection, modification, and emasculation of formal ecclesiastical institutions. The concept of cosmology places formal ecclesiastical structures, everyday ritual practices and attitudes, and political structures in a common frame, privileging none. Thai Buddhism, for example, is often characterized as a highly syncretic religion incorporating many older, indigenous forms, but—despite its failure thus far to achieve the formal status of official state religion—it is fully incorporated into all the pomp and ceremony of the Thai state. From the reign of Rama IV (1851–68), who attempted to reconcile Theravada Buddhism with Western science and to reform what he saw as a superstitious clergy, Thai religiosity has been troubled by the persistence of what—in true survivalist mode as practiced in the colonial West—are usually described as "animist" beliefs and practices, mostly associated with the veneration of ancestors. Rama IV's reforms were part of a larger, modernizing shift that has had only limited effects on ordinary ritual practices.

Under his successor, Rama V, the rupture is manifested in the urban landscape. It appears in the evident disjuncture between Rama I's wall (which included the Mahakan citadel, fig. 5.2) and Rama V's modern roadway, Rachadamnoen Avenue, touted in his day and subsequently as the "Champs-Elysées of Asia." Rama V was particularly concerned to replace the shape-shifting moeang with the inflexible national boundaries of a sovereign state. That rupture, however, was never absolute, either in religion or in the way the polity has been understood.

FIGURE 5.2. The Citadel at Pom Mahakan. Photograph by author.

Even the present regime, confronted with intractable problems, prays for enlightenment at the temple, the *lak moeang* ("city pillar"), that remains the deeply revered symbolic center of the ghostly moeang of yesteryear.

Thus, even the bureaucrats show respect for supposedly non-Buddhist elements in Thai religiosity. They, too, are caught in the cosmology of the everyday. Despite the fear that the demolition squads would smash the remaining house shrines during the final destruction of Pom Mahakan, the municipal workers sent to carry out the destruction left the shrines, leaning as though drunk among the shattered remnants of the residents' homes, isolated in the wreckage. Even those who were prepared to exercise brute force would not willingly commit such ultimate sacrilege. They also left trees deemed by the residents to be sacred, but treated them, by ornamenting them with formal labels, as horticultural specimens: science replaced religion as the overt cosmological ground of bureaucratic intervention.

Perhaps the bureaucrats' fear of the dead was reinforced by the knowledge that the spirits to which the shrines were dedicated were in most cases not the ancestors of the current residents. They represent spirits associated with the original settlement licensed by Rama III, whose imposing bronze statue sits enthroned on its stone plinth in the temple complex on the other side of the busy Mahachai Road. The residents frequently invoked Rama III's charter; for them, it was irrelevant that few if any of them were descended from the original householders, since they portrayed themselves as holding in trust the houses still supposedly haunted by spirits from that bygone time. Continuity, they argued, lay in the fact of community itself, a trust that they took as a sacred duty. They airbrushed the genealogical rupture out of the site's history in a way that mimicked the strategy of royalist historiography. By evoking the authority of Rama III as creator of "their" community, they appealed to a royal Siam that existed before ideals of Thai identity began to mimic European models.[57] They thereby threatened to expose the official airbrushing of the radical rupture between moeang and modern capital city while simultaneously removing the discontinuities from their own narrative of inhabitation.[58] An opportune way of turning the state's strategy of smoothing over the inconveniences of historical reality to their own advantage, their stance exemplifies the pragmatic tactics of subversive archaism.

Until 2004 the Chao Pom had their own communal shrine at which residents prayed for good fortune. When the area in which the shrine stood was occupied by the authorities, the Chao Pom reconstructed the shrine in the new community center, a space for meetings and displays that had replaced the home of the original shrine (fig. 5.3). In this way, the community reproduced the logic of the *moeang* as an analog of both the house and the encompassing polity, as a place centered on a *genius loci* (vaguely considered as ancestral), and as highly adaptable to changing external conditions and represented as simply one among many (*tua lek*, "a small body," as one resident put it to me, in an expression that refracts the body politic through the moeang structure). These are exactly the characteristics of the moeang throughout its many transformations across the time and space of the Tai ethnic world.[59] They provided a formidable framework—reinforced by frequent knowledge exchange with other such communities—for resisting the municipal modernizers.

Bourgeois supporters of the military regime, terrified at the prospect of an already insurgent proletarian power, worship Rama V as the architect of their bourgeois paradise, and attempt through acts of veneration to eternalize that historical period to their collective advantage.[60] To them, absolute monarchy and modernization are not mutually incompatible; to the contrary, it was the absolute monarchy that modernized the country and, in the official account, thereby saved it from the colonial yoke. The widespread acceptance of this version of events also perhaps predisposed them to accept an implicit equation of Thainess with a capacity for adapting European fashions to Thai materials, thereby excluding from the true Thai world those who stuck to the older dress modes (or, as in Pom Mahakan, affected them as a cultural strategy). In this context, modernization that destroys an old community and makes its space available for the activities of the leisured class seems acceptable—even morally imperative—to many middle-class Bangkokians.

FIGURE 5.3. Communal Religiosity. Photograph by author.

Intimations of the Polity in Greece and Thailand

Communities like Pom Mahakan and Zoniana enjoy cosmologically distinctive identities, identities that, when conceptualized as concentric with the nation-state, effectively both mimic and challenge the state's legitimacy and thereby invite official violence. For the people of Pom Mahakan, that identity is bound up with the classic Siamese moeang. The edges of the moeang, as Andrew Alan Johnson notes, are areas of ambiguity, inhabited by intelligent actors aware of their own capacity for loyalty and defection alike.[61] What goes for Pom Mahakan also threatens the edges of the nation-state itself, challenging the crypto-colonial model of the absolute national frontier and hinting at the ineradicable possibility of reversion to the pulsating moeang. Could the destruction of Pom Mahakan serve as a warning against subversion of state authority at this larger and more inclusive—and hence more dangerous—level of collective action?

The modern nation-state that emerged from the colonial experiment treats its frontiers as absolute and nonnegotiable, and national cultural identity as a fixed standard. The modern Thai state is defined by a single Thai ethnicity, enshrined in the name of the country; its relation with variously labeled Tai and Dai groups in neighboring lands is not only the basis of cultural irredentism, which occasionally flickers into life at moments of transborder tension, but an affirmation of the majoritarian status of the dominant ethnos within the national territory.[62] The country's old name, Siam, while hardly redolent of an egalitarian polity, carries no strong implications of a unified ethnic identity but rather suggests the pulsating power of those who ruled over the flexible kingly domain.

Pom Mahakan sits at the point of rupture between the moeang and the nation-state's capital. That rupture is fully visible today. Where Rama V smashed his way through the old walls, the sidewalk steps—high, clumsy, and unevenly spaced—show very clearly that the transition from the physical incarnation of the moeang to that of the modern city was brutally abrupt. Visitors can feel it in the strain of their legs as they either awkwardly mount the stairs or surrender to modernity and creep along the side of the asphalt road, wary of the motor traffic rushing by—those cars that ironically echo Rama V's lone motorcar, the only one in Bangkok at the time, which he was wont to parade up and down the King's Progress Avenue (Thanon Rachadamnoen). The avenue symbolically and materially links the old capital with the entire kingdom, and especially with the northeastern frontier of the nation-state where, in Johnson's analysis, the same tension between the two forms of polity is still being played out.[63] The offense of the Chao Pom was above all to have materialized, however inchoately, the spectral presence of the older polity in the heart of the new polity's capital.

In Zoniana, the most obvious cosmological arena of subversive archaism lies in the segmentary clan structure. While some might wish to see in the clan a survival of ancient patriliny, its centrality to the life of western Crete's mountain villages carries a more important message. It threatens not only to wrest control of violence away from the state but also to reveal the segmentary assumptions that underlie the nation-state and even the European Union. It is also linked to decades-long histories of patronage and vote-buying that continue to haunt the histories of some of the country's most distinguished political families.[64] Such tiny communities pose an existential threat to nation-states and to their pretensions to modernity, transparency, and probity. Villagers know that their clan structure is what makes them a particularly attractive target for the politicians' exercise of parasitical hegemony. At times, in the past, this Hegelian bargain has benefited large groups of villagers, sometimes even the entire community.

Within the ordered democratic polity lies a set of social realities that is at odds with its fundamental principles, but without which the state would falter. The state actually depends on the traces of archaic kinship allegiance, and on the patron-client relations that it sustains. Calling such relations corrupt or nepotistic does not explain their persistence any more than do the usual stereotypical assumptions about "mentality" or "national character." Despite the huge differences that separate the two communities and the two nation-states on which I have based the foregoing discussion, recognizing the issues that are common to both productively challenges assumptions that spring from methodological statism and methodological nationalism. Focusing on the idea of polity, rather than on a single type of polity, has been especially revealing of some of the more evanescent aspects of sociopolitical life. In the next chapter, therefore, I turn to a more systematic examination of what is at stake when, at one and the same time, we accept the possibility of multiple polities and challenge the conventions of anthropological comparison.

Polities in Conflict: Sources and Trajectories

Subversive archaists challenge the moral and cultural authority of the state. The stakes become clearer when we ourselves subversively shift perspective to comparisons that transgress orthodoxies such as culture areas and institutional similarities.[1] Such a move is not entirely random, and comparisons are not as structured by pure logic ("controlled") as their authors would often like them to be. The approach follows specific global historical trajectories and moments in which the lack of fit between disparate understandings of the polity become apparent. They emerge when competing interests, suddenly increased wealth or poverty, or strong external pressures undermine the tacit discretion with which each side engages the other, just as shifts of anthropological focus may similarly respond to geopolitical change.

With the arrival of drugs in Zoniana, some local people rapidly became wealthy, and this, I was told, created jealousy, which led to the competitive involvement of yet others—a revealing comment on the relation between local values of self-regard (*eghoismos*) and receptiveness to capitalist models of economic expansion. What had been a reasonably stable economy suddenly sprouted new inequalities, made glaringly visible by the construction of ostentatious new housing by those who were suddenly able to afford it. Abruptly, a new comparison emerged between the struggling many and the wealthy few. While such disparities exist in the larger society, their scale was a new experience for the village. Even successful animal thieves in past decades were only marginally wealthier than other shepherds. The competition among shepherds had largely been an equal-opportunity struggle. Injecting cannabis and also perhaps more dangerous drugs into the local economy caused a more substantial and lasting shift in the social landscape and brought new visibility to Zoniana.

That visibility, like the heightened identity so sadly noted by the president of Pom Mahakan, could hardly have failed to attract the authorities' interest. Moreover, their violent handling of the resulting crisis may have been prompted in part by the need to put on a performance of moralistic outrage, thereby obscuring the means by which a few villagers first became involved in cannabis cultivation. It seems likely that *someone* in authority played a part, thereby upsetting the roughly egalitarian composition of the community and developing a new and particularly insidious form of patronage—and creating the conditions for a direct comparison, as well as a conflict, between the polity of the nation-state and that of the clan-based community.

In Zoniana, this eruption of inequality exposed the contradictions of egalitarianism among highly competitive villagers. In Pom Mahakan, by contrast, the diehards who remained to the bitter end were all ultimately reduced to poverty. Status increasingly devolved from individuals' contribution to the community's cultural campaign. The president became the residents' knowledgeable and articulate public face. Others contributed through their specialized interests: the former palace police officer (who actually lived in a neighboring community) had a houseful of documents, photographs, and other memorabilia; one of the committee members had a younger brother who was able to study and become a lawyer, offering his services to the community; the treasurer worked for an insurance company and had professional experience as well as a real income; the former petty thief whose transformation into an acknowledged expert in traditional Thai massage attracted many visitors to the site. While there were rumors that one or two of the leaders had embezzled community funds, these seem to have been malicious, enhancing—and perhaps planted in the course of—the barrage of vilification. None of the holdouts became rich, or even economically self-sufficient. Self-sacrifice for the community conferred internal status. In the cruelly competitive larger city universe, it counted for naught.

Comparison is not merely an academic operation. Local people and state officials also compare, and their comparisons are consequential. City bureaucrats articulate hierarchies of value that can determine what happens to entire groups of residents. At the meta-level of comparing Zoniana with communities in Italy, Kenya, Thailand, the United States, or Yemen, moreover, we may discern the concealed role of powerful actors in shaping the new economic order at the local level. Such comparisons also expose the contingency of what are presented as obviously commonsensical official decisions and actions. The nation-state depends on obviousness because, in reality, its own primacy is not an obvious or logical necessity at all. It is presented as a given, and most people accept it as such. Implicitly or explicitly, subversive archaists question it.

Perhaps the most extreme example of a defense of the obvious is the U.S. government's reaction to armed millennialist movements such as, spectacularly, the Branch Davidians of Waco, Texas, studied by James D. Faubion.[2] He argues that the key character of his ethnography "was not setting out to repeat the obvious [but] to subvert or, in any event, to controvert it."[3] In short, he was challenging the hegemony, in Gramsci's terms, of received wisdom.[4] The U.S. political leadership embraces a rationalist and (in Weber's [1930] sense) Protestant form of Christianity despite assertions regarding the separation of church and state. The Branch Davidians spoke to the antiquarian model of Judeo-Christian culture, essentially the same one as that deployed by the national establishment, but their interpretation was different enough to be seriously unnerving. They were, as Faubion acknowledges, conservative and traditionalist.[5] Their stand against the U.S. government was indeed a full display of subversive archaism, and the response was one of terminal violence.[6]

If the example of a millennialist sect such as the Branch Davidians of Waco seems far removed from the cases of Zoniana and Pom Mahakan, as in some respects it is, it remains important not to allow official discourse to preempt our understanding of common sense or of what makes for a commonsensical comparison. If the people of the two communities described here seem somewhat eccentric, Waco comes across as much further removed from the mainstream. But these are differences of degree, not of kind; the comparison should not be dismissed as illogical. These are all cases in which a group of people disturbs an officially sanctioned sense of how the world should be ordered. Officialdom denies that these communities, despite labels ranging from "informal" to "insane," entertain powerful notions of order.[7] It is just not the order of the European-derived nation-state.

One difference, however, remains important for this analysis. The Branch Davidians of Waco rejected the authority of the state out of hand. The Zoniani and the Chao Pom, by contrast, have always tried to engage pragmatically with the state, through the concealed arrangements of patronage as well as the more open strategy of engaging the authorities in ways that ideally would educate both the bureaucrats and the residents about each other's logics and ethics.[8] They are not millenarian rebels; nor is their stance resistance in Scott's sense of refusing to cooperate with those in power.[9] They sustain a different understanding of cultural identity within a territory over which the state's suzerainty is acknowledged. Their eventual failures reflect the risk to the state both from the exposure of its ramified patronage networks and from the embarrassment of negotiating with people it has already declared to be beyond the legal pale.[10]

States treat local forms of archaism as dangerous throwbacks to a primitive past. The logic of racism frequently equates primitivity with criminality. Antonio Sorge has shown how Italian so-called criminal anthropology sought and claimed to identify survivals of archaic attitudes in the shepherding community of Orgosolo, a village not unlike Zoniana in its adherence to codes of male agonism and animal theft, and used these pseudo-scientific allegations to justify the hostility of the newly created Italian nation-state to the community.[11]

Such attitudes also inform the prejudices of present-day Greek bureaucrats and police officers toward Zoniana, but the Zoniani turn accusations of archaism back against the state by finding in them sources of legitimacy that seem not to have been vouchsafed to the Orgolesi. One important contextual difference is that, whereas the Orgolesi inhabit a nation-state that many Sardinians reject and that has never depended heavily on classical history as a legitimation of the national project (except under Mussolini), the Zoniani operate in a context where antiquity is the ultimate source of legitimacy within a national identity that they do accept and claim as their own. Recall here that the Greek state has developed a far more unified image of national culture than has the Italian, which must contend with strong regionalism at many levels, including a popular separatist movement in Sardinia. Internally, Zoniana is considerably less varied in occupational terms than Orgosolo, where Heatherington describes a perspective that "envisioned the revitalization of community, entailing the reinstatement of relations of trust, collaboration, mutual respect, and reciprocity across different occupational groups in the town."[12]

There are some occupational differences among the Zoniani, and a few modernizers—mostly no longer resident in the village—bemoan what they see as the backward attitudes of the shepherding majority. Overall, however, the force of segmentary logic in Zoniana is still strong enough to generate a generic attitudinal solidarity in relation to the state. In Zoniana subversive archaism is not a self-abnegating profession of backwardness (which it all too easily becomes in Orgosolo), but, on the contrary, a thoroughly modernist and proactive appeal to antiquity as a national resource betrayed and misappropriated by the bureaucrats.

As a result, the Zoniani have been more successful than the Orgolesi at reclaiming the official historiography of the nation-state for themselves. They have a clearer sense of themselves as a polity both politically distinct from, and yet also culturally related to, the official, bureaucratic state, and it is precisely the latter dimension, replete with intimations of corruption and collusion, that makes them a target for state representatives, operating within the same system, but representing different political and economic interests. Similar factors operated in Pom Mahakan, but under political conditions in which the residents had fewer protections than the Cretan villagers. Pursuing the comparison with Orgosolo for a moment will also help to clarify the particular weakness of Pom Mahakan at the historical moment of its demise.

Antiquity and Civility: A "Mediterranean" Comparison

At one level, the comparison between Orgosolo and Zoniana seems self-evidently useful. It fits the Mediterraneanist paradigm perfectly: two highland pastoral communities on islands famed for their lawlessness and agonistic masculinity. Superficially, the treatment meted out to each was more or less the same; the police and military attacks on Orgosolo, however, seem always to have focused on individual "bandits," whereas the 2007 confrontation with Zoniana and its aftermath resulted in an attack on the entire community—a crucial difference.

Sorge has tellingly anticipated my coinage of subversive archaism: "As holdouts to modernity in a now thoroughly interconnected world, pastoralists cannot be unselfconscious actors within their encapsulated universe. Theirs is a traditionalism that undermines the dominant order."[13] His statement holds generically true for all such communities. But whereas the Orgosolo shepherds seem totally anachronistic in relation to Italian cultural politics, being neither law-abiding enthusiasts for the values of urban civility (*civiltà*) nor efficiently cruel members of the Sicilian *mafia*, the Calabrian *'ndrangheta*, or the urban Neapolitan *Camorra*, the Zoniani would not regard themselves as having been "left behind" (Italian *arretrati*); they strut values and attitudes—or, indeed, "attitude"—in which urban Greeks can also see themselves with relative ease. Certainly there are Athenians who sneer at the Zoniani as backward, but the charge carries its own liabilities in a country that depends for economic survival on traditionalism and antiquity. The village as concept and entity remains an integral part of modern Greek identity even in official discourse.[14]

Italy claims as much of a lien on modernity and urbanity as on antiquity and tradition, its investment in aesthetic products "made in Italy" acting as a point of fusion between the two temporal planes.[15] Within Orgolese society a faction of cosmopolitans projects a vision that generally entails rejection of old ways of doing things. The Italian term for reciprocal animal theft, *abigeato*, has in fact become a legal term in Italy, but is yoked to the status of Sardinia as an island of exceptional violence rather than to nationwide practices. The abigeato is incompatible with Italian notions of civilized behavior.

The Greek nation-state, while culturally unified as the result of a carefully engineered process of assimilation to a central model, has never fully emancipated itself from the role of survivalist relict within the larger European arena. Non-Cretan Greeks do see Cretans as somehow different, but view Cretan mores as an internal eccentricity rather than an alien presence. They see Cretans as lawless and uncivilized, forgetting that many Cretans (including, today, many Zoniani) live in cities; they also sometimes admit to a sneaking admiration for the Cretan highlanders' sense of pride and autonomy—values that, as Ernestine Friedl noted in early days of ethnographic research in Greece, link all Greeks in a shared celebration of personal and collective independence.[16]

This stereotype, which more strongly resembles the ambiguous status of indigenous populations in Latin America than that of Orgosolo in its celebration of nationalistic essentialism, has its converse in the stance of the villagers themselves.[17] Like the Maya of Guatemala, the villagers claim for themselves a paramount ethical and historical position in a nation the majority of which, while lauding their traditionalism as a general principle, treats them in practice as uncouth and dangerous. From the villagers' point of view, the ambiguity is simply the product of jealousy on the part of those government upstarts in Athens. In the same spirit they tout the village's indisputable success at being well represented in the legal, commercial, and academic professions as a triumph of the old masculine ethos, a tribute to ancient skills and toughness that supposedly antedate even the vibrant Athenian polity of Pericles's time, rather than as a fortunate escape from anachronism by an exceptionally astute few.

Some of those commercially and educationally successful Zoniani, those who appear to correspond to Sorge's Orgosolo "cosmopolitans," do decry as hooligans (*daïdhes*) the younger village men who, they think, are wantonly courting disaster through their aggressive machismo, and they lament the weaknesses of an educational system that allows young boys to grow up with such attitudes. Unlike their Orgolese counterparts, however, they see the deepest failure as that of a state that is unwilling to compromise with local custom and, in so doing, to cooperate with the nation's most loyal representatives in restoring civility. At most, they will concede that the parents of these particular youths have failed to instill traditional values of respect and self-control in their offspring. Even those Zoniani who are willing to work with the state—such as the son of a former village president who became the regional education czar and wanted to encourage an improvement in youth attitudes to authority—do not offer unconditional rejection of local mores, but instead seek to educate villagers in those performances of civility that will get them the desired recognition by the state bureaucracy.

Their stance conserves a consistent pattern in past decades whereby it was precisely the most self-consciously traditional shepherds who, from time to time, would form committees and vigilante groups to stop the practice of animal theft for commercial rather than social profit—an inexcusable departure, in their view, from the traditional order. These shepherds went into action not because they thought ill of aggressive masculinity but, to the contrary, because they wanted to protect it from the opprobrium with which unrestrained youths threatened it. The young hotheads, their elders thought, were jeopardizing both the traditional practices of reciprocal theft and the equally aggressive entrepreneurialism that had led some of the most traditionalist villagers to colonize impressively large swaths of lowland and city.

The Zoniani remain deeply attached to their self-image as carriers of the true spirit of antiquity in a corrupt modern age—corrupt, because, as they well know from their own interactions with it, the state is a mechanism that depends on deeply embedded patronage. If, from the perspective of official legality and historiography, the villagers represent a criminal rejection of ancient values, from the villagers' standpoint it is the state that has corrupted the ancient values and national character. Such turpitude can be opposed only by a vision of pure tradition—the very basis of subversive archaism.

Their deliberate social and cultural archaism would probably never have succeeded in Italy. For all the glories of Etruscan and Roman antiquity, and even of the Renaissance, the modernity of the country has never depended on claims of continuity with those epochs, and has certainly not done so in terms of the nation as a whole. Alternative visions of antiquity therefore emerge as nothing more threatening than the expression of Italy's enormous internal cultural diversity.[18] Mussolini's extravagant celebration of Romanness (*romanità*) at the national level is today usually seen as a self-indulgent aberration from the general indifference to the imperial past—a past, moreover, associated with a capital city despised for both its detested bureaucracy and the crude speech and uncouth ways of its denizens.[19]

Such an attitude to the national capital's past and present would make no sense in Greece. Despite some grumbling about its problems, Athens—the ancient *polis* dragged in modern times from its long-faded past to serve as the capital of the nation-state—calls the tune of language and national culture. In Athens, any archaism that differs from that of the state still potentially threatens the sometimes tawdry but always unifying modernism of the archaeological bureaucracy, which has at best been indifferent and sometimes hostile to recrudescences of local expressions of antiquarian pride.

I do not want to exaggerate the contrast between Greece and Italy. Antiquity *is* important in Italy; Sardinians not only, for example, point to their island's prehistoric nuraghic culture as evidence of a distinctive local antiquity as venerable as that of Crete's so-called Minoans, but invoke that antiquity as a justification for disrespecting the nation's laws.[20] One difference, however, remains sharp: Italy's survival as a nation-state was never predicated on claims to direct continuity with the ancient past of its capital city, and was never framed in this way by foreign powers as a condition of national independence, whereas Greece's fragility is evident from the frequency with which its so-called European partners still upbraid it for its alleged failure to live up to the promise of "its" glorious antiquity. That antiquity, moreover, is specifically Athenian and associated with the European aspirations of the capital, in contrast to the conventional Italian view of Rome as a cultural and social backwater. For Greece, any challenge to the monochromatic antiquarianism of its official self-presentation represents an existential challenge the gravity of which most Italians would find hard to comprehend.

When we compare Zoniana with Orgosolo, the differences that lie below the surface of an apparently shared tradition of pastoral life are striking. In the sphere of economic production and subsistence, for example, Orgosolo looks much more like one of Scott's cores of resisting swidden agriculturalists than does Zoniana. It is not insignificant that Sorge is able to apply Scott's framework so easily to Orgosolo. The Orgolesi find themselves particularly at odds with a state bureaucracy that disapproves of the way they over-graze national resources and that fences off as a national park (Gennargentu) a zone that many of them consider part of the natural habitat for their pastoralism.[21] These conflicts are not unlike those that pit swidden farmers against virtually all the national governments of mainland Southeast Asia, and they are framed in very similar terms as conflicts between indigenous cultural rights and practices on the one hand and scientific environmental protection on the other.

While the Zoniani deeply resent European Union directives demanding the uprooting of their beloved vines, the Greek state, by contrast, has never demanded a reduction in their flocks. The proud indigeneity of the Zoniani—to invoke Tracey Heatherington's felicitous observation of Orgolese identity—is presented not, as the Sardinian sometimes is, as separatism, but, to the contrary, as quintessential Greekness.[22] To be sure, the Zoniani have limited choices of subsistence in their own territories, and they also have strong economic reasons for remaining loyal to their pastoral traditions. Meat and cheese are valuable products, and the uplands provide little in the way of fertile arable land. To adapt to the realities of the modern economy, however, the Zoniani have also diversified their activities and expanded their reach far beyond their own village, while always recognizing that it was their pastoral economy that provided the jumping-off point for these developments.

Maintained in their pastoral lifestyle by politicians whose parliamentary survival may at times depend on maintaining the support of large clans operating in pastoral mode, the shepherds of Zoniana are nevertheless quite willing to turn their hand to agriculture and commerce. They do so, however, as an extension of their mountain lives, diversifying their economy through part-time migration to lowland and urban settings. Not for a moment do they abandon their stance of traditionalism or view it as anachronistic in the larger national context. One of the last Zoniani to continue wearing the characteristic Cretan turban (*bolidha* or *sariči*) and jodhpurs (*čilotes*) is a wealthy entrepreneur operating a tourist enterprise on the coast; many years earlier, he had argued passionately with his slick German-inflected cousin in defense of animal theft as the basis for the survival of Zoniana as a community, and his subsequent successful trajectory exemplifies and supports his claim.[23] Back then, too, more than one of his political patrons still sported local dress at a time when Sardinian politicians would never have sought to present themselves dressed like the Orgolese bandits of yore.

The contrast I have drawn between Zoniana and Orgosolo should warn against any temptation to assume that all mountain-dwelling pastoralists, even in neighboring countries, archaize in the same way. Sorge's thoughtful remake of the old discourse about a common Mediterranean culture shows us precisely why areal generalizations cannot serve as a reliable guide to how specific communities will exploit their cultural resources.[24] Greece and Italy have developed as nation-states in strongly contrasted ways. While they both devote considerable energy to claiming high civilizational status for themselves, the fact that the model of urbanity, or civiltà, has so deeply permeated the furthest reaches of rural life makes traditionalism of the Orgosolo variety unsustainable in the larger national context. In Greece, by contrast, the village remains a core component of the modern national identity.

Parenthetically, it is worth noting that the Sicilian mafia operates on a distinctive and internally diverse plane. Some of its more media-savvy representatives, eschewing images of rustic simplicity altogether, perform and exaggerate the supposed attributes of sophistication. They adopt extreme formality and elaborate etiquette—urbanity in both senses of the word—as the menaces of choice. While the very real threat of physical violence does underwrite such performances, it is always a last resort in practice, because a mafioso who kills demonstrates in that very moment that he has failed to achieve his goals by subtler and less final forms of intimidation. Like Hegel's master who has killed his slave, he has destroyed the very source of his hegemonic social position. Far better, if a mafioso wants to develop a fearsome reputation, to show that he does not need to lift a finger in order to enforce compliance, simply permitting an oleaginous smile and an elaborately polite offer of unwanted but unrefusable help to drive home the message. The Orgolesi, too, and the Zoniani for that matter, do value verbal dexterity. But theirs is the dexterity of a local idiom in each case, whereas the verbal skill of mafiosi, while also sometimes in dialect form, more often entails a parodic mastery of urbane etiquette that casts fear into listeners' hearts.

Local meanings of civility cannot be understood independently of national discourses of civilizational development. Sicilian mafiosi have cynically and instrumentally latched onto that discourse; the Orgolesi, by and large, have failed to recognize it as a resource. When we turn to the Thai case, we will see that in this respect middle-class civilizational aspirations do not clearly coincide with Greek and Italian attitudes. Greek and Thai discourses entail adulation of recent foreign models and the correct use of the language of the capital, neither of which is central to the Italian concept of civiltà. Italians appreciate a more diffuse urbanity in its double meaning of long-established urban lifestyles and smoothly polite and accommodating interaction—the latter a quality that many rural Greeks view with suspicion but that Thais generally admire.

Italians have little doubt that civiltà is the key to their country's cultural life. It is grounded in an ethos of *convivenza*—of cohabitation with others many of whom might be quite different from oneself.[25] It also means that an indigeneity founded in violence and separatism can always be treated as foreign to national values. Many Sardinians collude in their exclusion from that national project; they do not wish to be considered Italian, and their traditionalism does not lay claims on the larger cultural universe of the nation-state, which to them is an alien presence. In some sense, they have made themselves irrelevant to Italy, except, perhaps, as a tourist oddity, a lair of separatists, and an episodic but sharp thorn in the side of the environmental authorities.

The Zoniani and the Chao Pom exhibit an understanding of their place in their respective national projects that contrasts radically with the experience of Orgosolo. Both the Zoniani and the Chao Pom consider themselves good nationalists. Traditionalizing Orgolesi are certainly at loggerheads with the state environmentalists, and their rhetoric is about saving an archaic way of life. But theirs is not a way of life that claims any centrality to Italian cultural identity, and the state's hostility is directed at particular individuals and to groups of shep-herds who oppose its activities. The most violent Orgolesi present no threat to the state's weakly defined model of *italianità* and they certainly do not repre-sent what it views as *civiltà*. By contrast, the Zoniani are as much at pains to emphasize their fealty to quintessential Greekness as the Chao Pom are to the ideal of Thainess.

Civiltà is one variant (or a set of variants) of what we might broadly call either urbanity (a question of form) or, more productively, civility (the actual performance of political relations). While the Greek and Thai cases illustrate very different kinds of civility from the Italian, taken together all three show clearly that models of civility are the outer representation of the polities in which they occur. What kinds of civility are represented by different kinds of polity? This question is especially important when, as in the cases I have been discussing, polities are both engaged in conflict with each other and yet also mutually entangled in the complexities of shared cultural identity.

The Social Roots of Subversive Archaism

Civility, as we saw in the case of Zoniana, does not necessarily imply an egalitar-ian ethos on the part of state or community. In Bangkok, a far more hierarchical place than Crete, the possession of good manners and—increasingly—of wealth is a claim to moral superiority within the karmic framework.[26] The spaces of the physical city are strongly marked as appropriate to particular social classes.[27] Bodies move through these spaces in ways that often call for adjustments in clothing and comportment according to each individual's perceived standing and relation to others. Although the people of Pom Mahakan expressed deep resentment at being treated as though they were lowly dependents in a feu-dal system, they themselves, for all their insistence on democratic procedure at their meetings, implicitly reproduced in physical space the Thai hierarchi-cal cosmology expressed through height above ground.[28] In this sense, they conformed much more closely to official norms than did the Zoniani and Or-golesi. In part, this difference reflects a series of contextual contrasts: on the one side, two fiercely independent communities, frequently romanticized in their defiance of the law and operating within the relatively safe setting of a parliamentary democracy; on the other, a tiny urban enclave, sitting on land earmarked for a royalist project in a city dominated by royal symbolism and in a country where even the bureaucrats must contend with the fear generated by a sometimes violent social hierarchy, where the romanticism of "community" often looks suspiciously like a foreign privilege, and where mere *phrai* can expect little mercy or compassion once they have been painted as villains. The Zoniani, moreover, only had to contend with the police. The Chao Pom had to contend with the army, and the army, in a real sense, was the state itself. In that context, the polite indirection of the highly formulaic palavers with the Bangkok administration thinly concealed, and thereby generated, a deep and realistic existential terror in the community that may well also have reflected a corresponding fear on the part of the less powerful city bureaucrats toward their superiors.

The Chao Pom were experienced in reading pretensions of egalitarianism as expressions of potentially violent power. The old *moeang* was never an egalitarian space. Like the ancient Athenian polis, it possessed a center that was invested with hierarchical authority, and it had the potential, at least, to exclude as well as to exalt. What Setha Low and Neil Smith argued for the polis and the agora at its center was also true for the moeang and its kingly pillar: "the publicness of the agora was . . . circumscribed . . . and stratified as an expression of social relations and inequalities." They go on to remark that "the narrow definition of public space that obtained in ancient Greece may therefore be an unintentionally appropriate inspiration for the present"—by which they principally intend the present of powerful, largely Western megacities.[29] While the meetings of the Pom Mahakan residents were hardly exclusive of any portion of the community's already tiny population, hierarchy was maintained both through the control of the community's managing committee and especially by the hectoring tone often adopted by its president. It was also highly visible, as we have seen, in the physical spacing of age and gender. The leaders were therefore well qualified even on the basis of their local interactions to read the more obviously top-down, condescending politeness of the bureaucrats as expressions of unyielding force.

For this Southeast Asian community, there was no logical contradiction in the coexistence of egalitarian politics with authoritarian forms of social organization, a common pattern of political engagement in the region.[30] The Chao Pom had a relativistic—or, indeed, segmentary—understanding of hierarchy. Within the community, differences, especially between leaders and followers, were recognized. But such hierarchies melted into strong solidarity before the authoritarian attitudes of the city and state bureaucracy.

Rural communities may, as in Leach's famous example of the Kachin, oscillate between egalitarian and hierarchical modalities.[31] City communities have no choice but to operate in both modalities. This necessity holds true for the capital city as a whole and for a minuscule community like Pom Mahakan, which viewed itself as a microcosm of the nation.[32] The internal hierarchy of age, gender, and leadership fuses into a solidary bloc that opposes, as a moral community, any sort of bullying from the outside. That capacity to unify in the face of external threats is equivalent to the segmentary solidarity that obtains in Zoniana. The attitude of the Chao Pom was that of stalwart royalists who reproached the bureaucrats for their un-Thai and un-Buddhist failure in their assigned role as servants of the kingdom.

Serving the people *is*, in this sense, serving the kingdom. The identification of the symbolic leader of the national moeang with his people in its local microcosm is consistent with, and explains, the residents' loyalty to the palace; it is the hierarchical social contract that underwrites the archaic moeang. The community leaders' constant emphasis on civility—on polite dealings with the despised bureaucrats, on inclusive ethnic attitudes inside and beyond the community, and on a mastery of formal manners (Thai *marayat*)—expresses the logic of that contract. The residents' archaism, thus couched in civilizational and urban terms, threatens the authority of the monochromatically autocratic state bureaucracy. The bureaucracy fails the test of Thainess precisely because, in performing its authoritarianism with such aplomb, it demonstrates its inability to treat the king's loyal subjects with due respect and compassion.

The Art of Looking Governed

The social groups that practice subversive archaism necessarily belong to a world in which claims to antiquity have traction. Such claims are, at least in part, the ideological legitimation of their chosen lifestyles. They therefore cannot dispense with literacy, standards of civility, or the other paraphernalia of urban culture or "civilization." The men of Zoniana, for example, are notable for their formal politeness, chivalrous attitude to visiting women, and elaborate rituals of drinking and other forms of commensality. During my early fieldwork, one elderly man made a point of reading virtually every word of the day's newspaper and was revered by politically more powerful villagers as a wise repository of historical knowledge. Etiquette also plays an important role. Toward government officials, villagers often display elaborate politeness. The Chao Pom, as I have noted, are past masters of political rhetoric. They value education for their children; observe the whole panoply of ritual etiquette in hosting monks, officials, and academics; and follow the procedural conventions of a formally recognized community.

Thus, neither group fits Scott's concept of "the art of not being governed."[33] Zoniana's early settlement may have been achieved by fugitives from state control many centuries ago, but today the Zoniani prefer to engage with the state, with which they actively contest the locus of governance. What sets them apart from the state-shunning groups described by Scott, but also makes them representative of a very widespread form of resistance to state hegemony, is their demand for reciprocal respect and their capacity to play subversive games with the state's own rhetoric and symbolism.

The Chao Pom, whose management of local heritage adopted all the trappings of state museum aesthetics, exhibited impressive skills in this regard. No separatists they, they included cultural elements from around the land, not as regional peculiarities, but as constituent elements of Thai culture as a whole. Until they were destroyed, their mastery of the arts of urbanity allowed them to parody and mock the unimaginative formality of the bureaucrats, always in a polite register that left formally ambiguous—but entirely clear to insiders—the all-important question of what they were really trying to imply.

Scott's argument is nevertheless important here inasmuch as it concerns the significance of civilizational discourses in the relations between states and local communities. He analyzes ways in which nonstate populations have consistently, at least in the region he has (following Heine-Geldern) labeled "Zomia" (roughly all of the uplands of mainland Southeast Asia and southwest China), evaded the all-seeing eye of state governments, resisting the audit-like gaze of the authoritarian state to live egalitarian lives in peace.[34] Scott's model arguably does work for many, if not all, of the upland societies of that region. There have been specific and telling challenges to his interpretation, however, and these suggest that his interpretation has been too generic. These exceptions include several groups in Southeast Asia.

That Scott's image of people scuttling for shelter does not apply to either Zoniana or Pom Mahakan rests on more substantive differences than the mere circumstance of being located outside the Zomian territory. The technique of both communities much more closely resembles an example held up as an exception to the Zomia thesis, that of the Phounoy, a Tibeto-Burman–speaking minority in the Phôngsali province of Laos, who regrouped in urban settings after fleeing the Lao state's enforced rural resettlement and sedentarization with the attendant abandonment of their traditional swidden agriculture.[35] The Phounoy's successful remaking of their communal identity in a diversified urban environment seems much more like the Zoniana colonization of the lowlands and cities than Scott's scenario of shy avoidance. This resonance with the Zoniana experience raises the question of whether such adaptations are as rare as Scott's analysis suggests.

Some separations between urban and rural communities, moreover, are by mutual consent, a culturally intimate complicity that is probably more widely recognized than can ever be publicly acknowledged. This is apparently what happened with the Phounoy.[36] Research by historian Andrew Hardy has similarly revealed that the Vietnamese did not unilaterally build a containing wall to isolate the Hrê minority; both sides wanted the separation, neither being desirous of deep involvement in the other's affairs.[37] The Phounoy rejected remoteness; the Hrê embraced separation, but in a way that suggests a cooperative relationship with the dominant urban ethnic group.

Scott treats remoteness as literally geographical. Approaching it instead as ideological, however, reveals the willful complicity of state and middle class— or, as in the case of the Vietnamese-Hrê wall, the national majority—in constructing remoteness as a condition of civilizational exclusion. In such cases it has nothing to do with mountains or with avoiding literacy; it is about creating a mutually convenient separation. Those thus banished want their reputed inaccessibility to be treated as factual because it affords them some protection. They do nevertheless know full well that it can turn into a dangerous fiction since state officials can use it to justify both inaction and violence. Both parties collude in perpetuating an image that serves their mutually opposed interests but may turn toxic at moments of conflict.

For decades the Zoniani rejoiced in their hypothetical isolation; it protected them from inspection and allowed cultural habits disapproved by the state to persist and flourish. With growing (literal) accessibility, moreover, the Greek state did much more than "see," to use another of Scott's preferred metaphors.[38] By actively reinforcing Zoniana's identity as an inaccessible and remote place, indeed as a place where the state could *not* "see," state and media together placed the village beyond the pale of civilization. But the villagers meanwhile belied the insinuations of remoteness, inaccessibility, and lack of civilizational and entrepreneurial resources. Their increasing visibility as entrepreneurs, some engaged in illegal activities, was their eventual undoing, just as the coalescence of a palpable identity hastened the undoing of the Chao Pom.

Yet these same villagers insist on their respect for national history and culture, which they often present with the self-deprecating insistence that they are "illiterate" (*agghramati*). That ironic disclaimer shows they have already fully mastered the rhetoric of the literate state. They would not understand the refusal of literacy that Scott has persuasively described for some upland Southeast Asian groups.[39] To the contrary, they prefer to employ the discourse of the state, including its various forms of documentation, as a context for contesting rather than accepting bureaucratic authority. What is more, they have urban ambitions. As I have already pointed out, the authorities themselves highlighted the illogicality of treating the Zoniani as remote by simultaneously attacking the Zoniana enclave in the already-mentioned Iraklio suburb of Ghazi, hardly a remote location by any stretch of the imagination.[40] The Zoniani are virtually everywhere already; and the state, by colluding with the media onslaught, has enabled their virtual presence to transcend even their zone of commercial expansion by occupying a disproportionately large space in the popular imagination. In this regard, we may consider the Zoniani as more successful at adapting to urban conditions than the Chao Pom, whose community, enclaved within the city, became a too-visible sitting target.

7. CIVILITY, PARODY, AND INVECTIVE

Civility, Incivilities, and the Politics of Respectability

In the preceding chapters, I explored the modalities of subversive archaism as I encountered them in fieldwork in both Greece and Thailand and enlarged the analysis through some other selected comparisons. I now turn to the discursive styles of confrontation between the subversive archaists and their respective state authorities. These encounters play out in two dominant, overlapping modalities: civility (or politeness) and parody (or clever subversion). The modalities overlap because parody often places the formal civility of the state, as well as its pretensions to academic knowledge, in a framework of absurdity, reversing the gaze of the state so that the state itself becomes the object of a discomfitingly critical perspective. Parody serves to demonstrate mastery over the forms of civility, a true social poetics of citizenship.[1]

These idioms of interaction, however, may also break down into a third, decidedly uncivil modality: the invective that state officials, often with help from the media, unleash against local communities. That breakdown usually follows a period of stilted formality, and, while officials represent it as fair warning of their intentions, it may be a sign that the battle is nearing its predictable end and that the bureaucrats are only pretending to negotiate. The residents also complain that these attacks are highly selective, targeting single communities for alleged crimes that in reality are endemic to entire areas. These generalities fit the situation in both Pom Mahakan and Zoniana.

Vilification requires an ethical and aesthetic framework to be effective. That framework is complex, compounded of the rationalism and developmentalism of the state; middle-class criteria for both moral excellence and seemly behavior; and a rejection of practices that usurp the state's exclusive right to decide between right and wrong. The state also arrogates to itself the power to define those paradoxically modernist concepts, heritage and tradition, and to dismiss as irrelevant—and possibly dangerous—whatever distracts attention from the project of national culture.

In both Greece and Thailand, the power of state cultural institutions has been spectacular—spectacular, that is, both in the sense of an impressive capacity to enforce their will and in the sense of being responsible for creating spectacles intended to inspire loving acceptance of their vision for the future of the past. These institutional displays, often backed by carefully orchestrated media campaigns, create an internal aesthetic hierarchy. In Thailand in particular, the spectacular has long been a favored instrument of cultural management—a "regime of images," as Peter Jackson calls it.[2] In Greece, a more democratic political system has encouraged a considerable amount of critical play, so that even the once-sacred images of the classical past may now become objects of public parody and satire. Such comedic treatment of national history would be unthinkable—and dangerous—in Thailand.

Against the neoclassical aesthetic of official Greece, moreover, there is a tendency both to romanticize and to excoriate its antithesis—the working-class and rural image of tough masculinity. In Greece, and especially in Crete, images of rebellious masculinity abound, as do those of bandits (*nakleng*) in Thailand. In both countries, such self-presentations have reinforced regional political careers but also been associated with the downfall of local political operators at the national level; and both are at odds with the bourgeois sensibility that attempts to co-opt and absorb rude eruptions of the local in the modalities of social interaction.[3]

Konstantinos Kalantzis, in a series of recent publications, has explored how the visual aspects of this self-presentation reveal the political dynamics of life in the far west of Crete (Sfakia district), in partly depopulated villages that have long enjoyed the reputation of being the original home of Cretan masculine pride. He has shown that in response to austerity, the debt crisis, and, especially, the pressures exerted on Greece by its German "partners" in the European Union, some Sfakian men play creatively—though far from uncontroversially—on "the motif of Cretan indigeneity clashing with the urbanite establishment and bourgeois manners."[4] In this phrase, Kalantzis has captured the social poetics of the clash that the Zoniani similarly emphasize. The difference is that in Sfakia the level of violence and of clan solidarity has been substantially limited by steep demographic decline; the Milopotamos region, notably including Zoniana, has now largely inherited the aura of lawlessness.[5] As Kalantzis's work demonstrates, the battle with the state and the bourgeois

FIGURE 7.1.
Decorum and Order
in Thailand.

establishment over the ownership of tradition is fought out as much in the realm of appearance—of self-performance—as it is through the weapons of verbal discourse and economic prosperity.

In Thailand, "looking good" (*du di*) is attributed to "good people" (*phu di*), whose karma is exhibited in their capacity for excellent self-presentation.[6] "Good culture" is culture that fits the dominant, state-enforced Thai ethnic aesthetic, as Alexandra Denes has demonstrated for the Khmer minority in Thailand's Surin province. The positive adjective, *di ngam*, combines the moralistic "good" (*di*) with a bourgeois aesthetic of beauty (*khwam suai ngam*) that shows its most destructive face in the rejection of working-class communities.[7] Enormous efforts are devoted to sporting the most elegant silk clothing and golden ornaments (preferably of recognizably Thai design and material) and the latest consumer accessories. Politicians and the advertising industry alike have long exploited this impassioned pursuit of elegance and modernity.[8] Success lies in appearing always-already in command of everything necessary to be elegant, beautiful, and wealthy. Such is the nature of karmic predestination.[9]

There is a clear parallel here with Weber's "Protestant ethic," in which visible prosperity constitutes evidence that its fortunate exemplars are the elect of God.[10] In that sense, middle-class Thais are protestant Buddhists, closely aligned with the administrative structure and ethos of the bureaucratic and militaristic nation-state. From the infamous instructions that the Phibun regime issued on how to dress (fig. 7.1) to offensively self-congratulatory official posters celebrating the "return" of Pom Mahakan to the people of Bangkok, the emulation of Western models speaks to the continuing disparagement of vernacular culture and of working-class and provincial Thais (figs. 7.2, 7.3).[11] Slum communities inspire voyeuristic horror in middle-class urbanites, who

FIGURE 7.2. The Bangkok Metropolitan Administration Thanks Itself.
Photograph by author.

FIGURE 7.3. The Authorities
Imagine "Everyone."
Photograph by author.

generally approve of the authorities' attempts to remove them in the name of beautification.[12]

The aesthetics of "looking good" includes "sounding good," both musically and in terms of linguistic criteria of elegance. Working-class protest in Bangkok is often associated with the dialect of Isan, the country's northeastern region, which Bangkokians frequently, and dismissively, reject as "Lao" rather than seeing it as a dialect of Thai itself. Admittedly the politics of Thai language are complex; Lao, along with minority languages spoken in much of Southeast Asia and southwestern China, is both a national language (of Laos) and, in a slightly different form, a dialect of Thai—which is itself a variant of the Tai language group. Rather than embracing the northeastern dialect as a refraction of the national language, however, Bangkokians tend to reject it as foreign and inferior, especially as its users tend not to ornament their speech with the polite particles and status-marked pronouns that are a requisite of polite speech in the capital.[13] There are Isan migrants among the Chao Pom, but the leadership's particularly unpardonable offense was that its members had mastered the etiquette and rhetoric of the Bangkok middle class—and that they sometimes appeared to be parodying as much as adopting it.

The sounds of working-class protest similarly offend the delicate sensibilities of the polite elite. Benjamin Tausig, who has emphasized the political implications of such dimensions of etiquette as the choice of pronouns in protest songs and commercial touting alike, has richly described Bangkok's sounds of protest.[14] One prominent dissident group, he noted, did not seek ever more intense amplification but exhibited "a turn toward de-electrification, a powerful mode of powerlessness." And he comments, "The trajectory of Thai dissident music was not one of increasing volume or intensity."[15] Adopting the relatively polite device of quiet protest, especially in conjunction with the use of "impolite" pronouns in the lyrics, approaches subversive archaism in that it adopts the nonconfrontational ethos of the Thai ruling classes. As in Pom Mahakan, however, performances of polite restraint failed to engage bourgeois sympathies or to trigger the desired social revolution.

In Pom Mahakan, amplification was usually very loud, notably when a new community meeting was announced. Here, however, the pronouns and particles were the polite ones, and the message they conveyed was of an ordered polity with effective leaders and democratic procedures. The Chao Pom were not a riffraff of squabbling dissolutes, despite rumors of bitter factionalism within the community. From within the comforting intimacy of their communal space, the Chao Pom projected into the streets of the royal city verbal, sonar, and visual images of loyalty, gentility, and compassion—images that were reinforced by numerous media reports, including extensive television report-age (notably by Thai PBS). They challenged the authorities to a duel of im-pression management in hopes that the municipal bureaucrats would lose face through overt anger or rudeness. By refusing the challenge, however, and maintaining an air of glassy-eyed tolerance, the bureaucrats also played the game with consummate skill—not, in the end, that it mattered, since they were carrying out orders from above and would not have dared to deviate from the predetermined outcome.

Visual, sonar, and olfactory effects constitute a politics of respectability. Against middle-class renditions of antiseptic spaces and the genteel sounds of polite conversation and discreet music, local communities project an intimacy that is profoundly different, and that often offends middle-class sensibilities. But the battle of images, invested though it is with strong moral overtones on both sides, provides culturally shared cover for the collusions and complici-ties that I have adumbrated in the preceding chapters. Visually, the images also frame a competition over how antiquity should be used in the present. Against the tidy fencing-off of old buildings, subversive archaists attempt, like native vegetation, to integrate those monuments into their lives, recognizing as cul-turally significant—as heritage—much more than meets the firmly censored and delicately nurtured eye of the bourgeois citizen. In so doing, they attempt to reclaim the very essence of what the state projects as national culture.

The Discourse of Alternative Heritage

The state's heavy investment in the past carries an inbuilt risk. When an entire population is educated in a carefully cultivated and regulated version of his-tory, where the very idea of a different interpretation is treated as treason, and where the slightest expression of anger can brand the speaker as undeserving of consideration, conformity with the dominant norms—looking good—can become a protective shield for dissidence. Behind it, communities can craft a divergent, subversive past. Moreover, they can play the game of imagery, espe-cially of loyalty to the national heritage, with a skill that by turns parodies and inverts the state's self-vision.

Such tactically useful ambiguity is a frequent consequence of nationalism. The premise of nationalism that in some sense all citizens are culturally the same and politically equal provides an effective disguise for hermeneutic diver-gence.[16] This is not the stuff of revolution, of regime change, or of tectonic ideo-logical shifts. It is, rather, the huge ambivalence of sameness—of what seem to be straightforward systems combining symbolism, identity, and belief in a single unchanging package that disguises the complexity and the ramified potential for discord within. Subversive archaists are outwardly conformists, although their conformity can often take the form of parody—a strategic move that it is hard for bureaucrats to counter without looking either foolish or brutal.

Parody and Pomposity

Subversive archaists' imitation of the formal rhetoric of historic conservation and heritage management counters official dismissals of their alleged ignorance and lack of culture. Their insubordinate conformity exposes the vulnerability of officials' institutionally encrusted interpretations. The bureaucrats' formalism offers these adroit parodists the easiest of targets: pomposity. Not all the rhetoric of the archaists is parodic; Greek villagers' etymologizing, for example, often sounds deeply earnest. But parodic effects may result even when parody is not intended. Connecting Zoniana with Greek prehistory fits the official ideology of unbroken continuity with antiquity. But it also defies the primacy of Athens.

In the same way, the Chao Pom, in ornamenting an old house with an elegantly styled plaque announcing that the building was "ancient" (*boran*, a label much favored by art historians and archaeologists), were not obviously poking fun at anyone, least of all at their own desire to achieve historical significance as a community. But their choice of label was potentially threatening nonetheless: it challenged the state bureaucracy's monopoly over the meaning and use of a word closely linked to the epistemology of cultural nationalism. Moreover, adding the age of the house ("200 years"), but only in English, shows that the intended primary audience may have been the international community (see fig. 7.4). UNESCO-style universalism uncompromisingly speaks English. These archaists were not seeking to subvert the capital city itself, a city that was also their home, but they were questioning the competence of its official guardians on a larger stage.

Subversive archaists' parodic performances are occasionally hilarious. In place of official signage solemnly celebrating dynastic power and the building of the city wall, for example, the Chao Pom adopted a very similar design to celebrate everyday local activities such as food production ("fish maw soup") and gold smelting. They created a "heritage" museum that aped the official museum discourse but seemed to suggest that they had something different and more domestic to offer.

The Zoniani, who celebrate tradition in the form of cultural activities such as local dance forms (also at one point a favorite heritage activity in Pom

FIGURE 7.4. Domesticating Antiquity at Pom Mahakan. Photograph by author.

Mahakan), also adopt more direct forms of defiance. They use official signage for target practice (fig. 7.5), thereby thumbing their noses at a law that nominally forbids them to bear arms. One large red "STOP" sign, riddled with bullet holes, leaves particularly little to the imagination.[17]

To bureaucrats, such exquisite parody ("archaeological" labels) or blunt disrespect (shooting at public signage) is unamusing. Some of the archaists' devices may intimate an antiquarian feel—archaeological museums in the first case, the heroism of the swashbuckling nineteenth-century independence fighters in the second; that is their sting. They express a mockery that cannot be countered without the risk of looking ridiculous. That is the force of subversive archaism. It is a performance of conformity with ideals of national heritage, but one that deliberately sets a trap and tempts the state to fall into it.

By the time of the final demolition of Pom Mahakan, the community museum, which had the design of a simplified, stereotypical version of a formal Thai house, had evolved. Early on in the community's struggle, it had served as a storage space for materials pertaining to the struggle itself. At that time, it was graced by a red and gold shingle with elegant formal lettering announcing that it was the "pavilion of the community's local knowledge" (*sala phumipanya chumchon*). That label was already a potentially parodic act. "Local knowledge," a term adopted by middle-class NGO and academic activists to indicate their respect for community thinking, had begun to sound condescending, as if "local knowledge" could somehow be distinguished—much as Akhil Gupta has argued for the distinction between indigenous and "scientific" knowledge—from

FIGURE 7.5. Target Practice in Zoniana. Photograph by author.

the real thing.[18] Now, on the eve of demolition, the building had been designated (in English) as the "community heritage museum"—a term that contradicted the state's monopoly of the past. During the demolition, as municipal workers trudged grimly past carrying the planks and boards that were all that remained of the stately old houses, the ironic claim to heritage—proudly proclaimed on a signboard overlooking the disaster—became a tragic rather than parodic reflection. If the house had previously looked like a caricature of the stereotypical Thai house or even of the National Museum, it now stood as an eloquently silent comment on the destruction of a vernacular cultural heritage and its devoted denizens.

From Civility to Vituperation, from Vilification to Violence

Officials' initial espousal of civility, usually in the form of corrosively condescending courtesy, lays the groundwork for the pious justifications of the violence that follows. This pattern transcends the radical political difference between Greece and Thailand, although the outcomes are different. Zoniana still exists, a significant segment of its population pleased that tough government intervention has cleansed the village of the taint of narcotics and criminality; its former dirt roads are now carefully paved and lined with formal ornamental lamps, courtesy of the central government. Those lamps illuminate the residents' movements through the village during the night hours.

Pom Mahakan, by contrast, has been eradicated, a once-vibrant community replaced by a soulless municipal park. Here nothing moves at night—and, it must be said, very little moves during the day. The empty site has fallen silent, bereft of voices with the knowledge and passion to challenge official invective. The authorities' public relations campaign against the community, which failed to persuade the educated middle-class people who formed the backbone of the civil society movements of the day, ultimately did gain plaudits from some neighbors of the community who claimed—revealingly, only after the community had been removed—that the residents had received their just deserts. One, who had requested anonymity because of his "personal connections with the former residents," declared, "Everyone around here hates them. . . . They also took the money [i.e., the initial compensation]. They just had to go." Another was reported as saying, "Everyone here thinks it served them right. . . . They formed a gang, acting like they were mafia. No one dared mess with them, even police."[19] This statement reveals a telling misapprehension. The unfriendly neighbors had failed to realize, or perhaps viewed with envy, the long-standing mutual support that local police and the residents had built up over the years.

The reported remarks do illustrate the impact of official propaganda, especially on small shopkeepers with much to gain from an influx of well-heeled visitors. No such negative comments had been reported in the press until after the eviction. Municipal officials thereafter drove their triumphant message home relentlessly. The campaign of self-justification continued even after the destruction of the community's physical presence, through the propaganda posters in which the city administration unctuously thanked itself—surely a rather "un-Thai" gesture of pridefulness by the elite's own standards—for "returning" the place to "everyone." The "everyone" in question, as the visual imagery made clear, was strictly middle-class and conspicuously Western-looking (figs. 7.4–7.6); the posters appeared not only in front of the citadel wall but also in other parts of the city, including the business district. The eviction was represented as a victory for the people of Bangkok rather than a blow against them. The question that remained unasked in this public campaign was nevertheless crucial to understanding the dynamic of events: *which* group of Bangkok people was the real beneficiary?

The comment that "everyone hates them," an after-the-fact judgment that may have reflected the speaker's own true feelings but for which there is no generic evidence, is suggestive of how hard the authorities worked to shape public perception. While it is true that some male residents dressed like underworld toughs, these are ordinary expressions of working-class masculinity in Bangkok. More remarkable was the unflagging politeness and restraint shown by the residents to all visitors. The Chao Pom often offered bottled water along with the formal *wai* greeting, the palms pressed respectfully together to suggest both equality (indicated by the chest-high positioning) and respect (shown in a drooping of the eyelids and a considerable pause over the gesture).

Their civility was in this sense the exact analogue of the comportment of the Zoniani, similarly bearers of an aggressive masculinity that offended bourgeois gentility but that also entailed gravely courteous respect to visitors: an invitation to be seated and drink a coffee or a glass of the local liquor, a polite questioning about where the visitors had come from and what they were looking to find, and a display of delicate amusement that the visitors could have imagined them as such fearsome villains. Despite the fear inspired by Zoniana surnames among urbanites now contesting their rapid expansion within the city, no evidence suggests that Zoniani actively use their names to terrorize the neighbors. They do not need to do so; their reputation has turned its poison against its instigators and carriers, who apparently believe that all Zoniani are dangerous and thus avoid risking any sort of confrontation with them. And so the Zoniani continue to be regarded as both throwbacks to a patrilineal past and successful modernists who have known how to play the capitalist economy to their advantage. The Chao Pom, by contrast, have retreated into scattered makeshift arrangements in which, as one of them told me in a message dank with intimations of deep depression, many of them were living far from their old homes and where their socially and economically impoverished life was *lambak*—full of difficulty and suffering.

Civility and Control

Aside from the difference in the political context between significantly degrees of democracy, there is one cultural difference that might also explain the difference between the two outcomes.[20] Indeed, these two sets of circumstances are interrelated. In Greece, whatever bourgeois urbanites might think of Zoniana, the concept of the Greek village is itself something of a sacred topos in middle-class discourse. To destroy an entire village would have been unacceptable. Pom Mahakan did not enjoy a comparable status.

Another cultural difference works to the advantage of Zoniana. In Greece, the language of protest, even among sophisticated urbanites, is blunt, caustic, and aggressive. In Thailand, expressions of anger signal a loss of control, and therefore also of face. On only one occasion did I see the Pom Mahakan community president erupt in untrammeled despair and anger, at a last-ditch meeting with the Association of Siamese Architects to try to save the old houses. He immediately apologized and covered his face with his hands, expressing deep, horrified shame at the sudden collapse of his once steely self-control.

If residents of Thai working-class communities allow themselves to be goaded into anger or violence, they lose their last chance of even partial success. Skilled parodists themselves, they recognize the formal civility of the bureaucrats toward them as a euphemistic assertion of hierarchy, a thin mask for the calumnies that these same officials are meanwhile assiduously pumping into public opinion. They know that the authorities also see civility as a useful delaying tactic and as a weapon in a war of psychological attrition. They recognize, in short, the incivility of official civility. By showing themselves to be the parodic masters of the performance of civility, they reproduce as irony the state's unintentionally parodic imitation of Western culture as the way to be "civilized" (*siwilai*).[21] Any outburst of anger, by contrast, would merely confirm the officials' assumption that these people were inadequate as Thais.

The internal civility of Pom Mahakan, in contrast to the politeness they showed such unwelcome visitors, was one of explicit inclusiveness. In that respect, it more closely resembles the Italian ideal of *civiltà*, as when, in the aftermath of the 2004 tsunami, the Pom Mahakan president emphasized a community of suffering that included the Muslim victims with the Chao Pom. Perhaps the fact that there were two Muslim-headed households in the community played a role; perhaps, too, the appearance of a Muslim city council member on an evidently sympathetic tour of inspection in 2003 had paved the way. More impressive yet, however, was the echo of the same sentiments a day later, in the poems recited by schoolchildren as they celebrated National Children's Day.[22] The Chao Pom were invoking a prenationalist model, that of the Siamese polity that had included people of many religious, cultural, and ethnic identities under a single encompassing but flexible mantle.

The authorities put on their own performances of civility. I attended meetings of city bureaucrats with the Chao Pom in which each side outdid the other in uttering profusely polite phrases signifying, in reality, total mutual intransigence. As the drumbeat of calumny—of which the residents were always aware—increased in the larger public sphere, the orotundities of polite speechmaking simply held the residents at bay and perhaps challenged them, if they would so dare, to erupt in rude anger. They steadfastly resisted the temptation. Nevertheless, the growing volume of libel prepared the ground for the eventual pronouncement that, since civility had not achieved an acceptable outcome, the authorities would finally have to resort to eviction and demolition.

Libels as Labels: Appealing to the Bourgeoisie

Calumny, perched like an evil goblin on the back of displays of smooth etiquette, is especially effective in this age of rapid and wide media dissemination. The poor and underprivileged are rarely able to find the legal resources to counterattack. Hence the calumnies that officials have heaped on both the Zoniani and the residents of Pom Mahakan.

The Greek authorities have repeatedly made stereotypical accusations of endemic violence against Zoniana, a community that rejects such an image by arguing that in reality it has displayed a far lower incidence of homicide than any Greek city precisely because the threat of vendetta is an effective deterrent.[23] The Thai authorities' treatment of Pom Mahakan revealed similar contradictions between local interpretations and official claims. The Bangkok municipality mounted an unrelenting campaign of vilification against the community, accusing the residents of immorality and drug use when in fact they had achieved an unusual, even spectacular level of success in suppressing drug use and holding their community to a common code of conduct. For long years not a word reached the wider public about the extraordinarily effective management skills shown by the residents—in active cooperation, moreover, with the local police—in addressing the issue of drugs, or of their more general skill at collective self-administration. The fact that some local people in the immediate vicinity continued to speak of the community as a drug-infested criminal lair indicates how successful the official libel campaign had been.[24] History, or at least the history the public gets to hear, often does seem to belong to the victors. But the media refused to be browbeaten. *Matichon*, a daily newspaper known to be critical of the current regime, and the relatively conservative English-language *Bangkok Post* both published extensive and notably sympathetic reportage on the residents' struggles.[25]

In their treatment of Zoniana, the media inflated popular perceptions of village criminality to the point where even mentioning to an urban Greek that I had been there would usually provoke an outburst of vituperation against a population of which the speaker clearly had no knowledge.[26] When Zoniani go down to the major towns and mention the name of their home village, the reaction is almost always negative, a toxic compound of disgust, fascination, and fear. The Zoniani continue to face this hostile response, of which they speak with considerable bitterness. They constantly mention a particularly offensive exclamation (a heavily emphasized, abruptly cut off "Oh!") they associate with urbanites' recognition, both moralistic and voyeuristic, of their name. Even a moderately sympathetic taxi driver in Athens, himself of Cretan descent, recited a verse that nicely captures the popular-bourgeois view of the village:

Δε φταίμ'εμείς στα Ζωνιανά μα η Μητέρα Φύση.
Εμείς κουκιά εσπείραμε μα φύτρωσε χασίσι!

(We Zoniani are not to blame; it's Mother Nature's bash.
We Zoniani sowed lima beans, but what came out was hash!)

The driver produced this ditty, of a type well-known in Zoniana, with huge amusement. It nevertheless represents the thin end of the wedge that has led to violence voyeurism.

The people of Pom Mahakan and Zoniana are often seen as marginal. But "marginalized" is a better term; it describes the process whereby powerful social actors *create* the conditions for which they then criticize those who emerge as weaker. People are never inherently marginal, nor are they inherently outlaws. Just as Nicholas De Genova and his associates have argued that migrants—or people in general—are never illegal in some essentialist sense, but instead are politically and socially *illegalized*, I suggest that the negative image of these two communities is the product of a historically and ethnographically observable process through which the wielders of power defined center and periphery.[27] To put the matter in the language of Mary Douglas, it is they who define the "place" to which all matter must be related as either inside or outside, and who define those who do not fit their concepts of order as "dangerous populations" living in remote or inaccessible fastnesses.[28] Community members' arguments to the effect that "we have two laws" (in Zoniana) or that "they [the bureaucrats] lack [the essential Buddhist quality of] compassion" (in Pom Mahakan) may serve to bolster their own conviction of their moral rightness, but politically they are powerless against the self-defining righteousness of the state and its laws.

As Teresa Caldeira has argued in a related vein, stereotyping constitutes an imperious form of knowledge: a willful form of ignorance that creates in public attitudes what walls produce on the ground, it justifies invasive action against the riffraff. As demarcation, it works in parallel ways to create conceptual and spatial separations; in the hands of police and other armed authorities, it also facilitates targeting.[29] The vilification of the communities in Zoniana and Pom Mahakan was a pragmatic prelude to the violence that eventually assailed them. It prepared the ground effectively. For Pom Mahakan, the vilification was also a postscript, intended to ensure that a retrospective tide of distaste would cover the community's traces in neighborhood memory as soon as the last wooden slats and planks had been carted away.

Civility and the Ethnographer

What happens to the ethnographer in the field can be a useful indicator of the dynamics in motion. In my case, this statement is arguably truer for Thailand, perhaps because my foreignness is more obvious there, than for Greece.[30] In Greece, local government officials and police officers talked openly to me about their work, attitudes, and experiences. In Thailand, by contrast, I often experienced official civility as defensive and dismissive. At one open meeting at which I expressed my views at the request of the residents, a senior official stiffly told me, "Thailand thanks the professor"—a clear refusal to engage further, and an equally clear self-identification with the majesty of state, both couched in the kind of politeness against which it would be disastrously self-defeating to retort.

In another confrontation, between a senior administrator and journalists discussing the status of a threatened market, after I had dared to ask a probing question, the administrator called me over and loudly, and in execrable but unmistakable English, offered to provide me with lessons in the Thai language—an offer of friendly assistance that others interpreted immediately, as I had, as a calculated insult. Again, any riposte I might have made would have caused me to lose face. In this particular case, however, an eventual reversal reveals the dynamics even more clearly. I decided to take him at his word and went to see him, asking for his views on the situation in that market. I also suggested that we do the interview in Thai rather than English. Suddenly faced with a situation where he was unsure what I would report, or to whom, he spoke to me in English only when his secretary was in the room, clearly intending her to be impressed and me to play along, which I did. When she left he immediately switched back to Thai, clearly happier in that language, and proceeded to speak very eloquently about his office's plans for the market.

This incident illustrates the miasmatic terror that plagues Thai bureaucrats, who must operate within an unforgiving hierarchy while facing an often hostile public. Some of my encounters with officials were, as in the incident just recounted, intended to be humiliating, but were usually couched in irreproachably polite and friendly language. In more private encounters, by contrast, some city bureaucrats were more helpful and courteously agreed to discuss their reasoning. The main architect of the final destruction, an outcome for which he had labored hard for well over a decade, even took me for a drive in his car so he could explain his feelings to me in detail. Later, as the sorry endgame played out, and in the course of a chance meeting on the street, he went to further trouble, over a bowl of street-food noodles and in full view of the wrecking crews and their depressing load, to justify the destruction. At no point did he accuse me of fomenting resistance or stirring up the seeds of rebellion. He did not need to accuse me of anything, and it would have done him no good; I had already heard that some administrators—well before the advent of military rule—had canvassed the possibility of my being banned from entering the country only to conclude that any attempt to do so would fail. It was enough for them to stonewall, to insist on the rightness of their cause, and to treat me in public with a condescension that never entailed the face-losing error of expressing anger or any kind of direct insult. Their tactics were much more effective than direct offense would have been and ran no risk of backfiring.

The basis of this dynamic lies in the historical relationship between Thailand and a West nebulously defined but painfully experienced. Working in two crypto-colonial societies, I faced issues less related to class position—such as Caldeira experienced it in her native Brazil, for example—than to the ambivalence Greeks and Thais alike have evinced in dealing with the old colonial powers (although the two issues of class and colonialism are both refractions of a larger pattern of inequality).[31] In Thailand, that ambivalence produced corresponding ambiguities in social interaction, never collapsing into outright confrontation. Even when, in a terminal meeting with the community, the military-appointed deputy governor of Bangkok intervened to put an end to my impassioned plea for the community's salvation—couched as incomprehension of the city authorities' reluctance to consider the views of external observers—etiquette reigned supreme. The ambiguity was reinforced by the fact that technically I was a guest of the community, not of the authorities, and it was the community president who invited me to go ahead.

With a formal expression of polite embarrassment (*khaw aphai*, instead of the more usual *khaw thot*) and a Western-style handshake, the deputy governor made it clear who was really now in charge. He essentially silenced me as quickly as he could without being directly rude. I could thus hardly complain without myself losing face. The handshake was surely a courteous gesture to my own cultural identity! Yet his intentions were clear to all; touching another person with whom one does not have a familiar relationship is impolite in Thailand, as is interrupting another's speech. His elaborate display of "Western" manners seemed to be a deliberate performance that local observers, including several journalists, had no difficulty in interpreting as a clear expression of disdain. It was a decisive rejection of any pretensions I might have entertained of serving a useful purpose in Thai society, or of having the slightest impact on a carefully prefabricated endgame. Had the deputy governor wished to treat me as more of an insider, a formal *wai* (pressed palms) gesture would have sufficed, perhaps suggesting that the conversation could continue in a more private setting. But he offered no such hint of interest. The community's doom was sealed, and nothing I could say or do would change that.

The scenario I have just described fits the crypto-colonial situation to perfection—not that a snub masquerading as etiquette is unique to crypto-colonial societies.[32] In Thailand, however, where affectations of Western habits (such as the use of forks and spoons) are laced with rules that Westerners often accidentally violate, the dynamic carries a particularly poisonous blend of respect and contempt, of openness and entrapment, that is entirely compatible with the egalitarian-authoritarian ambiguities of ordinary Thai political interaction.[33] In this crypto-colonial contact zone, local residents, state and municipal authorities, and the anthropologist are all entangled in mutually discomfiting ways.

After the Apocalypse: The Politics and Parodics of Signage

The defunct communal life of Pom Mahakan has now been distorted beyond recognition by the nostalgic signage of an imperious municipal bureaucracy. Civility here works as repression—in this case, repression of vernacular memory. Where once there had been simple but well-maintained homes and socially lively alleys, and where the signs put up by the community both parodied the pomposity of the state and yet also celebrated the familiar and the ordinary, now formal signs put up by the municipal authorities have recreated a sanitized memory of neighborhoods long ago destroyed. Not a word appears about the bureaucrats' own role in forcing through that final disappearance. Such signs are to be found throughout Bangkok, and they seem to signal a common pattern of destruction followed by the authorization of a carefully constructed simulacrum of memory.

There is no parody here, only the uncontested reassertion of official power to define the past. The bureaucrats can claim to have exercised civility in commemorating a way of life now lost. No one can compel them to announce how it was lost or who engineered its end. Just as colonial ethnologists sometimes practiced what Renato Rosaldo has called "imperialist nostalgia," claiming to have saved the remnants of former cultural glory for posterity after first destroying its political and religious foundations, so too the Bangkok bureaucrats perpetrated a similar deceit against a lived past—a deceit we might call *bureaucratic nostalgia*.[34]

Bureaucratic nostalgia is a forced eviction from the present, which evacuates the community from historical time just as the authorities have banished it from space. Subversive archaists are not nostalgic; they are firmly convinced that they live in those faded polities that to the uninitiated appear merely spectral. What outsiders call traditions are living aspects of their polity in the sense of a way of life. For a brief while the Chao Pom played with the idea of becoming a "living museum," for which they significantly used the English term as an appeal for middle-class and international support. The bureaucrats' nostalgia is a weapon of structural violence; they use the mockery of those monumentalizing little notices about vanished streets to exorcise any trace of the lived reality and to deny it any hope of return.

Such crocodile tears for a lost past resuscitate the formal civility that preceded the march to destruction. It is as if nothing has changed: the past was always doomed to disappear, the new signs of that perpetual civility already primed to usurp the real memories of real people. Bureaucratic nostalgia erases the memory of that unfortunate period when the state, its two faces turned toward different audiences, ramped up the parallel rhetorics of vilification and etiquette and then, when the calumnies were at their most strident, quickly destroyed the community that had dared to claim a morally and culturally superior status. Now, all that remains on the site is the polite acknowledgment that some human activity had occurred there, its complex everyday realities folded away with the asphyxiating mothballs of official historiography. And as a final insult, the only substantial new construction on the site is a public toilet.

Only the wisps of sacred cloth and the tiny headless statuettes buried in the gnarled trunks of venerable trees remind us that the ghosts of Pom Mahakan remember a different story. Perhaps the placement of these headless statuettes in trees deemed sacred by the now-departed residents is an act of appeasement for the damage done to them in the final horror of demolition.[35] We may never know. They certainly suggest that the trees themselves have, in the eyes of the former residents, resisted their conversion into botanical specimens and remain as living and sacred testaments to what used to be.

In Zoniana, there was no final act of destruction. There was, however, a renewed flurry of signage construction by the state. While some of the new signs offered target practice to the villagers much as their predecessors had done, it is notable that most have so far escaped attack and lack the distinctive scarring of bullet holes that decorated virtually all the old road signs. The new signs mark a new order, one in which there is no place for gunplay. This civility, it is clear,

FIGURE 7.6. Preparing for the Feast in Zoniana. Photograph by author.

will not tolerate reversion to the older and more rambunctious traditions, and there are many villagers who today willingly endorse the new order. They are pleased that the village is cannabis-free, delighted with the paving and school services that have arrived as civilizing devices, and proud that some of their own now staff the bureaucracy as well. The neat appearance of the village main street speaks to a collaboration between village and state that is totally absent from Pom Mahakan.

Yet even the most respectably law-abiding of the Zoniani maintain some of the elements of their archaism. They remain firmly attached to their clans, reproducing the logic of a segmentary system radically opposed to the centralizing authority of the state. The retired teacher's elegant diagram of his clan's genealogy is an officializing device, to use Bourdieu's term, that masks the reality of a political vision radically opposed to that of the state.[36]

The villagers also aggressively uphold the antiquity of the village and its linguistic and material links with the ancient world. In that respect, they could be viewed as simply falling into line with the learned scholars whose work underwrites national doctrine. But they also continue the tradition of massive meat consumption at baptisms and weddings (see fig. 7.6), which suggests that other values are also operative; some believe that these gargantuan carnivorous displays are only possible because a significant proportion of the meat is from stolen animals. Who knows? It is unlikely, given local ideas of propriety, that the host—be it the father of the groom or of the child to be baptized—would have checked on the sources of all the meat brought in by his kin and neighbors or refused any he guessed might have been stolen. As we have seen, the host may also not be able to stop inebriated guests from firing off their weapons in the usual way, especially if the feast is unusually rich and well attended.[37] Under the surface of respectability, the volcano of rebellious traditionalism slumbers uneasily, ready, if relations with the state deteriorate again, to erupt anew.

8. DOES A SUBVERSIVE PAST HAVE A VIABLE FUTURE?

Vicarious Fatalism

Why do some communities faced with overwhelming state hostility and contempt continue to fight for their collective survival and familiar way of life,
even emphasizing what places them increasingly at odds with the modernist
nation-states in which they are located? Why do they not simply fade into
tactical silence, perhaps to fight another day? The Red Shirt motorcycle taxi
drivers studied by Claudio Sopranzetti, stalwart communications runners of
a would-be revolution suppressed by the Thai military, did exactly that.[1] Why,
then, did the Chao Pom not simply give up, hoping to regroup elsewhere?
In the last months before the final demolitions, they knew that they had no
chance of a last-minute reprieve; their final efforts were directed at saving the
houses rather than themselves. In that campaign, they were supported by an
academic architect, Chatri Prakitnonthakan, who had participated in some of
their family events and is fighting a rearguard action against what he sees as the
authorities' cultural vandalism.[2] A few still hope to recreate their community
in another location but they face terrifying economic and political odds.

Even in their desperation, they are not fatalists. Fatalism is less a belief system than an orientalist and colonial fantasy, a vicarious quality wished on a
colonized or downtrodden people by oppressors seeking to justify their domin-
ion.[3] In modern nation-state terms, it underwrites the indifference and structural violence that, in extreme cases, allow poor people to die. It determines, in
Akhil Gupta's powerful phrase, "the categories of poor who are deemed appropriate to neglect."[4] Fatalism, in short, is a convenient rhetorical instrument of
power, a weapon vicariously turned against the weak.

Neither the Chao Pom nor the Zoniani are fatalists. They are familiar with concepts of fate: *mira*, the ancient *moira*, in Greece, karma (*kamma*) in Thailand. Their use of it, however, is almost entirely proactive and retrospective: not "what will be, will be" but "what was to have happened has come about." Virtue always offers the possibility of improving one's lot.[5] The struggle of the Chao Pom was constantly expressed in terms of Buddhist compassion, the virtuous education of children (especially on National Children's Day, when it could be linked to nationwide and royally approved celebrations), and Thainess. The claims to Buddhist virtues were manifested in ritual acts such as collective merit-making ceremonies attended by a group of chanting monks from a nearby temple, who would then, as a further demonstration of the community's devotion, be treated to an elaborate feast. The residents' Thainess was expressed mostly through the energetic promotion of traditional arts and crafts, but also through these religious devotions.

To such stances of virtue, the authorities counterposed an image of squatters exhibiting the predictable wickedness of the lowly. In these ethical tournaments, concepts of destiny served as instruments of blame and self-exoneration on both sides. They might have provided useful explanations of incontrovertible failure, but they did not induce community members to accept abuses of power in advance. Indeed, residents resisted attributions of inevitable failure—and, as the tragic story of Pom Mahakan reveals, some fought to the bitter end and even beyond it.

Official calumny creates the pretext for physical violence by insinuating a vision of peaceful order threatened by fractious internal enemies—enemies who have not graciously accepted the fatalism wished upon them and who consequently deserve the karmic justice that awaits them at the hands of the authorities. Their very insistence on resisting confirms their lowly karma.[6] Yet they do resist. While nothing guarantees their ultimate survival, many such groups have been proactive in protecting their right to be different. Had they been true fatalists, they would have surrendered to the perceived inevitability of their failure.

In the modern nation-state, these groups face daunting opposition. Appadurai's attribution to the ethnonational state of an "anxiety of incompleteness" risks substituting a psychological explanation for a social one, but it may, precisely for that reason, explain the willingness of majority citizens to participate in violence against minorities.[7] Subversive archaism, however, seems instead to provoke an *anxiety of unmodernity*, which feeds a specifically middle-class moral panic. Already an easy target because of their communities' small size, working-class residents do not resemble prosperous consumers.[8] Obvious working-class identity is especially damning in Thailand, where personal style is carefully calibrated to an ethnonational ordering of appearances as markers of karmic standing.[9] Bangkokians who chanced to wander into the Pom Mahakan community encountered tough-looking men stripped to the waist in the steaming heat with their elaborate amuletic tattoos in full view, or sitting carefully daubing themselves with skin whitener in a vain attempt to climb a social scale partly calibrated to skin color. Although the visitors would have seen no evidence of drug use in a community that had successfully put an end to it, they might, especially during New Year's celebrations, have encountered some men drinking *lao khao*, a powerful liquor that quickly intoxicates the drinker, or raucously dancing to deafening amplified music as fireworks exploded into the sky around them. And the signs of poverty were everywhere: the weather-beaten wooden houses, the cheap clothing, aged television sets, simple pushcarts used only by poor food vendors. Vilification plays on a cultivated fear of working-class communities, which a recently emerged middle class sees as an existential threat to its still fragile modernity.

Despite the differences between Zoniana and Pom Mahakan, there is a crucial similarity in their relations with their respective nation-states. In both cases the archaic forms of polity—patrilineal clan affiliation in Zoniana, the mandala-based *moeang* in Pom Mahakan—defy the faux historicity promoted by officialdom and consumed by the moneyed classes.[10] Spectral visions of a past order do not reassure the new consumers and their political allies. The moeang has no fixed borders and offers no fixed ethnic identities. The segmentary clan seems the antithesis of stability and reliable authority. Unfettered from the artfully reimagined and airbrushed past, these old polities inspire only fear and disgust in the bureaucratically nurtured, to whom they look like the vengeful spirits of anarchy and chaos. They have risen from a disordered past to trouble a complacent present, and they are not welcome.

When the state attacks subversive archaists, as we have seen, it does not usually begin with brute force. A sustained campaign of vilification prepares the way, not as a warning to the subversive archaists themselves, but as a means of creating a cynically useful self-fulfilling prophecy for the general public. To use another unpleasant state metaphor, it creates, or rather performs, "facts on the ground."[11] It presents a failure of understanding as a triumph of legality and reason.

In Zoniana, vilification preemptively served political interests ranging from those of politicians hailing from rival villages to the higher government officials who found themselves in the grip of these wily local dispensers of patronage. The press was a willing accomplice; even in the early days of my fieldwork, there was much coverage of "mafia" and "Wild West" scenes, exacerbated by a sudden escalation in the level and intensity of the raids on flocks, a breakdown of reciprocity in favor of purely commercial motives, and the use of radio equipment to escape police traps.[12] By the time of the events of 2007, Zoniana's reputation had taken a further beating through the involvement of some of its wilder menfolk in attacks on government offices and participation in international crime rings. Those involved in such activities were (and are) still a minority, strongly criticized by most villagers. Nevertheless, a poisonous combination of sensationalist journalism and growing police insensitivity to internal differences prepared the way for the village's collective transformation into a national bogey.

Where the Thai authorities crafted Pom Mahakan's evil reputation without significant press support, the Greek authorities could count not only on a largely complicit press but also on public incomprehension of the traditional forms and purposes of reciprocal animal raiding. Both the earlier shift to commercial raiding and its transmogrification into cannabis cultivation fueled ill-informed generalizations about "*the* Zoniani," who were caricatured in the press as backward and violent. One cartoon in a conservative but generally reliable Athens daily showed a group of men dressed in stereotypical Cretan mourning garb and speaking a generalized Cretan dialect. When a newcomer asks why they were in mourning, they say "Kalashnikov has died!"[13] In the background, clearly visible, is the bullet-riddled road sign proclaiming the presence of Zoniana—a sign that has repeatedly appeared in media coverage of Zoniana since the original raid. What neither the press nor the police cared to notice was that blanket calumnies of this kind are especially likely, following the logic of segmentation, to generate strong solidarity at the collective village level. That is indeed what has happened.

By provoking this dynamic, the authorities generated a virtually inevitable outcome. One media cartoon even suggested that the law against terrorism, the one the police invoked to justify the raids on Zoniana (and that more liberal Athenians opposed in their own environment), had outlived its usefulness because there was now no one left who could be characterized as a terrorist ("It's time for the *tromonomos* [antiterrorism law, literally "terror-law"] to be annulled; it's no longer creating guilty people!").[14] This perfect illustration of the self-fulfilling character of illegalization also reflected the widespread belief, certainly shared by the Zoniani, that a democratic state that uses such legal instruments is betraying its own principles.

The state's logic displays the tautological self-confirmation of much bureaucratic thinking: these people are bad; therefore, they had to be removed, and we have removed them; therefore, they must have been bad; and so, now, it is clear that we have done our job well. Once the temporality of the state's own use of language is obscured—the transformation that representing *illegalization* as *illegality* performs—that circularity also disappears from view and is replaced by established facts. A performative process transforms the temporal contingency of state-building into eternal truth—the classic nationalist sleight of mind.

The vicarious fatalism of the state also, and consequentially, recurs in scholarly analysis. It is what leads even so astute an observer as Scott to predict that all surviving rebels against the order of the state will be driven into the mountains, there either to achieve a safe oblivion or, if conditions are hostile, to succumb to extinction.[15] As Jonsson rather pointedly hints, Scott thereby, no doubt inadvertently, reproduces the wishful thinking of the state.[16]

Vicarious fatalism ignores the mutual entailment of state and local community. Phounoy society, for example, "is not defined by opposition to the state . . . but by an innate intimacy with it."[17] That entanglement is an integral aspect of the cultural intimacy of both the state and the local community. Subversive archaists engage in deep intimacy with the state, whether through quiet deals with police officers or sustained patron-client relations. They can never confidently count on these dear friends and protectors for help, however, even in good times; when their patrons fall from power, they are doubly exposed.

Performance, Place, Proactivity

Pom Mahakan has never been inaccessible. It was not only situated in a plain; it was located in a capital city and indeed based many of its cultural claims on a special historical relationship with that city. "We live in the moeang," insisted the inhabitants, utilizing the rich ambiguity of the Thai word as both "city" and "moral community." Concomitantly, they emphasized their identity as ethnically Thai—as members, in other words, of the dominant, governing majority. Unlike the Zoniani, however, they never succeeded in placing community members in positions of authority in the municipal administration or in a major political party. They were not fatalistic, but nor did they succeed in penetrating the power structure to the extent achieved by the Zoniani, and that weak political performance certainly contributed to the community's eventual demise.

At least the plan to reconstitute the community in another site that some residents and NGO activists were contemplating in the aftermath of the final demolition was certainly no fatalistic resignation to oblivion. It would not preserve the spectral relationship of the community with a complex piece of national history and with the architectural evidence for the destruction of that vanished older polity. But it would also hardly represent passive acquiescence in the destruction of the community.

The residents of these communities were acting in ways that their respective states regarded as troubling. Their members were performing images intended to evoke deep historical antecedents, as with the adoption of earlier dress styles and traditional arts in Pom Mahakan. Such traditionalism ostensibly lays claim to cultural membership in the nation—the outward mark of the good citizen. To *behave* like good citizens, however, is not necessarily to *be* good citizens—to act as the state would wish. It is to perform roles that fit a national image, but these roles may carry alternative interpretations. They constitute a rhetorical claim to national as well as local identity, a lien on history but not necessarily an acceptance of official ideology and practice. The Chao Pom seemed very much at ease when called on to present a historical face to the world.

Zoniani, too, are consummate performers; their concept of aggressive masculinity is grounded in being "good at being a man," not, in the conventional sense, in being "a good man."[18] Male performance, moreover, is locally interpreted as a validation of clan identity and pride. Like the Chao Pom, however, with their ostentatiously Central Thai and formal diction at meetings, the Zoniani, too, use highly formal (and occasionally even neoclassical) variants of the Greek language, and code-switching with a sometimes disconcerting agility analogous to the stylistic switches made by the leadership at Pom Mahakan.

It is when their performances are directed not only at each other but at a larger public and at the state itself that subversive archaists become a source of official anxiety. Their attitude to the state is rambunctious and insubordinate, yet it is also a deeply reverent and respectful resuscitation of the core notion of *polity*—of a way of life representing a different ethos and a different age, a return to paths intentionally not taken by the bureaucratic nation-state in its idealization and realization of the status and security of modern middle-class life. When subversive archaists perform their social and cultural roles, they are not only creating new social paths for themselves at home; they are also reshaping their community's role in relation to the state.

The challenge these marginalized communities pose is not, however, to the legitimacy of the nation or of the idea that the nation should be embodied in some form of political structure. It is to the legitimacy of the Western European–derived model of the national state as an exclusive cultural and administrative entity. The very presence of such rebellious traditionalizers as the Zoniani and the Chao Pom foregrounds the culturally intrusive and historically recent arrival of the modernist nation-state. In its most overt form, traditionalizers' claim to greater antiquity is the challenge that indigeneity movements pose to settler states and their postcolonial successors. When the challenge comes from members of the national majority, it undermines the state's legitimacy at its core.

In an important sense, subversive archaism is an inversion—or perhaps a special case—of cultural intimacy. It is a way of suggesting that the state's claims to authority rest on flawed assumptions and on the tutelage of foreign powers. In beleaguered enclaves like Zoniana and Pom Mahakan, we find very different assumptions about what an ideal polity should be. It is a far cry from the official, European-derived nation-state perspective, and the aspirations that animate it persist in collective discourse as templates grounded in historical experience.

Citizens chafe relatively little under a state authority that does not interfere too much in the pleasant pursuit of minor illegalities. But that tolerance has clear limits. Above all else, it does not yield to the state's claim to ultimate moral authority as the entity that represents the nation to the outside world. The state thus also insists on citizens' complicity in protecting the spaces of cultural intimacy from exposure. For related reasons, it keeps firm control of the nation's past. Any claim to alternative readings of antiquity, and especially to deeper historical roots than those of the state, is a serious threat because it exposes the relative newness of virtually *all* bureaucratic state structures. In an age when claims to heritage have proliferated exponentially, heritage claims themselves become a danger sign for state authorities.

Antiquity, materialized as "heritage," is a source of legitimacy that the nation-state has therefore always tried to monopolize, much as it has expropriated the idiom of kinship and attempted to replace clanship or other large local loyalties with nationalist fervor.[19] In both Greece and Thailand, the archaeological and fine arts administrations have long been powerful players in national politics, and any suggestion of alternative readings of the past have been considered tantamount to treason. The communities that I am discussing here, while professing loyalty to the nation, are appealing to a sense of polity that competes with the nation-state for legitimacy on precisely the terms on which the nation-state has always established its own claims.

Such communities are not only conservative; they are often also, as in these two cases, decidedly nationalistic. But their nationalism makes them all the more potentially threatening to the officials to whose own hold on power they attribute a suspiciously "foreign" feel. Locals are quick to seize on any hint of foreign domination. When I said to a Zonianos that he was facing the wrath of a foreign-imposed government, thinking of the origins of the Greek state in the early nineteenth century, he agreed fervently with the description—but what *he* had in mind was the antiterrorism law that had been invoked to justify the police action against the village. He saw the promulgation and enforcement of this law as typical of Western meddling in his country's affairs, meddling that had turned its leaders against his community. His view of the matter echoes a widespread perception that the special antiterrorism law (187A of the Greek Penal Code), the "terror-law," is a device imposed on Greece by the European Union and that it is frequently used inappropriately to target those—anarchists, far-left social activists, and cultural outliers such as the Zoniani—whose views and actions discomfit the state even when there is no evidence that they were plotting anything more violent than a protest.[20]

Despite the irritation that their cultural posturings pose for governments, communities of subversive archaists are not necessarily destroyed or humiliated solely because they have had the effrontery to challenge the state's monopoly of national cultural discourse. Subversive archaism is far from rare. Suppressing its every eruption would be an impossible, self-destructive undertaking for the state. Moreover, it is not clear that officials always understand the challenge to their cultural legitimacy that subversive archaists pose. In addition, the loyalty of these rebellious citizens remains an important strength in times of national emergency.

Sometimes, however, a catalyst makes subversive archaism significantly more dangerous. Not only does subversive archaism contest the cultural legitimacy of the state—a defiance that the state could ordinarily ignore with ease—but, given a sufficiently combustible situation, it may contribute to igniting an explosion. Such factors include open defiance of official orders, injury or insult to a government official, refusal to vacate expropriated land, and shifts in the balance of power among political patrons. Faced then with a serious public questioning of its authority, and with illegalities that have begun to put their competence in question, the state's officers may feel the need to act with decisive, exemplary force—as they did in both Zoniana and Pom Mahakan.

Mutations of Subversive Archaism

Subversive archaism is by no means always as benign or constructively intentioned as the cases presented here. Appeals to the past against a plodding bureaucratic state, or to "a new order" and "law and order" against the bureaucracy's classificatory obsessions and the complex and slow-moving operation of its legal apparatus, can generate the very opposite of Zoniana's warm hospitality to strangers or Pom Mahakan's generous embrace of minority groups in a shared community of suffering. Invoking ideologies of the purity of racial blood and the rejection of demonized outsiders, traditionalizing movements—from the militant monks of Sri Lanka and Myanmar to the neo-Nazi groups of Europe and the increasingly visible white supremacist militias in the United States—re-create national culture and tradition for far more destructive ends. Some have achieved significant parliamentary representation, even, in Europe, at a supranational level.[21]

Those who rampage on the streets in the name of protecting a white European heritage and religious roots that antedate Christianity are opposed to any degree of civility, especially of the open-handed and open-minded kind. For these groups, concessions to generosity toward outsiders amount to national betrayal. In some cases, such fears are explicitly cosmological: open-ended civility betrays the old gods such as those once invoked by some Nazi leaders, or the Roman glories invoked by Mussolini—ghostly intimations of the past that are repeatedly resuscitated by the ultrarightists of today. These groups therefore directly contest the state, not to save purely local interests as happened with Zoniana and Pom Mahakan, but ultimately to wrest power from the current elite and take over its machinery for themselves and for the exclusively defined ethnic entities they claim to represent. While their antimodernism might merit consideration as subversive archaism, they also threaten a return to the politics of their twentieth-century predecessors.

The subversive archaists we have met in the earlier chapters had no such ambitions. What they wanted was an accommodation with the formal polity, accompanied by mutual respect. But a community that has already been lured into activities involving drugs and encouraging a masculine pride in the use of guns, or a community that has been scattered to the winds, cannot but be a target for recruitment by more dangerous forces. And if those forces are willing to subscribe to the principles of subversive archaism, we cannot altogether exclude the possibility that even these hitherto generous and welcoming places will learn the lesson of resentment from the founders of their nation-states and develop more destructive forms of subversion in the name of an ethnically, religiously, and spatially cleansed archaism.[22]

In this book, I have focused heavily on two groups of people who rejoiced in an affective attachment to specific physical places. But other groups have emerged as "communities" in a spatially transcendent sense, especially since the advent of social media. Among these we might number the "antivaxxers" (opposed to any kind of vaccination for religious or other reasons) and the "antimaskers" (libertarians opposed to regulations requiring the use of masks and self-isolation during the COVID-19 pandemic). The antivaxxers are archaists only in the sense that they reject the authority of modern science. But the antimaskers are more intent on subversion of the social; not so much Luddites as libertarians, they invoke an idealized historical model of "freedom" against what they claim is the dead hand of bureaucratic government. Their conspiracy theories, moreover, supply the vague specter of some mysterious external force that is humiliating the nation by imposing "foreign" authoritarian governance on it. Their nativism may seem to match the Zoniani's rejection of the European Union's antiterrorism law, or the insistence of the Chao Pom that the laws used to justify their eviction required rewriting because of their inherent unfairness to long-established communities. Inasmuch as the antimaskers' actions place individual rights above the common good, however, they bear little resemblance to the subversive archaists of Pom Mahakan and Zoniana. Where both of those communities look to a segmentary polity that represents their social reality, the antimaskers subordinate any semblance of social contract to an altogether individualistic autonomy.[23]

The antimaskers do nevertheless represent a version of subversive archaism. Like the Bangkok and Cretan communities, they deploy national watchwords— "liberty" and "democracy"—against the bureaucratic state. They seek to transform the present into an idealized national past. If the official American narrative can rest symbolically on an irrelevant date and a bogus pictorial representation of the signing of the Declaration of Independence, and if similar questions can be raised about the Magna Carta, new readings of the concept of liberty may yet play a large and potentially destructive role in the fight against the COVID-19 pandemic.[24] The demand for the freedom to lie on a beach or to circulate heedlessly in shopping malls and restaurants suggests an antisocial perspective leading to a completely atomized world of individuals. As of mid-2020, these libertarians had already enlisted powerful allies at the very head of government in the United States and in other countries. They had brought subversive archaism to the institutional structure that has most to fear from it and had either infected its bearers or taken their lead from the top.

These self-absorbed libertarians join other, even less sympathetic actors in the fringes of subversive archaism. There they meet the ultrarightists or so-called integralists, whose goal is a racially and ethnically cleansed, gated, and white territory, a culturally and socially monochromatic dystopia. They are prepared to defend that exclusive universe with horrifying violence. In their claims to greater purity, they resemble religious fundamentalists, whose exclusions follow other criteria but who similarly invoke a textualized antiquity. Instead of so-called strict constitutionalism, fundamentalists seek—and, again, are prepared to impose—literal adherence to a single theological script.

All these groups are seeking polities other than that of the bureaucratic and modernist nation-state, and in that sense are also invoking a retrospective cosmological order. At the same time, they generally imagine that order as an ethnonational or orthodox religious polity. They conflate the alleged foreignness of the authority they are resisting with the perceived foreignness of potential new arrivals in their territory—migrants, refugees, heretics, infidels, "communists."[25] What the two communities I have placed at the core of this analysis teach us, however, is that rigid boundaries and categorical exclusions are not a necessary condition of cosmological redemption or of the emergence of a polity. Whether through a vision that refracts social and theological reality through the experienced divisions of social life, or one that reproduces the divine order diagrammatically on earth, both these perspectives escape the logic of the rigid, bureaucratic, ethnonational state.

In contrast, the other alternatives briefly mentioned here are devastatingly less accommodating of difference. Aspiring to create a distinctive way of life within a larger and more pluralistic national territory, the integralists pursue— with apocalyptic rhetoric, stockpiled weapons, and safe houses—the destruction of all who do not conform to their goal of ethnic, racial, and ideological purity. They are not subversive archaists willing—indeed, seeking—to work with flexible national authorities to build a space for local difference. On the contrary, their activities, some of them conducted with the chilling matter-of-factness of those confident of success, are oriented to a culturally arid vision of the future. Even when they speak the language of nationalist patriotism, their goal, in collaboration with other groups, is global racial and ethnic domination and the annihilation of otherness. They seek to exterminate human diversity.[26]

Future Prospects

The Zoniani and the Chao Pom challenged official authority over long periods of time. Pom Mahakan has disappeared as a community, perhaps never to emerge again or to reappear in a venue far removed from the place that gave its cause historical valency. Zoniana, at least, has survived, and today is increasingly vigilant so as not to give the authorities excuses for further violent interventions. Zoniani will continue to organize their social life in patrilineal clans for the foreseeable future. This form of social organization has proved effective as the villagers spread their economic tentacles into the plains and cities of the island. A generation of schoolchildren is exhibiting some of the same rebellious, cheeky attitudes that informed their parents' and grandparents' maintenance of a lifestyle disapproved by the state, but perhaps without the grasp of etiquette and self-control that was an essential component of the village's success in remaining free of official pressure for so long. There are danger signs when young boys make rude remarks to visitors and scamper off before any of their elders can chastise them. There are even more worrying danger signs when drunken youths defy their hosts to shoot off reverberating fusillades of gunfire at celebratory events. Even if there are no more direct confrontations with the police, it is possible that there may be active recruitment of the next generation to ultrarightist movements, perhaps with the connivance of elements within the police forces themselves. We have seen that there is greater intimacy between the police and archaizing communities than either group would find it politic to admit. For the moment, however, there may be a much closer connection between members of the police and the disgraced remnants of the ultrarightist Golden Dawn movement, as the attacks on the claims of the Zoniani to Greek identity would seem to presage. Moreover, the murderous violence that led to the conviction and sentencing of leading members of Golden Dawn exhibited none of the principled emphasis on social order that governs the Cretan vengeance code and the juridical mechanisms of the state alike.[27] As I have argued here, subversive archaists do share with the formal ideology of the state—if not always with its personnel—a commitment to the idea of an ordered polity. They differ solely, but fundamentally, on what that polity should be, as they do from totalitarian movements with which they may share little more than a distaste for the pedantries of bureaucracy.[28]

For the moment, a somewhat subdued truce seems to be holding between Zoniana and the authorities. With good luck the calumnies heaped on the villagers' heads will eventually fade to more realistic assessments, and the village majority, which condemns acts of unnecessary violence on both sides, will feel less exposed to ridicule either by the media or by the homegrown delinquents. At the same time, the aggressive archaism of the villagers will probably fade, its weakening prefigured by the disappearance of traditional male dress and representing one of the last phases in the gradual (if sometimes reluctant) nationwide acceptance of the primacy of the law-courts.[29] At a time of global economic crisis, the village will remain a haven for those who, unable to find other work, can still expect to make a living as shepherds. Zoniana will survive its terrible humiliation; and the local voices of accommodation are likely to prevail, if only because they can still reach back to trusted (if now somewhat weakened) sources of patronage, thereby demonstrating the practical value of relative moderation.

The last holdouts among the Chao Pom, by contrast, were all evicted from the place that gave meaning to their collective identity, with few or no protections against severe indigence as the Thai and the global economies threatened a precipitate downward plunge. The symbolic coffin they erected in their meeting

FIGURE 8.1. Final Rites: Burying the Soul of a Community. Photograph by author.

area, hard by the old moeang wall (fig. 8.1), expresses their sad plight. The replacement of the moeang by the nation-state has finally been effected in one of the few places where the older model still had some place-specific significance. The change is visually realized in the veneer of manicured lawns and largely unused pathways over a space that once hosted a living community and now stands as a vacuous monument to the unimaginative pomposity of municipal planning.[30] Oblivion, masked by the official celebration of some notional past community life, is almost complete except for those barely visible traces of community piety—broken religious statuettes and shreds of holy cloth—hidden in the bark of the old trees.[31]

If, like the Red Shirt motorcycle-taxi drivers, the Chao Pom can find a way of discreetly regrouping, the work begun as subversive archaism may yet recuperate some parts of that older, non-European polity far removed from bourgeois modernism. But the road ahead—if it exists—is not yet in clear sight, and in the present political atmosphere the chances of success seem to dwindle to the vanishing point, much as the broken community itself, the signs of its proud archaism reduced to rubble by the wrecking machinery of modernity, shuffles dejectedly out of sight, sound, and memory. The very "placeness" of Pom Mahakan is an important component of the erstwhile residents' claims to represent national heritage, and its absence would be hard to ignore in any future reconfiguration of their collective identity.

Subversive archaism intimates more flexible social and political arrangements than those of the nation-state. Whereas the state may espouse repressive and exclusive versions of ethnonationalism, as both Greece and Thailand have done at various times, subversive archaists do not necessarily follow suit. They can often see beyond the conflation of nationalism with racism or other forms of exclusion. In so doing, they also suggest ways of reframing the concept of national heritage.

Subversive archaists can reach back into the mists of time to recover earlier and more inclusive polities, mores, and idioms of belonging. Both the segmentary clan and the moeang are flexible models that separate social life from rigid demarcations of territory, identity, and legal rights. These, as much as palaces and poetry, are elements of a durable heritage in themselves. Their evanescence, a tricksterish quality that sits well with aversion to state control, may actually invest these elements with greater staying power than the more palpable materiality of monuments; it certainly makes them harder to pin down and attack.[32]

Archaists are thus well-equipped to question unilateral reifications of the past as the exclusive heritage of a monopolistic class, ethnic group, or political movement. Unlike ultraright populists, who also often appeal to a glorious past, they are not necessarily interested in excluding or humiliating people of different identity; what they demand is the respectful and reciprocal affirmation of shared humanity. Unlike many self-styled libertarians, they show their deepest concern for collectivities, from the nuclear family to the nation, rather than for purely individual rights. Despite their conservatism and narrowly local focus, they can teach us that there are innovative ways of reaching back into the past to find the building blocks, suitably repurposed, of a more sociable, communal, and inclusive future.

Not everything they have attempted is constructive, practicable, or even appealing. Nevertheless, their views deserve a sympathetic hearing. The bureaucratic, ethnicized nation-state has generally resisted or ignored their ideas as incompatible with modernity; its leaders cannot perceive, or afford to acknowledge, the durability and viability of pre-state polities. As a result, the world is a more conformist and less imaginative place. Within that constricting environment, however, the archaists still conjure up evanescent but persistent intimations that the world could, if it wished, be thoughtfully otherwise.

Preface and Acknowledgments

1. An intermediate presentation of the main argument appeared as Herzfeld 2019.

2. See Herzfeld 1991a (on Rethimno [locally called Rethemnos], Crete) and 2009b (on Rome).

3. "When karma takes on this ontological quality—a proposition of how things are rather than a guide to how to look at the world—it can present a barrier to the identification of both the proximate and root causes of social inequity" (Aulino 2019: 116; see also Bolotta 2021). By extension, those who actively oppose the monarchy have no rights because they "do not register as members of the polity or as human beings" (Haberkorn 2016: 244).

4. It is also true that the regime is not as discontinuous with Thaksin's legacy as it would prefer the world to believe. It pursued and even strengthened at least two of the major innovations of the Thaksin premiership: universal health coverage (the "30-baht scheme") and, with some modifications, the "One Tambon, One Product" (OTOP) scheme for the projection of local crafts and products. It has also continued Thaksin's assault on the homeless and on squatters in provincial cities (see Elinoff 2017, 2021) as well as in Bangkok.

5. For more detail, see Herzfeld 1985. For more information on neighboring villages with similar social institutions, see Astrinaki 2002; Saulnier 1980; Tsandiropoulos 2004.

6. Interview conducted by Yorghos Sakhinis, Kriti TV, for the program *Antithesis*, available at https://www.youtube.com/watch?v=IMrBXnbkHjo (accessed 5 August 2016). The interview was very briefly reported, without discussion of the Zoniana material, at https://www.neakriti.gr/article/eidiseis/1013418/o-maikl -xertsfelnt-stin-ekpompi-antitheseis-/ (accessed 5 August 2016). The first two comments to be attached to the YouTube URL are both favorable; neither was written by a person with a Zoniana name. One of them, self-named as Mitsosa Mitsos, praises the journalist for "understanding what journalism should be today especially as citizens need substantive information and not the little parrotings of [those in] power." The other, Voula Arapli, congratulates me on discovering "the human being" here (in the village? or in Crete?). These comments, especially in view of the fact that during the interview I was critical of the Greek government's refusal to acknowledge the presence of ethnic minorities, lead me to suspect that what I subsequently found as the political template in Zoniana might have a geographically and politically much broader resonance than anyone in the bureaucracy suspects.

7. I conducted the new fieldwork in the summers of 2016, 2017, 2018, and 2019, for a total of a little over two months in total. While I would not recommend such quick

encounters as the basis of starting up an ethnographic engagement, my long-standing relationship with the villagers made it possible to learn a great deal in the very short time permitted by other obligations. My earlier fieldwork in Thailand is documented in Herzfeld 2016c; I received new information about Pom Mahakan while conducting research in a nearby community between 2016 and 2020.

8. The transliteration of Greek and Thai, which I know from previous experience to be a politically fraught operation for both languages, has necessarily been inconsistent. I have generally opted for decent phonetic approximations but have respected existing conventions for specific names. No reader will be completely satisfied; I can only hope that no one will be deeply offended by my choices.

Chapter 1. The Nation-State Outraged

1. See Evans-Pritchard 1949; cf. J. Davis 1988; Hutchinson and Pendle 2015; Shryock 1997. Jordan has enjoyed relative peace, but the threat of fission is ever-present at multiple levels. Libya and South Sudan have been much less fortunate. For an earlier discussion of the segmentary structures underlying the modern nation-state, see Herzfeld 1987a: 158–66.
2. Herzfeld 2016a: 8.
3. This argument is spelled out in Herzfeld 2016a.
4. Steinmüller (2013) offers an especially insightful ethnographic account of such accommodations in China.
5. L. Smith 2006: 54.
6. Ferguson's (1994) critique of the politics of development is germane here.
7. For major critiques of this universalism and other aspects of official heritage discourse, see especially Meskell 2018; L. Smith 2006.
8. Tambiah 1990.
9. See Weber 1930; cf. Baehr 2001.
10. Nation-states are themselves far from uniform. Here, for example, we will focus on a very robust democracy in one country and a thinly disguised military dictatorship in another. That contrast makes what they have in common all the more striking.
11. Anderson 1991.
12. See Scott 2009, who cites Clastres (1987) approvingly in an epigraph. These are romantic interpretations of resistance and freedom from state control. Far more tenable anthropologically is Kapferer's (1988) ethnographically grounded demonstration that even the most benign ideologies can be transformed into their violent antitheses.
13. For a highly relevant discussion of how such emergent state-like entities can be damagingly misunderstood, see Ong 2018.
14. Scott 2009: 30, 48, citing Braudel 1973. Crete, with its contrasted coastal wealth and harsh mountain eyries, would seem to qualify for such treatment. See also Sorge 2015: 24, 49–53, on Sardinia.
15. See Abu-Lughod 1990. For other relevant critiques of Scott, see Reed-Danahay 1993; Gutmann 1993. For a nuanced critique of Clastres, see Wolf and Heidemann 2014: 5.

16. Fabian 1983; Danforth (1984) has shown that the states themselves commit allochronic categorizations.
17. Holston 2008, 2009.
18. It is to Maple Razsa (2015: 17) that we owe this apt description of anarchists. Scott (2009) uses the term "anarchism" to describe local rejection of the state in Southeast Asia. Razsa's ethnography vividly captures a particular local (Serbian) and global moment of anarchist activism. On Greek anarchism, see Vradis and Dalakgolou 2011. Subversive archaists do not fit the anarchist label because they seek accommodation with the state and mimic its heritage rhetoric.
19. As Hans Baer (2018: 175) notes, some reactionary social movements achieved enormous impact by disguising their goals in the rhetoric of very different ideologies; Nazism, for example, masqueraded as a genuinely socialist movement through adroit symbolic and rhetorical manipulation. See also Kertzer's (1980) insights into the communist adoption of Catholic symbolism in Italy.
20. Durrell 1957: 159.
21. Rakopoulos 2015b: 63; see also Schneider and Schneider 1994, 2003: 109, 163–64.
22. See especially Di Bella 2008; Rakopoulos 2018. Both authors demonstrate that there are many tactical and strategic variations on the ideology and practice of silence in Sicily, indicating a broader social basis for the supposed code than a simple correlation with mafia activity.
23. See Herzfeld 2009b: 181.
24. On the antimafia movement, see Rakopoulos 2017; Schneider and Schneider 2005.
25. See especially Belew 2018: 206–8.
26. On Gush Emunim, see especially MacGillivray 2016. After the electoral triumph of rightist parties under Benjamin Netanyahu and the inclusion of religious movements in the government, the group's influence on Israeli politics increased substantially, and its settlements were legalized. If its members are subversive archaists, it is the sense of being opposed to the secular state against which they have forged numerous pragmatic alliances with rightist politicians. If the Israeli right remains in power, Gush Emunim may eventually represent a rare instance of *successful* subversive archaism.
27. Brownell 1995; on Falun Gong, see especially Palmer 2003.
28. See especially Chun 2017: 35.
29. Peutz 2018.
30. See Peutz 2018: 49.
31. Peutz 2018: 64, 94. On the role of patronage in other instances of subversive archaism, see especially chapters 2, 3, and 4.
32. Peutz (2018: 128) suggests that the state's attribution of ecological damage to the depredations of goats may be inaccurate. In this regard, her remarks recall the many other critiques of allegedly environmentalist arguments against both pastoralists and swidden agriculturalists. For an insightful treatment of the conflict between state environmentalism and traditional practices, see especially Heatherington 2010.
33. Greenland 2021: 179–80.
34. Greenland 2021: 184, 190–91.

35. Herzfeld 1985: 107.
36. Apostolakis 1993.
37. On comparable instances of local archaeological knowledge and cultural manage-
    ment, see Hodges 2013; Odermatt 1996.
38. I am deliberately restricting the term "movements" here because not all rebellious
    impulses or resurgences of older models are fully developed social movements in the
    strict sense of the term. They often follow the appearance of those inchoate "blank
    banners" that Edwin Ardener (1971: xliv) identified as emergent forms of political
    awareness, but they may remain in a relatively passive form that nevertheless does
    give state authorities cause for concern.
39. Fallmerayer 1830, 1836. See Danforth 1984; Herzfeld 2020b: 71–82 for extended
    discussions.
40. See Heine-Geldern 1956; Jory 2016; Tambiah 1976.
41. See Charnvit 2019; Jory 2016: 20, 107–26.
42. This allusion to the god Ram also suggests continuity with a high-prestige, Sanskritic
    tradition that is not formally part of Buddhism. I have mostly adopted this conven-
    tion (e.g., "Rama I") precisely because, in the context of a more critical historiog-
    raphy, it highlights the tense disjuncture between the official narrative and a more
    complex historical reality.
43. In recent years, the most dramatic instance was the reinstatement of the previously
    disgraced royal consort with this pronouncement: "Henceforth, it will be as if she
    had never been stripped of her military ranks or royal decorations" (*The Guardian*
    2020).
44. See, e.g., Anderson 2014: 155.
45. Heine-Geldern 1956: 9–10. In Laos, the erection of statues of long-deceased kings
    may represent a similar process in a culturally related but ideologically very different
    context; see "Facts and Details" 2014.
46. A more generic alternative to calling someone a Fallmerayer is the label *anthellinas*,
    "anti-Hellene." In Thailand, the relevant charge is that of *lèse-majesté*; unlike accu-
    sations of Fallmerayerism, however, it has the force of law and conviction can bring
    heavy prison sentences.
47. Wyatt 2003: 43.
48. Reynolds 2006: vii–viii.
49. Horn 2010; Ünaldi 2014: 395–98.
50. Barrow 2015; but cf. Ünaldi 2014: 397.
51. Suppression, however, does not guarantee silence: the plaque has widely reappeared—
    as a fashionable clothing emblem. For useful coverage, see Ruiz 2017; Khaosod English
    2020a, 2020c; for a more comprehensive and scholarly treatment, see Subrahmanyan
    2020. Furthermore, the statues of the 1932 revolutionaries were quietly removed
    from a military base in Lopburi (Pravit 2020a). One of these leaders was Phibun
    Plaeksongkhram, whose doctrine of "Thainess," discussed elsewhere here, has nev-
    ertheless been heartily endorsed by the military-controlled government (with some
    tweaks aimed at foreign and especially tourist consumption; see Farrelly 2016). This

is yet another example of how official Thai historiography airbrushes inconvenient dissonance out of the narrative of national unity.

52. Dhani (1947: 93–94) more generally traces the father metaphor back to the Sukhothai period (1238–1438); on p. 91, the prince invokes Malinowski's metaphor of tradition as a collective treasure, thus demonstrating the functionalist implications of state traditionalism. On the persistence of royal paternalism as the legitimating model for the "despotic paternalism" of even the 1932 putschists as well as loyalist military leaders, see Thak 2007: 2–3. This schema also fits the karmic explanation of royal charisma and its refraction through the lesser orders; see especially chapter 2.

Further changes in the status of the monarchy are carefully orchestrated. The tight control of public ceremony surrounding the funeral rites for Rama IX illustrates, as Isaacs and Renwick (n.d.) point out, how a "unifying aesthetic . . . was structured within a larger system of surveillance, cementing political hierarchy and re-fashioning post-democratic authority." They also note the particular emphasis placed on requiring mourners to be *riap roi*, or appropriately self-disciplined in their appearance. The entire performance, which (in their carefully observed analysis) disguises shifts in the power structure of modern Thailand attendant on the passing of Rama IX while emphasizing continuity of style and symbolism, contributed to the process I have identified here as historiographic airbrushing.

53. On ethnic hierarchy, see especially Denes 2015.

54. Englehart 2001: 32 discusses the writing of laws affirming this relationship in the reign of Rama I.

55. Dhani 1955: 23–24.

56. See Baker and Pasuk 2016: 31. The prince's views are laid out in Dhani 1947.

57. On the long history of impunity in Thailand, see Haberkorn 2018.

58. See, e.g., Ellis-Petersen 2019; Panu and Patpicha 2019.

59. On rachasap, see Diller 2006. Thai is in this sense diglossic, like modern Greek, but instructively for my argument the Greek "high" register (*katharevousa*), unlike the Thai royal language, was technically available to all citizens—though it was used to exclude the masses—and symbolized *cultural*, not monarchical, continuity. On the fate of purist Greek (*katharevousa*) after its formal abolition (which followed that of the monarchy some two years later), see Moschonas's (2004) provocative discussion; see also Kazazis 1982. Because rachasap is specifically tied to the institution of monarchy, it does not directly affect the ordinary language, and would be unlikely to do so in any postmonarchic scenario. Katharevousa forms are often still used ironically; ironizing rachasap would be dangerous.

60. The fact that some kings were of partly Chinese ancestry gave their critics useful propaganda material but made no real difference to how they were popularly perceived or represented.

61. Constantine I (reigned 1913–17, 1920–22) had similarly been formally considered Constantine XII in the Byzantine line of succession. Greek monarchs were not "kings of Greece" but "kings of the Hellenes," a name both intended to assert continuity with the ancient past and suggestive of irredentist designs on Greek-speaking populations still living outside Greek territory.

62. See, e.g., Triandafyllidou and Kokkali 2010 for an overview. Danforth (1997) offers one of several anthropological accounts of the origins and effects of this policy on specific groups.

63. See especially Pinkaew 2014; Reddy 2015.

64. See Barmé 1993; Farrelly 2016; Kammales and Patcharin 2018; Saichon 2002: 134–48.

65. On Greece, see Bakalaki 1994; on Thailand, Porranee 2018; Woodhouse 2012; see also fig. 7.1.

66. The term *authorized heritage discourse* (AHD) was coined by L. Smith (2006: 29–34). It suggests the reduction of heritage (or tradition) to a predictable routine in the Weberian sense suggested by Niezen's (2003: 141) comment that "it is in the nature of bureaucracy to challenge the arbitrariness of tradition and dim the luster of charisma." Bureaucracy responds to local tradition by attempting to nationalize and routinize it through the exercise of AHD.

67. Summer visits by people of local descent and election laws that require voters to cast their ballots in their registered domicile (which is often not where they currently live) complicate the calculation of population size.

68. Pashley 1837: 82–83 (especially note 2).

69. Tsandiropoulos (2007: 171) correctly notes that villagers often invoke tradition to justify such acts of bellicosity. The temptations of sudden wealth, invoked by the more law-abiding villagers and helpfully analyzed in Tsandiropoulos's important article, are a major contributory cause of the new lawlessness. But neither explanation exhausts the complex of causes fueling the involvement of some villagers in organized crime, and Tsandiropoulos provides persuasive evidence of the role of external sources of wealth as well. The social organization of the village, which remains an important element in the maintenance of its distinctive sense of collective identity, also sustains the ideology of aggressive masculinity that underlies the villagers' invocation of tradition, and leads to a defensive—if often reluctant—solidarity with the miscreants in the face of official over-reaction.

70. These police officers are known as EKAMites, from the formal name of their elite division (EKAM, or Ειδική Κατασταλτική Αντιτρομακτική Μονάδα [Idhiki Katastalktiki Anditromaktiki Omadha, Special Suppressive Antiterrorist Unit]).

71. This summary of village perceptions is based on both what I have heard in Zoniana and a relatively balanced newspaper account (Lambropoulos 2008a).

72. I use the word "real" advisedly, as also in the subtitle of the third edition of *Cultural Intimacy* (Herzfeld 2016a; see also Herzfeld 2018b); the hidden realities of political practice rest on the mutual dependency of local villagers and national politicians. Official discourse is designed to conceal such realities, and it is so designed by those who most stand to profit from it. That observation, often paraded as an excuse for the replacement of parliamentary democracy by military dictatorship, is equally (and perhaps even more) applicable to the dictators themselves, particularly as they dispose of vast means to conceal their own corruption. See, for example, a remarkably courageous critique of the Thai military dictatorship by an (anthropologically trained) journalist (Pravit 2018).

73. For an account of my original fieldwork there, see Herzfeld 2016c.

74. The name specifically means "the people of the fort [*pom*]."

75. On the inculcation of hierarchy and morality in "slum children" (*dek salam*), see Bolotta 2021; Mahony 2018.

76. The quotations in this and the preceding paragraph are from internal documents obtained from the community.

77. See Lipat-Chesler 2010; Suchit 2003. Apparently a retired palace policeman who had once been a community member and continued to visit it and maintained a private museum was the first to discover this information in an older newspaper report.

78. See especially Chatri 2012. Thongchai 2001 and Reynolds 2006 provide some important historiographical context. See also Sirinya's (2018) scathing critique of the prevalent attitude to vernacular culture in the specific context of the destruction of Pom Mahakan.

79. In listening to the residents' views, we are not thereby, condescendingly, giving the Other a voice. We must, however, listen to the multiple other voices that the generalized and top-down focus of our sibling disciplines has blurred or silenced. I make this plea with a strong sense of the responsibility that stems from the role of Lewis Henry Morgan's own ethnographic observations in reshaping the Western world's understanding of society, both in his own influence here in the United States and through the writings of Friedrich Engels. It is a heavy charge, and I am deeply appreciative of the trust and honor implied in the invitation to deliver the Lewis Henry Morgan Lectures—all the more so because, when Bob Foster asked me to give them something of a retrospective slant in terms of my research history, he and his colleagues also graciously agreed to an extra year of preparation so that I could conduct new fieldwork in Greece for the express purposes of this event.

80. Zoniana (for which I then used the pseudonym Glendi) is described in Herzfeld 1985, a monograph that appeared in Greek (with Alexandria Publications) in 2012. After discussion with the villagers, I decided to abandon the pseudonym, as the villagers apparently now prefer to see their village named in work that they understand to be sympathetic to their perspectives. Pom Mahakan no longer exists as a physical community; before its destruction, which I recount here, its central location, symbolic significance, and increasing visibility would have rendered the use of a pseudonym pointless.

81. John Osburg (personal communication, 2018) has usefully suggested that these libels operate very much like conspiracy theories in modern populist politics.

82. For a comparable and geographically close example ("Where are your guns?"), see Kalantzis 2020: 63.

83. "The growing attraction of the Pom Mahakam [*sic*] community is, however, indicative of the potential of tourism to highlight the value of 'alternative' heritage. While we consider that the community has a right to its place regardless of its ability to generate tourism revenue, this is clearly an important bargaining tool in the ongoing conflict with the BMA [Bangkok city hall]" (Kisnaphol 2012: 213). The well-meaning attempt to project community life onto the white citadel wall on the street side clearly engaged the community members and a local NGO, but such efforts—and

there were others—may also have stiffened the authorities' resistance to compromise. King and Dovey (2012) focus, with hope rather than optimism, on the effect of slum tourism on international awareness of the inhabitants' problems.

84. On voyeurism in "slum tourism," see, variously, Dürr and Jaffe 2012; Frenzel, Koens, and Steinbrink 2012; Kieti and Magio 2013; Nisbet 2017; on "dark tourism" and crime, see Robb 2009. Robb's (2009: 58) remark that "dark tourism occupies a tense intermediary zone between voyeurism and social justice" also applies to slum tourism.

85. The substitution of the name of a drug (hashish) for the plant (cannabis) from which it is produced exemplifies the orientalism and sensationalism of media, official, and bourgeois discourses about these mountain villagers.

86. These quotations are taken from Lambropoulos 2008b; the ellipses are in the original Greek. This report suggested that the police command had already taken a decision not to use locally stationed officers when raiding the village for fear that these officers were already engaged in profitable arrangements with the miscreants.

87. Kalantzis (2019: 59–63), discussing media representations of the raid and its aftermath from the perspective of his own fieldwork further west, detects a more general ambiguity in the public response: a discreetly growing sympathy for actions that defied not specifically the police but the government and the foreign powers to which it was beholden. This accords with the villagers' own resentment of the way in which the European Union has, through its local political and bureaucratic representatives, extended the country's humiliatingly crypto-colonial condition.

88. See *Newsbomb* 2011.

89. Kalantzis (2019: 61–63) usefully discusses the ambivalent response of urban Greeks. On the social dimensions of animal theft in Zoniana, see Herzfeld 1985: 163–205.

90. This is also sometimes understood by celebrities and others reaching a broader public; see Kalantzis 2019: 61.

91. See *The Nation* (Thailand) 2020.

92. McCargo (2019: 212–13) sees the judiciary as restricted in imagination and agency by its role as the representatives of royal authority rather than as independent arbiters of justice. While he is writing mainly of the Constitutional Court, his analysis pertains to the Thai judicial situation more generally.

93. Claiming too much familiarity with royal personages, for example, can be considered subversive. Handley (2006: 439; see also 455n14) noted that a predecessor's book (Stevenson 1999) had been attacked for excessive familiarity—specifically for using Rama IX's nickname; Stevenson's book and Handley's own account of the late monarch's life and political attitudes were both suppressed in Thailand. Handley (2006: 439) describes Stevenson as "liberal with style and careless with facts to the point of embarrassing the palace," while Stevenson (1999: 3, 125) questions the accuracy of *The King and I*, which is also banned in Thailand. I well remember during one of my earliest visits to Thailand that Stevenson's book was in clandestine circulation and a source of great interest to political activists despite their apparent loyalty to the throne. Successive attempts to suppress these works have clearly failed. Stevenson's (1999: 3) account of the humble origins of Rama IX's mother would also have been seen as a direct act of defiance against the presumed karmic order of Thai society.

Chapter 2. National Legitimacy and the Illegitimacy of National Origins

1. For Greece, see St. Clair 1972: 75–77; for Thailand, see Anderson 2014: 34–35; Reynolds 2006.

2. On crypto-colonialism, see Herzfeld 2002.

3. Complaints about corruption in Thailand have been rife for decades, but it seems likely that their prominence in public discourse today is the result of direct American concern to strengthen democratic institutions against communist influence during and immediately after the Vietnam War. See also Connors 2007; Ockey 2004.

4. Herzfeld 1985: 22.

5. This astute observation by Aulino (2019: 133) about the morally appropriate relation between status and obligation seems broadly applicable throughout Thailand; a similar moral principle—without the karmic framework—theoretically obtains in Greece, where its prospects for realization are widely viewed with comparable cynicism.

6. Especially in the aftermath of the 2007 raid on Zoniana, "Cretans offered people of both leftist and rightist self-images nativist inspiration to rail against the political elites that, in the view of many, had led to Greece's financial meltdown and its subjugation to outside lenders" (Kalantzis 2019: 60).

7. They are thus not the "primitive rebels" of Hobsbawm's (1959) celebrated coinage; rather, they build on the romantic-nationalist image associated with those rebels and claim a spiritual identification with them.

8. It also, as Kalantzis (2016) argues, means that in the larger geopolitical context Greeks from other parts of the country may invoke the image of the heroic Cretan resistance fighter, endowing that image with a conditional but potent moral authority. This ambivalence is the direct consequence of the segmentary worldview that also replaces agonistic relations with the rhetoric of solidarity in the face of foreign pressure (see also chapter 4).

9. Gallant (1988: 275–76) explicitly points to this structural similarity.

10. Souliotis 2007.

11. On the Greek case, see my discussion of the management of the vocabulary of national revolution (Herzfeld 2020b: 55–67).

12. Morgan (1877: 512) lays out this evolutionary sequence with dogmatic clarity. In fact there is some evidence to suggest that in Europe, at least, cognatic kinship did (as he claimed) progressively displace agnatic descent as the organizing principle of property transmission—although this was reversed for a while in some areas during the nineteenth century (see also chapter 4).

13. Most commonly, this takes the form of recognizing a bride's surname as indicating her *yenos* (patriline, ancient Greek *genos*).

14. Gallant 2015: 38; Herzfeld 2016a: 157.

15. There are hints of a connection with the "Saracen" occupation of Crete that ended with the brutal invasion of the island in 961 by the Byzantine emperor Nikephoros Phokas, notably the place-name *Sarakina*. Local legends that attribute the origins of the Zoniani to "Arabs" (perhaps meaning Berbers) are potentially significant in con-

nection with the right-wing dismissal—especially common among police officers—of the villagers' claims to Greek and Cretan identity. Berber society is strongly patrilineal and clan-oriented, although, as with all such societies (including Zoniana and the Nuer), cross-cutting ties are also significant, especially in the forging of alliances; see, e.g., Hart 1970.

16. The most famous example of this intellectual modality in Greece is a brief booklet on matriarchy by Panayis Lekatsas, who explicitly declares that "the most ancient social arrangement mirrored in those [remnants of antiquity] lies in what we will call the Maternal Lineage. Its characteristics are genealogical reckoning in the maternal line, female-to-female inheritance, and the primary position of the Mother. . . . In the genuinely Maternal Lineage, the father is only a recipient of hospitality [*filoksenoumenos*]" (Lekatsas 1970: 16–17). In true survivalist mode, he then claims that Morgan (1887) demonstrated matrilineality among the Iroquois ("American natives") in confirmation of what Johann Jakob Bachofen, in *Das Mutterrecht* (1861), had already shown for Greek antiquity and, indeed, for all humanity in its ancient beginnings (Lekatsas 1970: 20–21).

17. Notably Kavadias 1965. Campbell's (1964: 42, especially note 6) terminological evidence strongly contradicts that position: the term *soi*, which on Crete usually refers to the patriline, among the Sarakatsani meant *kindred* (i.e., Ego's kin through both male and female links). See also chapter 3 for further discussion of kinship terminology on Crete.

18. See Humphreys 1978 for further discussion.

19. Despite strong male authority in public, matrilocal residence and matrilineal ties among women confer enormous influence on the latter during elections (Bowie 2008).

20. This convention is reflected in the practice, adopted here in accordance with *The Chicago Manual of Style*, of listing Thai authors under their given names.

21. Ferguson 1994; on "lateness," see especially Thomas 2016: 232–42. In Thailand, the achievement of modernity has a date: the long reign of Rama V (Chulalongkorn) (1853–1910), a cult figure for the bourgeois establishment of today (Stengs 2009). In Bangkok, the name of the first significant road, Rachadamnoen ("royal progress[ion]"), fuses dignified progression in the royal (and sole) motorcar by Chulalongkorn himself with the forward march of national modernity (see Herzfeld 2016c: 75–76). On Thai historiography, see especially Charnvit 2019; Reynolds 2006; Thongchai 1994, 2001.

22. In invoking the image of postcolonial grotesqueness, I follow the formulation of Achille Mbembe (1992: 3).

23. On the modern refiguration of the *hajduk*, see especially Bracewell 2003; Pavlaković 2010: 2017–19, 2029–32.

24. I am deeply indebted for this insight into the significance of the term *rebel* in the United States to an unpublished paper by the late Allen Walker Read, "The Persistence of Verbal Symbols of Emotion in Charged Contexts" (composed in 1978; the present location of the manuscript can be found at https://collections.shsmo.org /manuscripts/columbia/c4033.pdf).

25. After failing to reach an accommodation with the palace, the military junta of George Papadopoulos decided to hold a referendum on whether Greece would become a republic. To no one's surprise, the proposal garnered 78.6 percent of the vote despite suspicions of rigging. In fact, when the transitional government of Konstantinos Karamanlis decided to hold a new referendum, the result gave the pro-republic vote an only slightly smaller share (69.18 percent) of the vote. There is little popular enthusiasm today for a restoration of the monarchy.

26. Herzfeld 1991a: 227; Hamilakis and Yalouri 1996: 126.

27. Hamilakis and Yalouri 1996: 125–27.

28. On inchoateness in the early stages of emergent protest formations, see Ardener 1971: xliv.

29. Stengs (2009) attributes this transformation to Rama V (Chulalongkorn), whose Westernization of Siam, precisely because it was proclaimed as a radical move intended to guarantee Siamese independence, marked, in my own interpretation, the definitive re-fashioning of the country as a crypto-colonial nation. Her focus on the resurgence of the present-day cult of Chulalongkorn, coupled with the intense consumerism and the attempts of the middle classes to fend off its spread to the working-class and provincial segments of the population (see Sopranzetti 2012; see also Sopranzetti 2017), indicates that the current political situation in Thailand retains many of the features of crypto-colonialism.

30. Again, see Stengs 2009.

31. The nakleng style is common in southern Thai establishment politicians; see Askew 2008: 305.

32. Sirikit is the widow of Rama IX (Bhumibol) and the mother of the present king, Rama X (Vajiralongkorn). *Suan* means both "park" and "garden"; the garden was thus a clever parodic move.

33. See especially Strate 2015. The psychological relationship among humiliation, developmentalism, and a defensive cultural posture, which some writers have suggested for non-Western societies, is the subject of important reflections and critiques (see Sahlins 1992; Robbins and Wardlow 2005; cf. Moore 2007); socially, at least, the defense of cultural intimacy in modernist states often implies avoidance of collective embarrassment (see Herzfeld 2016a). Greece, like Thailand, was subjected to considerable humiliation by the Western powers over the past two centuries.

34. On this humiliation, see especially Strate 2015. Wyatt (1994: 273–84), by comparison, offers an almost hagiographical assessment of Rama V's reign, but at least acknowledges that Thai historiography invests the king with a virtually magical aura that occludes the opposition that his Westernizing provoked at home or the alarm with which some of his Western advisers viewed certain aspects of his reign.

35. Faster infrastructural development, and therefore greater prosperity, emerged from the greater pressure colonial powers were able to exert on those areas closest to the threatening presence of military invasion; such pressures clearly contributed subsequently to the high status of developmentalism in official Thai thinking. See especially Paik and Vechbanyongratana 2019.

36. Signs of a more independent critique are nevertheless now appearing. See Sopranzetti 2017; Tausig 2019; Ünaldi 2014. At the time of writing, street protests have

become bolder in their objections to royal privilege, a fact that arguably reflects a more sophisticated understanding of royal complaisance, at the very least, in the suppression of democratic freedoms by the military forces controlling the government.

37. Peleggi (2002) offers an astute analysis of Rama V's fascination with European bourgeois culture.

38. All historical writing is necessarily selective. See especially Collingwood 1946; Goldstein 1976.

39. On the Hmong minority, see Tappanai 2019. On the increase in Nazi-themed entertainments and the reactions to complaints, see Ruiz 2019). Comments critical of *farang* (white foreigners) by the Thai minister of public health in connection with COVID-19 (e.g., Khaosod English 2020b) were rightly criticized as racist.

40. The ethnonational model is trenchantly anti-diversity; see Tambiah 1989. Nation-states typically invoke a unified past, sometimes little more than a caricature, that absorbs and dissipates the evidence of multiple origins in order to promote the unity of the present and future (see, e.g., Dietler 1994 on French nationalism and archaeology).

41. Such niceties did not stop Cretan urban anarchists from hailing rebellious mountain villagers as resistance fighters (Kalantzis 2019: 67).

42. On these dynamics, see, notably, Campbell 1964.

43. We owe our understanding of this crucial difference to Hodgen's (1936) astute analysis of these discourses.

44. Kharalambidhis 2010.

45. See Caftanzoglou 2001; Dumont 2020; Herzfeld 1991a.

46. Danforth 1997; Hamilakis 2007: 125–67; Sutton 1997. Greece refused to recognize its northern neighbor as Macedonia until 2019, when an agreement, bitterly contested by hardcore nationalists on both sides, resulted in the compromise name of North Macedonia.

47. See Dumont 2020. The negotiations and pressures are beautifully documented in this important work, which illustrates in painful detail both the insensitivity of the archaeologists and their supporters and, at the same time, the helpless fury of the many residents who were directly affected.

48. See Allen 2013 for a comprehensive account of the espionage carried out by foreign archaeologists in Greece.

49. See especially Sutton 1997; Vernier 1991. The Hellenic Folklore Research Centre was created in 1918 by Nikolaos G. Politis and brought under the aegis of the Academy of Athens immediately after the latter's establishment as an official institution of state.

50. See Herzfeld 2020b: 74–94.

51. O'Connor (1990, 2000) offers an interesting comparison between the classical Greek city-state, or *polis*, and the Thai *moeang*.

52. See Herzfeld 2020b: 106–7. The Dodecanese, where Rhodes is situated, did in fact have a nascent separatist movement in the years following its incorporation into the Greek state in 1948, but the effects of that movement have been minimal.

53. On Rama VI's role, see Barmé 1993: 29.

54. See Julispong and Ittigorn 2000.

55. On Thai attitudes to conservation, see Byrne 2009.

56. On the Surin Khmer minority, see Denes 2015.

57. Dimitris Parasiris (see also Parasiris n.d.) has placed a helpful and detailed etymological account of this and related lexical items on the village website: http://www .zoniana.gr/name.htm (accessed 20 March 2020); the attitude of some educated urban Greeks emerges in the placing of another (and congruent) explanation of the phrase on a website devoted to Greek slang (or *argot*, as the site also calls it, the Gallicism suggestive of a supercilious attitude to local usage): https://www.slang.gr /lemma/15094-za (accessed 20 March 2020).

58. Wanjiru 2016: 264. The "civilizing" of Crete, which only became part of the Kingdom of Greece in 1913, entailed a cartographic transformation in which the topography lost its local points of reference and was recast in terms of street names and numbers and precise cadastral measurements (Herzfeld 1999). Local people will still sometimes use the older system to give directions to other locals.

59. See Parasiris n.d.

60. See Akin 1969: 1; Englehart 2001: 32.

61. They particularly emphasized their status as *phrai* but avoided any hint of antimonarchism. On the centrality of social hierarchy to Thai political history, see, notably, Sopranzetti 2017: 23–24, 192–95; Subrahmanyan 2020: 75.

62. On the constituent elements of this mutual engagement, so characteristic of Thai thought, of the karmic basis of class hierarchy and a Buddhist vision of equality, Bolotta (2021: 17, 65, 97, 182) provides especially interesting insights; see also Tambiah 1976.

63. One architect, holder of the title *mom rachawong* (the great-grandchild of a king), was an ardent supporter of Pom Mahakan and believed that the old houses on the site were important markers of Thai culture. Such individuals, protected to a very limited extent by their royal titles, are in any case few and far between, although some architects, notably the aristocrat Sumet Jumsai, have incorporated vernacular elements into their designs (see, e.g., Perera 2012: 91). In general, the story of vernacular architecture in Thailand is one of continual destruction; ordinary homes do not fit the official royalist narrative that Thongchai (2001) has critically analyzed. Conversely, ignorance of vernacular techniques and a lack of interest on the part of many professional architects generates a waste of available resources despite some attempts, in at least one case initiated by an official body, to incorporate vernacular elements in modern housing (see Poomchai 2010; Tongkao, Tanakarn, and Chinasak 2015).

64. I paraphrased the bureaucrats' ideal role as *phu rapchai prachachon*, servants of the people, in an attempt to gloss the English term *civil servants*; my comment that instead they treated the people as *their* servants was well received in Pom Mahakan, where it converged with local complaints about being treated as *phrai*. Again, the issue is less that of commoner status than that of being treated as predestined to subservience.

65. Reynolds (2006: 32) trenchantly exposes the inappropriateness of the European bureaucratic state as a model for understanding Southeast Asian polities; he also

draws parallels between the latter and what are sometimes called "segmentary states" (Reynolds 2006: 41–42), a perspective that is highly relevant also for the two alternative polities—the Thai moeang (see Tambiah 1976, 1977) and the Cretan segmentary clan system—that I am considering here. The crypto-colonial bureaucratic state is an intrusive mode of governance in both Greece and Thailand, a fact that, not surprisingly, has triggered strong resentment, however indirectly it may be expressed in political practice. The unresolved—and unresolvable?—tension between indigenous and imported models of governance surely lies at the heart of Thailand's continuing political instability; Greece has in this respect been more fortunate, perhaps because it would have been embarrassing for the European Union to tolerate a failure of fully fledged democracy in the European country credited with originating it. Instability plagues other societies in which violent segmentary feuding on a large scale continues to roil the weak new systems mandated by international intervention, as in South Sudan (see, e.g., Hutchinson and Pendle 2015).

66. An Archaeological Service official, for example, contemptuously dismissed migrant workers' house ornamentation as "not very pleasing aesthetically" (Herzfeld 1991a: 37).

67. On the nation-state's aspirations to immortality, see, famously, Anderson 1991; on the translation of this ideal into bureaucratic practice and on its vicissitudes, see Herzfeld 1992 and 2016a.

68. Thai democracy activists, however, have begun using the symbolism of blood as shared substance among the people, thereby inverting the royalist representation of "Thai blood" as an ever-ready symbol both of ethnic unity and of sacrifice for the throne (Elinoff 2020: 72–78).

Chapter 3. Belonging and Remoteness

1. Caldeira 2000; Herzfeld 2006. See also Arjun Appadurai's (2000) discussion of "urban cleansing" and Asher Ghertner's (2010) model of "aesthetic governmentality."

2. Guano 2004.

3. See Greenland 2021: 145–49.

4. Blok 1981: 438.

5. See also Ismailbekova's (2017) notably similar findings for patronage in Kyrgyzstan.

6. Delaney 1995.

7. The morality and operation of patronage constitute a central theme of Campbell's (1964) classic study.

8. For a fuller discussion of foreign involvement in Greek corruption scandals, see Herzfeld 2016b.

9. See Steinmüller 2015: 84, 95–96.

10. Delaney 1995; Özyürek 2004.

11. See, e.g., Steinmüller 2013: 218.

12. Elsewhere in the literature, readers will find the transliterations *muang* and *müang*; transliteration of both Greek and Thai is notoriously inconsistent and highly politicized. I have opted for a simplified phonetic approach that will allow Anglophone readers to arrive at a reasonable approximation in both languages.

13. Scott 2009: 59; and see Heine-Geldern 1956: 3–7; Tambiah 1976, 1977.

14. See the useful account in Navanath 2003, which should be read together with R. Davis 1984, Heine-Geldern 1956, and O'Connor 2000.

15. This process began under Rama IV (Attachak 2000: 81); Attachak's account, while somewhat hagiographic, is interesting for its recognition of the conjuncture of temporality, capitalism, the appeal of foreign goods, and the consolidation of centralized state control of the national territory.

16. This conditional transformation becomes especially evident at the time of a monarch's death. See Anuman 1957.

17. Gray 2006: 46–53.

18. Evans 2002: 163.

19. For one rendition of the section drawings showing the mandala format, see Arsomsilp Community and Environment Architect 2018. I am indebted to Taylor Lowe for sharing with me the results of his meticulous research on the history of the parliament building's design and execution.

20. A further issue with treating Pom Mahakan as an independent *moeang* is that the community lived *outside* the old mandala-shaped wall, although, from its perspective, it was the bureaucrats from the city administration who were the true outsiders. Thus, when the bureaucrats accused the Chao Pom of invading (*buk ruk*) the space, the latter simply turned the accusation back at the bureaucrats (Herzfeld 2016c: 135, 173).

21. One's native country is *ban moeang*; this is the sovereign national territory (see Attachak 2000: 77).

22. See Herzfeld 2016c: 41. For a more positive evaluation of building up a community's *tua ton*, see Nathapong 2005: 52. In Thai the usual word for identity, *atalak*, refers primarily to the external features that constitute recognized markers of group membership; *tua ton* signifies something more processual through which a group gains both self-recognition and external visibility.

23. On the metaphor of siblinghood, which blends familial equality with status differentiation by age, see also chapter 4.

24. On complicity, see also Steinmüller 2013: 219.

25. Konstantinos Kalantzis (personal communication, 2020) reports the version *gestapitis* (from *Gestapo*); in a regional news report I found the form *gestambites* (plural) in a context that clearly supports this etymology (*Rethemniotiko Vima* 2010: 3).

26. Lambropoulos 2008b. If so respectable a medium, with presumed links to the political establishment, could express such views, why would the villagers think otherwise?

27. "Eating" is often used in this way to connote bribery, as it also is, in Zoniana, for animal theft. See also chapter 2 on "eating the polity"; Peutz (2018: 103–4) recounts a view of the Yemeni state as "eating" at the expense of the people of Soqotra. What makes bribery so evil, even in the eyes of those who feel compelled to make such illicit payments, is that they undermine what the state itself claims is the right of every citizen to be treated as an equal.

28. Efetio Pireos 2010: 324–25 (my translation).

29. FlashNews 2011.

30. See Herzfeld 2016c: 179.

31. Society for Threatened Peoples 2004.

32. Military coups can also change the dynamic, as happened with Pom Mahakan. Elinoff (2017, 2021) shows how evictions from the railway tracks of the Thai city of Khon Kaen were aimed at suppressing dissent while also permitting a bourgeois takeover of potentially valuable urban spaces.

33. Wanjiru and Matsubara 2016: 267.

34. E.g., Gikandi 2018.

35. The concept of common good is itself problematic. See Cellamare 2008.

36. See the interview by Thanasis Niarchos (2012).

37. Ardener 1987: 50.

38. Greenland (2021: 119); she also remarks, "Blaming *tombaroli* for bleeding the nation of its patrimony is a crucial move because it masks state inefficiency and widespread mistrust of the government's process of cultural power."

39. Hage 1996: 481.

40. On the discourses of civilization, order, and beauty in Thailand, see Herzfeld 2017a; Stengs 2009; Thongchai 2000. On *khon ban nawk* and their "incursion" into the pale of Bangkok civilization, see Mahony 2018: 100.

Chapter 4. Cosmologies of the Social

1. D. Smith (1996: 279–84) offers an early and cogent historical exposition of this distinctive aspect of the nation-state among the world's many kinds of polity. For a treatment of the northern Thai moeang in cosmological terms, see R. Davis 1984.

2. Kapferer 1988; Kertzer 1980.

3. Heywood 2015, 2017.

4. Malarney 1996.

5. This topic has already generated a great deal of discussion in academic and other media. See, as a useful starting-point, Jiang 2018.

6. Wilcox 2021: 21–23. Evans (2002: 175) comments on the cultural values that have favored the survival of presocialist statues in Laos, an observation that resonates with Wilcox's analysis. On heritage politics in Luang Prabang, see also Berliner 2010.

7. Dakin 1973: 46, 58.

8. See, e.g., Yannaras 1972.

9. On rural moeang, see, e.g., Formoso 1990; R. Davis 1984; O'Connor 1990, 2000.

10. For Greece, see again Yannaras 1972, an exponent of the Neo-Orthodox response to what he regards as the Westernized and bureaucratized—even, in a Weberian sense, "protestant"—characteristics of the official national church. For Thailand, see Taylor 2008. In Thailand, dramatic confrontations between the Dhammakaya and the present regime (see Taylor 2017) illustrate this conflict particularly well. In Greece, religious adherents to the old (Julian or pre-Gregorian) calendar, notably in Crete, reject the moral authority of the official church.

11. See, e.g., Associated Press 2011.

12. Politis 1871–74; Zambelios 1859; see also the discussion in Herzfeld 2020b: 42–44, 114.

13. See, e.g., Aitamurto 2020: 11; *Alfavita* 2012; Mac Sweeney 2019: 6.

14. See, e.g., Gajek 1990; Koehne 2014.

15. Golden Dawn has since been declared a criminal organization by a Greek court and several of its leaders have been sentenced to lengthy terms of imprisonment. See Gatopoulous and Becatoros 2020; H. Smith 2020b.

16. J. Davis (1977: 197) writes of "residual patriliny."

17. Given how the identities of the competing Nuer and Dinka tribes solidified in mutual opposition with the emergence of South Sudan as an independent state, Greek officials' discomfort with Cretan clan organization is perhaps understandable. For the colonial period, see Evans-Pritchard 1940, 1956; for the period of state formation, see Hutchinson and Pendle 2015.

18. Herzfeld 1984b: 658.

19. Durkheim 1960: 295, 305. Evans-Pritchard (1956: 62) introduced the useful metaphor of refraction.

20. The phrase "and the God of Crete with us" was prominent in the 1978 local election propaganda of the Neoliberal party (Neofileleftheri), headed by no less a luminary than Konstantinos Mitsotakis (Herzfeld 1984b: 666–67); Mitsotakis was subsequently elected leader of the New Democracy party, and then became prime minister (1990–93). His son Kyriakos Mitsotakis became New Democracy leader in 2016; since winning the parliamentary elections of 2019, he also has served as prime minister.

21. See Shryock 1997.

22. Lamprakos 2014, 2015.

23. Herzfeld 1987a: 42–44.

24. Di Giovine, forthcoming. On the geopolitical implications of the mandala model in modern Asia, see Dellios 2003, 2019.

25. Herzfeld 2016c: 47–48.

26. Non-Cretans often fail to realize that this usage is explicitly patrilineal since in standard Greek it is used more generically to distinguish *any* category of insiders from the corresponding outsiders. Cretans use the terms in both senses, thereby disguising their distinctive perspective.

27. Revealingly, he was later forced by the rebukes of village women to add the names of female members.

28. This is also the historical relativism that, in the very different context of modern Jordan, has allowed sheikhs to make exclusive claims of historical accuracy for stories about their own segments of a shared patriline (or for their own patrilines against others), and to make that positionality the basis of what they mean by truth; see Shryock 1997: 148–52.

29. Watson 2004.

30. See Friedl 1962: 106. Rozakou (2012) and Voutira (2016) offer usefully critical accounts of the Greek state's expropriation (which Voutira calls "reification") of the ancient tradition of hospitality as the ideological cover for its exclusivist response to foreign immigration. Shryock (2019) debunks larger but related Western myths of hospitality in relation to Bedouin practices in Jordan.

31. Herzfeld 1987b; and see, again, Shryock 2019.

32. Herzfeld 1987b: 81–86; see also Cabot 2014; Kalantzis 2019: 143–45, 199, 238; Papa-taxiarchis 2014; Rozakou 2018. Friedl's (1962: 105–6) observation, based on her 1950s fieldwork, shows how even at that relatively early time the neoclassical obsession with cultural continuity had permeated the consciousness of rural villagers as much as—or perhaps more than—that of urban sophisticates, some of whom privately treated it (and increasingly today treat it) with considerable skepticism. Continuity with ancient traditions of reciprocal hospitality does not conflict with the view that hospitality often serves to express agonistic relations; such relations were no rarer in the ancient Hellenic world than they are in modern Greece (see, e.g., Nagy 1994: 23).

33. Friedl 1962: 105–6; Papataxiarchis 2014, 2017; Rakopoulos 2015a. It can take on decidedly segmentary qualities when a local community decides that the bureau-cratic "hospitality" of migrant detention centers is an affront to their own values (Quagliariello 2021: 27–28).

34. See Harney 2020; Rozakou 2012.

35. See the extended discussion in Herzfeld 1987b.

36. My hosts often seemed keen to make me feel at home; in this, they confirmed Peter Loizos's (1975: 89–92) insight that friendship (*filia*) can be altruistic and interest-oriented at the same time. Sorge (2015: 145), writing of Orgosolo, similarly observes that "a degree of instrumentality, along with a fair dose of selflessness, combined to produce the cohesive compound that holds members together." Only a Eurocentric post-Protestant ethos makes us view actions that are simultaneously self-interested and altruistic as impossibly self-contradictory.

37. Papataxiarchis (2014) notes that humanitarian displays of hospitality to refugees in Greece are consistent with agonistic coffeehouse interaction. See also Rozakou 2018: 174–201.

38. Thus, for Evans-Pritchard's (1949) Cyrenaican Bedouin, the catalyst that led to the emergence of the Libyan state was the comprehensive Italian invasion and bureau-cratic unification of their territories, which had been subdivided among the various clans at several levels of segmentation.

39. The Dublin III Regulation, which went into force in 2013, replaced the Dublin II accord of a decade earlier. These accords were designed to ensure that migrants did not move beyond the national borders of the European Union member countries in which they had arrived. They placed an intolerable burden on countries like Greece, which, being on the front line of arrival, found their already strained econ-omies subjected to enormous additional pressure. See Cabot 2014: 23, 26. On police attitudes, see Cabot 2018; on European Union unfairness in relation to Greece, see Herzfeld 2016b.

40. Even something as apolitical-seeming as coffeehouse sociability becomes an idiom of resistance, as Knight (2015: 121–31; see also Herzfeld 2016a: 201–2) has astutely noted. All of Greece became a stage on which people sat for hours with a single coffee cup or a glass of water, apparently oblivious to the crisis swirling around them. In fact, they were far from oblivious; and they were well aware of the sources of that crisis, which many saw as a repeat of the German Occupation during World War II

(Argenti and Knight 2015; Knight 2015). See also Kalantzis 2015. On coffeehouses as social stages, see especially Herzfeld 1985: 149–62; Loizos 1975: 92; Papataxiarchis 1991. Such performances, far from demonstrating endemic laziness, projected solidarity against the "blond races" that, centuries earlier, had similarly afflicted the Greek-speaking world with their false promises and hegemonic ambitions (see Herzfeld 1973).

41. Rozakou 2018: 24–27; see also Rozakou 2016: 191–92. Also of note is Mamoulaki's (2017) telling critique of anthropological ethnocentrism and the failure to acknowledge the centrality of solidarity in the Greek value system.

42. Rozakou (2018) sees in the shift to voluntarism and solidarity a self-colonizing act of inclusion in the European *mission civilisatrice*. If she is right, this process matches the internal coalescence of the Greek people to the more inclusive coalescence of a "European ideal"—further evidence of a segmentary worldview. In reality, models of solidarity existed long before the crisis; on Rhodes, for example, villagers I met in 1974 either admired the "mutual help" (*allilovoithia*) among the former Jewish population of the island or openly rejoiced in the Jews' deportation by the Nazis.

43. On the *sasmos*, see Herzfeld 1985: 82–83. I was fortunate enough to be caught up in one of my own; to this day, my erstwhile opponent and I are expected to address each other as ritual kin, with appropriate implications of reciprocal obligation and esteem. For an unusually sympathetic journalistic account of this peacemaking dimension of local violence, see *in.gr* 2021.

44. See Herzfeld 1987a: 152–60; Karp and Maynard 1983; Evans-Pritchard 1940. Segmentation occurs in many non-unilineal situations. Bestor (2003: 251–94, especially 266–67), for example, applied the model to practices designed to contain conflict in the Tsukiji fish market in Tokyo—a context to which patrilineal clans were irrelevant.

45. In countries where patrilineal clans are still important nationally, segmentation explains local ways of refracting historical fact that would make little sense to a literal-minded or Eurocentric historian (Dresch 1986; Shryock 1997). We also encounter segmentation, at least implicitly, in the Chinese concept of *guo jia*, nation, in which, like Greek *ikoyenia*, the element *jia* can also mean both household and clan. While the modern nation-state rejects segmentation as the basis of political life, the origins of many nation-states in societies organized according to segmentary principles continually generate tension and contradiction.

46. When it is directly yoked to patrilineality, it becomes more obviously foreign to the European state's official vision, but even then, as Astrinaki (2013: 364) notes for the specific case of Greece, the state finds it convenient (and ideologically consistent) to overlook local particularity and its specific historical formation.

47. See Herzfeld 1987a: 156, 204, 1991b; Rumsey 2004: 287.

48. See the related argument in Ben-Yehoyada 2016.

49. See Strathern 2020: 30, 39.

50. Sunait 1990. Tambiah (2013: 504) sees mandala-based polities as having first emerged with identifiably segmentary properties; these clearly persist, as Sunait shows, in pre-Bangkok Siam, and even, if in shadowy form, in the Chao Pom's understanding of community-polity relations.

51. Appadurai 2006: 4, 8.

52. Tambiah's (2013: 509–11; see also Tambiah 1976, 1977) metaphor of pulsation (and specifically of the "pulsating galactic polity") expresses an especially felicitous contrast to the territorial rigidity of the bureaucratic state.

53. Jory 2016: 18–19; my emphasis. Jory also notes that *barami* seems to be an exclusively male attribute.

54. The activists notably included representatives of the Centre on Human Rights and Evictions at the international level and the Four Slums Network at the national level; students, academics, a lawyer, and a former planning administrator also offered assistance at various times.

55. *Khun pen satru kap thahan*; this is an ambiguous phrase, since *thahan* means both "the [specific] soldiers" and "the military [in general]," the latter a potent threat during a time of military rule.

56. See Kitchana 2019.

57. Much of the information in this paragraph emerged at a desperate last-ditch meeting with the Association's representatives and NGO supporters; there, the president's despair was tragically apparent (see chapter 7).

58. These are described in Herzfeld 2016c: 136–39.

59. For a more detailed discussion, see Herzfeld 2016c: 115–18.

60. I have described this process in detail, as it emerged from the tragic days of the military junta, in my original ethnographic study of Zoniana (Herzfeld 1985: 106–22).

61. The nearest equivalent in Thailand would be the convergence of merit-making and vote-seeking one sees at village funerals (Fishel 2018), but in Pom Mahakan I did not encounter such obvious political patronage beyond the occasional involvement of influential academics in the residents' social activities. Bowie's (2008) account of the political clout matrilocality gave women in a northern Thai village suggests something analogous to the agnatic political contests of Zoniana, but again was not obviously operative in Pom Mahakan. Women did, however, wield great economic authority; in particular, women were the main operators of the Pom Mahakan rotating credit fund.

62. Numbers are often more symbolic than accurate in these villages. When narrating their exploits, for example, sheep thieves would sometimes simply double the numbers on each successive raid, or would produce a series of numbers ending in a single digit (e.g., 7, 17, 27, etc.). Short of accompanying the thieves on their raids, the best I could do was to assess these numbers as expressions of the general level of depredation.

63. Herzfeld 1985: 107.

64. See, e.g., Holmes (1989: 98) on the *onoranze* due to a local lord in northern Italy. Campbell (1964) remains the most authoritative study of how patronage operates at the local level. While some of the more egregious features of this system have fallen victim to a collective sense of national embarrassment, and while the disappearance of systemic patronage may be a matter of time, for the moment much of what Campbell describes exists to this day, albeit in muted and more genteel format.

65. On patronage and international relations, see Herzfeld 2016b.

66. I briefly alluded to this scandal in chapter 3.

67. This lawyer was also later accused of having connections with the "mafia" operating within the same Athens prison in which the convicted Zoniani were incarcerated. There has been no conclusive demonstration of his involvement to date, but the miasma of suspicion remains potent. The state, however, has also provoked suspicion of its intentions in this case; a distinguished constitutional lawyer, Nikos Alivizatos (2019), roundly criticized the uncouth and embarrassingly public way in which the accused was apprehended.

68. See the important discussions of Greek conspiracy theories by Panourgiá (2009).

69. In this instance, the celebration was for both a wedding and the baptism of the couple's two children. In this region of Crete, it is not unusual for a couple to have one or two children before formally marrying. In everyday speech, the engagement ceremony is termed a "wedding" (*ghamos*), implying that sexual relations are now considered licit for the couple.

70. Herzfeld 2016a: 89.

71. On "responsibilization," see Gershon 2011; on its impact on the production of volunteerism in Greece, see Rozakou 2018: 19–22; and on the moral dimensions of neoliberalism, see Muehlebach 2012. It is perhaps a sign of prescience that the political party based in this part of Crete in the early years after the fall of the dictatorship was called "The Neoliberals."

72. They had been locally manufactured in the past but now were apparently imported from China.

73. For the specific details of these rules, see Herzfeld 1985: 149–55.

74. See chapter 3.

75. See R. Davis 1984: 21. See also Sophorntavy 2017: 55.

Chapter 5. A Plurality of Polities

1. See Wimmer and Glick Schiller 2002.

2. My inspiration here comes from Giambattista Vico; see Herzfeld 1987a: 9, 21–25.

3. Thiranagama 2018: 39. In Vietnam, Erik Harms (2016: 4) encountered a strategic use of civility—understood as encompassing civilized attitudes—that seems to straddle the two extremes "as a surrogate [together with contestation of land use rights] for the kind of political life citizens in other countries normally enjoy."

4. Note that *politeness* has a different etymology, being related to the Latin for "clean, polished," and, as such, may signify varying degrees of repression through the imposition of a code of manners and social order. Being politic, on the other hand, does have a direct connection with civility; impolitic behavior is uncivil because it creates awkwardness.

5. Cf. *capital city* with *caput mundi*, "head of the world," the self-designation of imperial Rome.

6. Herzfeld 2009b: 181–217.

7. This inclusive vision is incompatible with the trend toward gated communities. See Caldeira 2000; Low 2001, 2003, 2008.

8. *Mission* is a bureaucratic term in French (being *en mission* can, for an academic, mean being on research leave). It does nevertheless seem to echo the role of *missionaires* (missionaries) in promoting colonial interests, and thereby reveals the persistent religiosity underlying France's self-declared secularism (*laïcité*, from Greek *laos*, "[a] people").

9. See, e.g., Hamilakis 2007; Plantzos 2012, both of whom, moreover, engaged with the concept of crypto-colonialism before many other Greek intellectuals were prepared to do so; and see now Solomon 2021.

10. Caldeira (2000), Feldman (2016), and Silverstein (2010) are rare exceptions. Political scientist James Ockey (2004) makes use of the term in writing of the Thai state and its bureaucracy.

11. It is in the second sense—of an urban center—that the Zoniani generally use *politia*. But we should beware of splitting apart its meanings into three distinct and mutually exclusive concepts, as this would simply return us to the logic of the bureaucratic state.

12. Steinmüller 2013, especially pp. 217–20. Legal systems are generally impossible to follow in their entirety. That impossibility, as Scott (1998: 8) points out, is the basis of the British work-to-rule, which on occasion can bring an entire transportation network, or even the civil service, to its knees in a matter of hours.

13. *Ta Nea* 2018: 11. The agreement to name the neighboring country "Republic of Northern Macedonia" did not satisfy Greek ultranationalists, for whom the Greekness of the name "Macedonia" was nonnegotiable, but the fact that the deal was done shows how far Greece had receded from its erstwhile espousal of such extreme positions. Mount Athos is the semi-independent, exclusively male monastic republic located within Greek territory.

14. Plika 2018.

15. See especially Campbell's (1964: 258) early acknowledgment of this attitude.

16. I am indebted to Michael Stuedli for the Swiss historical memory.

17. Feldman 2016: 515.

18. Balibar 2009: 24–25.

19. Tanabe 2016: 8–14; Turner 1969: 95–96.

20. I do not intend here to diminish the significance of Balibar's insights. On the contrary, he shares with Feldman a deep revulsion for the ways in which border controls have been used as a form of extreme violence, and seeks to discover the possibilities for the emergence of civility with which to resist that violence: "The (democratic) political order is intrinsically fragile or precarious; if not continuously recreated in a politics of civility, it becomes again a 'state of war,' within or across borders" (Balibar 2001: 19). Feldman, however, identifies the actual forms of a transient but important form of civility that short-circuits the rigid opposition between state and migrant, and sees *in such moments* the emergence of polity conceived not as a bounded entity but as a way of facilitating interaction across boundaries. See also Herzfeld 2018b.

21. For a defense of this translation of Weber's German metaphor as a "traveling idea" based on Weber's (1905) original insight, see Baehr 2001: 168–69.

22. His astute assessment reminds us that we should view reification not as an abstruse philosophical problem but as a social process that includes, but is not exhausted by, such formulations as Gayatri Spivak's (1989) well-known concept of "strategic essentialism."

23. Herzfeld 1985: 221–22.

24. His memory appears to have been accurate. A writer for the liberal newspaper *To Vima* commented, "The 'state of Zoniana' once again attacked the . . . powerless Greek Police" (Lambropoulos 2008b).

25. See Cabot 2018: 215, 224. She uses the classical transliteration (*politeia*); I prefer, subversively, to use the modern one as a reminder that its meaning is still under negotiation in Greece as elsewhere.

26. The "Gypsy" claim is doubly racist because it insults both the Zoniani and the various Romani groups now living in Greece and constantly in conflict with the police, who tend to regard them as habitual thieves. It may well reflect the high adhesion to the neofascist political movement Khrisi Avyi (Golden Dawn) among the police rank and file, a tendency for which there has been evidence for some time (see, e.g., Lambropoulos 2014). The irony of these claims lies especially in the fact that while some Zoniani did apparently vote for Golden Dawn, archrival Anoya claims that its residents have unanimously rejected it. This political pattern is an inversion of the time in World War II when the Zoniani could accuse Anoya of having nurtured supporters of the German occupying forces, whereas Zoniana evidently had none. Golden Dawn uses conventional stereotypes of all Cretans as *makherovghaltes* (knife-pullers)—that is, as uncontrollably violent—to justify its mockery of Cretan heroism against the Nazi invasion of the island in 1940 (P.K. 2018: 40). An analogous case is that of the Spanish Maragatos, deemed to be "racially" Berber in the dominant Spanish nationalist discourse (see now González 2016, 2019). Dismissing the Pom Mahakan community as not a "real Thai community" was not an official, public claim but one that a key municipal official offered me as a valid reason for evicting the residents (Herzfeld 2016c: 105).

27. Sovereignty includes the generic right to inhabitation but, as here, not necessarily legal ownership of a specific piece of land. In colonial situations, this distinction may be highly consequential for all parties; see Bacon and Norton 2019: 306. The systemic denial of Thainess is an exclusion from collective sovereignty, whether implicitly (as here) or directly (as in the treatment of immigrants and minorities; see Pinkaew 2014).

28. Bolotta 2021: 17, 98, 182.

29. Thai elite members often condescendingly view the Lao-speaking citizens of the independent Lao state as "younger siblings" (*nong*) of the Thais and in an arrested state of cultural development.

30. Although a large proportion of the residents had moved to Pom Mahakan from other Bangkok locations, or indeed were born on site, that did not grant them the same status as middle-class Bangkokians, and many remained highly conscious of their provincial origins.

31. Heatherington 2010: 223.

32. See Wilcox 2021: 107.

33. On police attitudes in Greece, see Cabot 2014: 14, 48–50, 56; Herzfeld 2011: 22 (and on a comparable phenomenon in Italy, see Herzfeld 2009b: 227–30). For Thailand the evidence thus far is mostly journalistic; the government reacts defensively to any

suggestion that the police have behaved with anything less than perfect professionalism; see, e.g., Jack Burton 2020.

34. Some Zoniana votes for Golden Dawn in the 2015 parliamentary elections seem, on the evidence of two informants, to represent a protest against the major parties rather than an endorsement of the group's neofascist ideology.

35. In earlier years, especially under the Metaxas regime, the Greek government used "exile" (*eksoria*)—that is, to a remote border area or island—as a punishment for both animal-thieves and political offenders. In this way, the state identified remoteness as removal from the community of humankind and established a clear parallel between the traditional practice of animal theft on the one hand and alleged political offenses on the other.

36. See Lefevre and Aukkarapon 2014. Thaksin had himself held lieutenant-colonel rank in the police until it was revoked by the military regime in 2015.

37. On Golden Dawn's popularity among the police, again see Lambropoulos 2014. It remains to be seen whether the movement's disbandment as a political party will change that situation or drive such sympathies further underground.

38. Herzfeld 2016c: 185.

39. Høyem 2018: 92.

40. In Crete, the media often suggest that villagers who deal in drugs are betraying their own claims to manly valor (Kalantzis 2019: 61).

41. On diversity in pre-Bangkok Siam, see Wolters 2018: 127–28.

42. This statement holds especially true as such communities unite to defend their rights across international borders; see Niezen's (2003) comprehensive account.

43. See Denes 2015; see also chapter 2.

44. Niezen 2003: 204–6. These relations are, as Bacon and Norton (2019) argue, ultimately colonial in nature, a situation that imposes massive constraints on governance reform but does not preclude, and may even encourage, "indigenous peoples' agentic, strategic responses" (2019: 305) that in turn reshape the colonial framework itself.

45. While Sunait (1990: 90) recognizes the segmentary proclivities of the pre-Bangkok Siamese polity, he suggests that patrilineality played no significant role there as authority sprang from individual charisma rather than clan solidarity. The moeang is thus a very different polity from the agnatic clan, although both exhibit strongly fissile tendencies at times of internal tension and a capacity for reaggregation to face external menace.

46. Gibson 2007: 5.

47. My coinage of "methodological statism" follows the logic of Wimmer and Glick Schiller's (2002) "methodological nationalism."

48. Caldeira 2000: 302–4, citing especially Jacobs 1993 [1961]. Her broad definition of the liberal tradition—which brackets Charles Taylor with Étienne Balibar and Chantal Mouffe, for example—is helpful in showing that even some of the more "revolutionary" writers operated on the basis of culturally shared assumptions about the meaning of urban space; those assumptions are totally at odds with the exclusivism of neoliberal governance.

49. O'Connor 2000: 442n13; see also O'Connor 1990: 65.

50. Chernela 2008; see also D'Orsi and Dei 2018: 117, 123. Evans-Pritchard's (1940) classic study of the Nuer has been widely discussed; see especially Karp and Maynard's (1983) use of the term "moral community," which distances it from Durkheim's (1960: 63) more restricted sense.

51. In Campbell's (1964: 9) description, the Sarakatsani similarly conceive of their community in moral terms.

52. See also John W. Burton's (1983: 112) discussion of the way in which a moral community may be generated through a ritual act that first connects a group of people to a place.

53. Yalouri 2001, especially 142.

54. Low 1995, 1996. On the complex of meanings surrounding the terms *lak* and *moeang*, see, usefully, Raendchen 2000, where the exclusive translation of the first term as "pillar" is questioned. Whatever its literal meaning, some sort of vertical structure—a tree, perhaps a phallic symbol, or a stupa—appears to be the common denominator across a wide variety of Tai-speaking groups.

55. On Rome, see Herzfeld 2009b: 102–8; on Thailand, see Siani 2020.

56. It is not particularly helpful, in this context, to distinguish between formal or ecclesiastical and informal or popular religion (see Stewart 1989). There is a continuum of *usage* that indicates the often unstable, shifting significance of such physical manifestations of religiosity for members of the local population.

57. That process was all the more notable for having been achieved without military violence; ironically, Rama I had built the fort at Pom Mahakan precisely to repel the expected French invaders sailing up the Chao Praya River. On Europeanization and its eventual, paradoxical conflation with Thai identity, Saichon (2002: 143) notes that at one point Thainess was equated with traits "of already advanced nations" such as wearing European-style trousers and celebrating the New Year on 1 January instead of 1 March. See also Thongchai 2000.

58. For relevant critiques of official historiography, see Reynolds 2006; Thongchai 1994, 2001. Another example of this smoothing of dynastic history is the canonization of King Taksin, the monarch whom Rama I—founder of the present dynasty—defeated in battle, killed, and supplanted; Taksin was subsequently assimilated to the national historiography as a worthy precursor and great king (Evans 2002: 165).

59. See especially O'Connor 2000: 433–34.

60. See the important discussion of the cult of Rama V in Stengs 2009.

61. Johnson 2020: 54.

62. *Dai* is a Chinese coinage that apparently results from the impossibility of distinguishing, in Mandarin, between the aspirated (ᴨ) and unaspirated (ᴨ) forms of "t" and a resulting tendency to confuse the unvoiced and unaspirated "t" (ᴨ) with voiced "d" (ᴨ).

63. See the more detailed discussion in Herzfeld 2016c: 61–62, 77.

64. The political families are often defined by patrilineal descent, itself indicated by surnames (Papandreou, Karamanlis) and organized to play the democratic framework much as the Roosevelts, Kennedys, and Bushes have done in the United States. In the United States, too, patrilineality is still marked by royal-sounding marks of dynastic succession ("John C. Brown III").

Chapter 6. Subversive Comparisons

1. This approach has long been my preferred strategy; see especially Herzfeld 1984a, 1987a, 2017b, 2019; cf. Candea 2019: 290–91. Candea (2019: 32) usefully describes the emergence of a loftily colonial comparativism that still sometimes underlies even apparently radical alternatives. In turning comparison itself into a *comparandum*, he begins to dismantle that conceptual imperium, and does so, albeit with somewhat different goals, in a way that resonates with the intentional transgression attempted here.

2. Faubion (1993) has also worked in Greece.

3. Faubion 2001: 11.

4. Gramsci 1971; see also Bates 1975; Herzfeld 2015.

5. Faubion 2001 :43—with the proviso, however, that the Branch Davidians recognized that the future might not reproduce past experience.

6. It might also be worth exploring the suppression of Dravidian-speaking Dalits in India—people whose claims on a greater antiquity than that of the Aryan *Hindutva* state must cause some anxiety in New Delhi. For a discussion of the complex relations of indigenous groups and the state in India, see Wolf and Heidemann 2014.

7. On informality, see, e.g., Thomas 2016: 53–54.

8. Walker (2012) describes Thai peasants who similarly try to work within the state system, but his account does not involve archaizing strategies as such. He does, however, discuss the active ritual engagement of local spirits—"an attempt to draw external power into more intimate and localized spheres" (110)—in exploiting the symbolic power of the state. We might instead, or complementarily, view that entity in cosmological terms as the encompassing moeang or segmentary polity.

9. Scott 1985.

10. The term *bandit*, especially in Italian (*bandito*), has precisely this sense of being "banned" from operating within the national territory.

11. Sorge 2015: 38.

12. Heatherington 2010: 220.

13. Sorge 2015: 77. Carta (2015: 91–125) sees in Vittorio De Seta's 1961 film *Banditi a Orgosolo* a genuinely ethnographic portrayal of the Orgolesi, which contrasts with the stereotypical images of peasants living in a past time characteristic of Italian films of earlier periods. The prevalence of banditry in Orgosolo led to severe repression by the state, but here the violent official reaction seems to have been motivated by genuine fears of separatism as well as the political and economic costs of banditry left unchecked. In Zoniana, by contrast, the politicians who had the most to gain from reciprocal animal-rustling, through the patronage they extended to the perpetrators, would then fulminate against the practice.

14. See my discussion of the place of the village in the construction of Greek identity today (Herzfeld 2020c); see also Kalantzis 2020.

15. Greenland 2021: 25, 150–80; Hom 2015: 186.

16. See especially Friedl 1962: 105–6.

17. See, for example, Thomas 2016: 235; Thomas shows how urban *ladinos* in Guatemala are convinced that there "are no indigenous people in the city." Here we encounter

an old European conceit that regards urbanity (in both senses) as a European (and colonial) prerogative. For Italians, this claim is uncomplicated: they see themselves collectively as the very quintessence of European urbanity. Urban Greek sophisticates, however, are often embarrassed by a rural population that does not necessarily share their ideas of civilized living, even though it does share with them values of obligation and pride.

18. I say "internal" cultural diversity because many Italian cities and regions have been resistant to recognizing the non-Italian (migrant) presence, in some cases seeing the proliferation of ethnic restaurants as a threat to the survival of distinctive regional cuisines or even of national specialties. See, e.g., Blogo 2008; Guerrisi 2008.

19. The major exception today, not surprisingly, is the attitude of ultrarightist Romans, for whom *romanità* still represents a hypermasculine and authoritarian ideal. Their public violence reciprocally fuels the anti-Roman prejudice in other parts of the country.

20. See Odermatt 1996.

21. On that struggle, see Heatherington's (2010) comprehensive account.

22. See Heatherington 2010: 53; her observation resonates with my own description, not of Cretan identity in particular, but of Greek identity in general as that of "aboriginal Europeans" (Herzfeld 1987a: 49–76). Sardinians often insist that Sard is not a dialect but a language, a distinction that has a basis in law; the regional government uses both in its official name (Regione Autònoma de Sardigna 1997). With this one striking exception, everyday Italian usage recognizes as "languages" only those speech forms that are not recognizably related to standard Italian (e.g., Alberësh, the Albanian spoken in southern Italy). On the other hand, even Romans will speak of their local dialect (*romanesco*) and standard Italian (*italiano*) as though they were entities of equivalent status, a conceit that would be incomprehensible to most Cretans. I have heard a Zonianos boast about me to visitors, "He speaks our language [*ghlossa*]!"—meaning what Greeks, including Zoniani, would more ordinarily call a dialect (*dhialektos*). Such statements, however, do not imply a political contrast between language and dialect, as they would for many Sardinians; the Zoniani are apparently unanimous and unambiguous in their intense devotion to Greek identity, a stance that is central to their subversive archaism.

23. See Herzfeld 1985: 40–45.

24. Sorge is clearly fascinated by the commonalities displayed by various Mediterranean societies, but his subtle interpretations largely escape the excessive generalization of "Mediterranean culture" about which I complained in some of my earliest anthropological writings (see especially Herzfeld 1980, 1984a, 1987a). As we will see later, what he says about friendship and hospitality in Orgosolo resonates nicely with Evthymios Papataxiarchis's analyses of male sociality on the island of Lesvos in Greece. But intra-Mediterranean differences do reflect the divergent historical and geopolitical trajectories of the various nation-states.

25. For an early and influential account of civiltà, see Silverman 1975. While Italian society has not been uniformly welcoming to foreign migrants (and while the same applies to the northern Italian reception of southern Italian migrants), the self-image of

mutual tolerance and "cohabitation" is deeply ensconced in the usual self-stereotype. On *convivenza*, see Herzfeld 2009b: 211, 223.

26. For a sophisticated account of the complex mutual entanglements of karma, status, wealth, merit (*bun*), and manners in Bangkok, see especially Sophorntavy 2017: 129–36. On the shifting relationship between moral status and wealth and the role of manners in cementing the bourgeoisie's mutual entanglement with royalist hierarchy as an affluent merchant class grew to dominance from modest beginnings in the eighteenth century, see Jory 2021, especially 33–34.

27. Sophorntavy 2017: 126–28.

28. On the clothing of bodies in relation to status and space, see Van Esterik 2000: 207; Sophorntavy 2017: 56. Sophorntavy (2017: 51–52) connects the symbolism of height as expressed in urban contexts to symbolic articulations long entrenched in the Tai-speaking cultural universe.

29. Low and Smith 2006: 4. See also O'Connor 1991, 2000.

30. Herzfeld 2016c: 27.

31. Leach 1956.

32. That perspective may itself have roots in ancient cosmological ideas; see Heine-Geldern 1956: 1.

33. Scott 2009.

34. Scott 2009: 179, 290.

35. See Bouté 2011; Decourtieux 2013; Rozenberg 2012.

36. Rozenberg 2012: 216.

37. Hardy 2015.

38. See Scott 1998. Scott's concern with the state's attempt to make communities "legible" has clear resonances with the concept of "audit culture" (see Shore and Wright 1999, 2015; Strathern 2000).

39. Scott 2009: 290.

40. See chapter 4.

Chapter 7. Civility, Parody, and Invective

1. I define social poetics as the capacity to control and play creatively with social conventions; it addresses the tension between convention and invention in everyday life (Herzfeld 2016a: 175).

2. Jackson 2004. See also the analysis of media production in Isaacs 2019.

3. Kalantzis (2012, 2014, 2016, 2019) provides valuable discussions of the *local* production of images of Cretan masculinity and situates these images in a political economy of representation. On the nakleng in provincial Thailand, see Askew 2008; Pattana 2005. On the bourgeois models that animate royal imagery, see Peleggi 2002. And on the fusion of such models with present-day consumer culture, see Isaacs 2019.

4. Kalantzis 2016: 25. But Cretan men do, in their own diamond-in-the-rough way, also perform elaborate courtesies, as Robert Pashley (1837) noted when traveling in Crete in 1834. See also chapter 1.

5. Kalantzis (personal communication, 2020) nevertheless reports that, with a demographic reversal through the arrival of new families, feuding has become more frequent again in Sfakia. For other discussions of Cretan masculinity, see Astrinaki 2002; Damer 1988; Machin 1983; Saulnier 1980.

6. While the concept of *du di* has some common ground with the Italian notion of *fare bella figura*, the latter is not as explicitly class-based and does not have the same implication of inevitability that the Thai focus on karma entails. On hegemonic Thai notions of "good culture," see Denes 2015; on manners, see Jory 2021; Sophorntavy 2017: 52–53.

7. Denes 2015; Herzfeld 2017a.

8. See Isaacs 2019; Sopranzetti 2012.

9. On the referents of *khwam suai ngam*, "beauty," see Herzfeld 2017a.

10. See Weber 1930.

11. There is a further irony in the persistence today of the *khwam pen thai* model so passionately advocated in his time by Phibun, who is now being quietly erased from the pantheon of authoritarian predecessors to the current military establishment. His participation in the 1932 military coup that attempted to reform the monarchy as a constitutional institution makes him an awkward predecessor to the present royal-military complex, especially at a time of increasingly vocal criticism of royal prerogative and military authoritarianism. On the political uses of Thainess since the military coup of 2014, see Farrelly 2016.

12. See the discussions in Elinoff 2017; Herzfeld 2017a.

13. The yoking of polite lexical ornaments to a provincial dialect in which they were not customary exposed supporters of the Assembly of the Poor to ridicule in the 1990s (see Missingham 2003: 166).

14. See Tausig 2019: 176.

15. Tausig 2019: 48.

16. The premise of national homogeneity rests on the "iconicity" principle that underlies much nationalism (Herzfeld 2016a: 100–106). Anderson (1991) argues that nationalism allows individuals to imagine themselves as sharing a set of characteristics with their co-nationals.

17. It also served as the main illustration in the poster for the 2018 Morgan Lectures. Interestingly, a nearly identical STOP sign appears in a picture of a caravan used by a group allegedly plotting to kidnap the governor of Michigan, Gretchen Whitmer, just before the 2020 U.S. national elections. This does not prove a kindred attitude on the part of the Zoniani and the alleged kidnappers, even if they have at times shown similar proclivities for violent self-expression; rather, it underscores the importance of seeing beyond coincidences of symbolism to distinguish carefully among widely varying—and differently motivated—shades of opposition to state authority.

18. Gupta 1998.

19. Jintamas 2018.

20. I write of *degrees* of democracy as being more expressive of the actual contrast than a simple binary of "democracy" and "dictatorship." The Greek democratic system still confronts serious shortcomings in controlling police excesses and addressing

the rights of migrants and minorities (see, e.g., Cabot 2014, 2018; E. Davis 2012; Rozakou 2012, 2017a, 2018; Voutira 2016), while the Thai government describes its polity as "Thai-style democracy" (Farrelly 2016: 333)—an exceptionalist appropriation of the concept of democracy that recalls the discursive tactics of the Greek military dictatorships of 1967–74. The two countries nevertheless today present a stark contrast, especially in terms of the representativeness of their respective parliamentary systems and of speech and press freedoms.

21. On being *siwilai*, see Thongchai 2000.

22. See the more detailed account in Herzfeld 2016c: 188, 198–99.

23. This claim, a nice example of local functionalism, recalls Max Gluckman's (1955) famous "peace in the feud."

24. Herzfeld 2016c: 34–35.

25. I was interviewed twice in *Matichon* (18 March 2017, 13; 2 February 2019, 13) and published op-ed pieces there (in Thai) and in the *Bangkok Post* (in English) during these final years. Earlier, I had written for *The Nation* and its Thai-language companion newspaper *Krungthaep Turakit*, but the *Nation* group became notably less willing to confront government after the military coups of 2006 and 2014. Many Thai journalists supported the Chao Pom; among these, Ploenpote Atthakor, writing in the *Bangkok Post*, was consistently staunch. While press freedom is severely limited in Thailand, courageous—if sometimes necessarily cautious—journalism continues to flourish in a few publications. Criticism of municipal authorities is also safer than even mildly critical commentary on national-level personages and institutions.

26. See also chapter 1.

27. De Genova 2017. On illegalization more generally, see Thomas and Galemba 2013: 211.

28. The phrase *matter out of place* is often vaguely attributed to Douglas 1966, where in fact it does not appear; Douglas did invoke it elsewhere, attributing it, perhaps incorrectly, to Lord Chesterfield (Campkin 2013: 47–48). I take the term *dangerous populations* from Foran (1998: 3–4), who opens an analysis of social movements in Iran by tracing a useful genealogy of the term to the nineteenth-century French concept of "dangerous classes."

29. See Caldeira 2000: 32, also citing Balibar 1991: 19 and Douglas 1966: 40. There is an obvious parallel here with racial profiling, which reproduces the logic of segregation.

30. In Greece I had the advantage, until Brexit, of being an EU citizen, in addition to looking less different from my interlocutors and being more comfortable in the language from the start. On changing Thai perceptions of my language and gestures over time, see Herzfeld 2009a.

31. See Caldeira 2000: 9.

32. See, for example, the respectful pronoun with which a powerful Roman lawyer snubbed an opposing, junior colleague, thereby denying him even a pretense of collegial recognition (Herzfeld 2009b: 35).

33. It is considered highly impolite to put the fork in one's mouth at all, although this happens with increasing frequency among young people or those wishing to exhibit

modern sophistication. The adoption of European-style eating utensils was one of Rama V's reforms; the code of etiquette that accompanied it can entrap the unwary.

34. On imperialist nostalgia, see Rosaldo 1989.
35. I am grateful to Paritta Chalermpow Koanantakool (personal communication, 2020) for suggesting this possible interpretation.
36. See Bourdieu 1977: 37–40 for a discussion of officializing strategies.
37. See chapter 4.

Chapter 8. Does a Subversive Past Have a Viable Future?

1. Sopranzetti 2017: 259–66.
2. See Chatri 2003; Pravit 2020b.
3. For an early discussion, see Herzfeld 1987a: 125–6.
4. Gupta 2012: 19.
5. Siani 2020: 107; Sophorntavy 2017: 134–35.
6. See also Sophorntavy 2017: 194.
7. See Appadurai 2006: 8–9.
8. On Thai consumerism, see especially Sopranzetti 2012.
9. See Isaacs n.d.; Sophorntavy 2017.
10. In Thailand many NGOs supporting poor communities are run by middle-class people, among whom academics and students figure prominently, but these groups represent a small and relatively privileged minority.
11. I take the term from the Israeli use of biblical archaeology—note the appeal to antiquity again—to justify the annexation of Palestinian land. See especially Abu El-Haj 2001. On the creation of self-fulfilling prophecies of material change, see especially Holmes's (2013) account of central bank officers' predictions, which overdetermined public expectations and thereby created the economic situation the bankers desired.
12. See Herzfeld 1985: 263, 267.
13. Cartoon by Andreas Petroulakis dated 23 December 2013 and published in *I Kathimerini*. It can be accessed at this (derivative) site: https://www.cretans.gr/2014/10/01/apothane-o-kalasnikof/ (accessed 21 March 2020). The site is a Cretan one, which suggests that some Cretans enjoyed the joke, though whether sympathetically or from Schadenfreude is unclear.
14. The cartoon, by Tasos Anastasiou, appears under the heading "Ο Τάσος Αναστασίου για τον τρομονόμο [Tasos Anastasiou on the terror law]" in 3point-magazine, 29 June 2018, https://3pointmagazine.gr/o-τάσος-αναστασίου-για-τον-τρομονόμο/.
15. Scott 2009; for a critique, see Jonsson 2014.
16. Jonsson 2014: 7–8.
17. Ducourtieux 2013: 452.
18. The term *kala'ndras*, more fully *kala andras*, literally means "well [performing] man," a gendered evaluation as opposed to being considered "a good human being" (*kalos anthropos*). A *kala'ndras* or *kala kleftis* (good at being a thief) is distinguished by

performative skills that highlight his masculinity and make it socially palpable. See Herzfeld 1985: 38–39, 47.

19. See, for example, Yanagisako and Delaney 1995; see also Herzfeld 2016a: 79–81, 114–16.

20. The text of the law can be found in Greek at http://www.coo.org/2013/01/greek -penal-code-article-187A.html (accessed 20 March 2021). "In theory, Article 187A of the Criminal Code was drawn up with the intention of confronting terrorist activity, but it ended up by criminalizing other activities as well, with the result that it condemned group actions that have no connection with terrorism. It was introduced into Greek legislation via international and European accords" (Stefou 2018). For a more general and equally scathing critique of the law, see Misos Taksiko 2015.

21. See especially Holmes's (2000) account of ultrarightists in the European Parliament.

22. On resentment as a motor of much modern nationalism, see Greenfeld 1993.

23. For further discussion, see Herzfeld 2020a.

24. On the Declaration of Independence, see Wills 1978: 341–45; on the Magna Carta, see Helmholz 2016; Radin 1947.

25. The specter of an invasive "communism" still haunts U.S. politics, while in both Greece and Thailand communism has often been treated as a foreign—and therefore dangerous—dogma (see also chapter 5). Right-wing libertarian ideas map all too easily onto ethnonationalism.

26. See, e.g., Bennhold 2020. Even Dyal's (2018) relatively sympathetic analysis, while offering a useful (and rare) recognition of the intellectual underpinnings of right-wing extremism, cannot disguise the violent and destructive consequences of any eventual political ascendancy on the part of these groups.

27. See H. Smith 2020a. In a searing indictment of police collusion with Golden Dawn members prior to their eventual conviction, Papapandoleon (2020) clearly distinguishes between the rule of law and a rightist establishment's passivity in the face of such collusion. Halkià (2015) had already presciently noted establishment collusion in Golden Dawn's impunity and in its members' brutal violence against racial, sexual, and ideological others—a stance that displays, we may add, none of the structured reciprocity fundamental to Cretan concepts of masculine vengeance.

28. On this, see especially Feldman's (2019: 21) astute comment on the "benighted sense" that one can perhaps identify in at least one instance of Nazism's intellectual appeal.

29. See Gallant 2015: 34. Many villagers are already disinclined to revert to violence as a way of settling disputes, although they still take pride in the local reconciliation ritual (see chapter 4) while also regarding some acts of revenge as morally legitimate.

30. An editorial in the English-language daily *Bangkok Post* (2020) offered this caustic comment: "After booting the old Mahakan Fort community out of their homes in 2018, and turning the area into a park intended for tourists, the Bangkok Metropolitan Administration (BMA) recently, for the first time, tacitly admitted to its mistake. The park, which was officially opened in July 2018, has been nothing short of a failure, and seen very small numbers of visitors." See also Sirinya 2020.

31. Many of the trees had been treated as sacred persons by the residents (for example, a *bodhi* tree [*ton pho*] would be considered descended from the original under which

the Buddha received enlightenment, and some venerable trees had been ordained as monks prevent their destruction [Herzfeld 2016c: 31]). On sacred trees, in a very different context, see also Siani 2020: 116.

32. Contrast, for example, what happens to monuments marked as "World Heritage" and consequently exposed to the destructive wrath of anti-Western revolutionaries (Meskell 2018).

References

Abu El-Haj, Nadia. 2001. *Facts on the Ground: Archaeological Practice and Territorial Self-Fashioning in Israeli Society*. Chicago: University of Chicago Press.

Abu-Lughod, Lila. 1990. "The Romance of Resistance: Tracing Transformations of Power through Bedouin Women." *American Ethnologist* 17:41–55.

AGFE. 2005. *Forced Evictions: Towards Solutions?* Nairobi: Advisory Group on Forced Evictions [UN-Habitat].

AGFE. 2007. *Second Report: Forced Evictions: Towards Solutions?* Nairobi: Advisory Group on Forced Evictions [UN-Habitat].

Aitamurto, Kaarina. 2020. "The Rise of Paganism and the Far Right in Europe." In *Oxford Research Encyclopedia of Religion*. Oxford: Oxford University Press. https://doi.org/10.1093/acrefore/9780199340378.013.681.

Akin Rabibhadana. 1969. *The Organization of Thai Society in the Early Bangkok Period*. Ithaca, NY: Cornell Southeast Asia Program.

Alfavita. 2012. "Οι 'ιουδαιοχριστιανικές' κωλοτούμπες της Χρυσής Αυγής" [The 'Judeo-Christian' somersaults of Golden Dawn]. 16 October. https://www.alfavita.gr/koinonia/3007_oi-ioydaiohristianikes-kolotoympes-tis-hrysis-aygis.

Alivizatos, Nikos K. [Αλιβιζάτος, Νίκος]. 2019. "Ελλείματα νομικού πολιτισμού" [Failures of legal culture]. *I Kathimerini*, 20 April. http://www.kathimerini.gr/1020521/article/epikairothta/ellada/n-alivizatos-elleimmata-nomikoy-politismoy.

Allen, Susan Heuk. 2013. *Classical Spies: American Archaeologists with the OSS in World War II Greece*. Ann Arbor: University of Michigan Press.

Anderson, Benedict R. O'G. 1991. *Imagined Communities: Reflections on the Origin and Spread of Nationalism*. 2nd ed. London: Verso.

Anderson, Benedict R. O'G. 2014. *Exploration and Irony in Studies of Siam over Forty Years*. Ithaca, NY: Cornell Southeast Asia Program.

Anuman Rajadhon, Phya. 1957. "The Golden Meru." *Journal of the Siam Society* 45:65–72.

Apostolakis, Andreas. 1993. Letter. *Rethemniotika Nea*, 31 December.

Appadurai, Arjun. 2000. "Spectral Housing and Urban Cleansing: Notes on Millennial Mumbai." *Public Culture* 12, no. 3 (Fall): 627–51.

Appadurai, Arjun. 2006. *Fear of Small Numbers: An Essay on the Geography of Anger*. Durham, NC: Duke University Press.

Ardener, Edwin. 1971. Introduction to *Social Anthropology and Language*, edited by E. W. Ardener, ix–cii. London: Tavistock.

Ardener, Edwin. 1975. "The Problem Revisited." In *Perceiving Women*, edited by Shirley Ardener, 19–27. London: Malaby.

Ardener, Edwin. 1987. "'Remote Areas': Some Theoretical Considerations." In *Anthropology at Home*, edited by Anthony Jackson, 38–54. London: Tavistock. Subsequently published in *Hau: Journal of Ethnographic Theory* 2 (2012): 519–33.

Argenti, Nicolas, and Daniel M. Knight. 2015. "Sun, Wind, and the Rebirth of Extractive Economies: Renewable Energy Investment and Metanarratives of Crisis in Greece." *Journal of the Royal Anthropological Institute* 21 (n.s.): 781–802.

Arsomsilp Community and Environment Architect. 2018. "Sappaya-Sapasathan." https://arsomsilparchitect.co.th/en/project/sappaya-sapasathan-2/.

Asia News. 2019. "Following Criticism of Muslim Students 'Profiling,' Prayut Defends the Police," 18 September. http://www.asianews.it/news-en/Following-criticism-of-Muslim-students-%27profiling%27,-Prayut-defends-the-police-48040.html.

Askew, Marc. 2008. *Performing Political Identity: The Democrat Party in Southern Thailand*. Chiang Mai: Silkworm.

Associated Press. 2011. "Greek Protesters Decry Mark of the Beast ID Cards." 6 February. https://www.cvtnews.ca/greek-protesters-decry-mark-of-the-beast-id-cards-1.604456.

Astrinaki, Ourania [Αστρινάκη, Ουρανία]. 2002. "Ο Άντρας κάνει τη Γενιά ή η Γενιά τον Άντρα: Ταυτότητες, Βία, Ιστορία στην Ορεινή Δυτική Κρήτη" [The man makes the clan and not the clan the man: Identities, violence, history in mountain western Crete]. PhD diss., Pandio University of Social and Political Sciences. http://thesis.ekt.gr/thesisBookReader/id/15610#page/1/mode/2up.

Astrinaki, Ourania [Αστρινάκη, Ουρανία]. 2013. "'Παράδοση Βίας' και ιδιώματα κρητικότητας στις ορεινές κοινοτητες της δυτικής Κρήτης" ["A tradition of violence" and idioms of Cretanness in the mountain communities of western Crete]. In *Ελληνικά Παράδοξα: Πατρωνία, Κοινωνία Πολιτών και Βία* [Greek paradoxes: Patronage, civil society and violence], edited by Eleni Gara and Katerina Rozakou, 363–401. Athens: Alexandria.

Attachak Sattayanurak. 2000. "The Intellectual Aspects of Strong Kingship in the Late Nineteenth Century." *Journal of the Siam Society* 88:72–95.

Aulino, Felicity. 2019. *Rituals of Care: Karmic Politics in an Aging Thailand*. Ithaca, NY: Cornell University Press.

Bachofen, Johann Jakob. 1861. *Das Mutterrecht: Eine Untersuching über die Gynakokratie der alten Welt nach ihrer religiösen und rechtlichen Natur*. Stuttgart: Krais und Hoffmann.

Bacon, J. M., and Matthew Norton. 2019. "Colonial America Today: U.S. Empire and the Political Status of Native American Nations." *Comparative Studies in Society and History* 61:301–31.

Baehr, Peter. 2001. "The 'Iron Cage' and the 'Shell as Hard as Steel': Parsons, Weber, and the Stahlhartes Gehäuse Metaphor in *The Protestant Ethic and the Spirit of Capitalism*." *History and Theory* 40:153–69.

Baer, Hans A. 2018. *Democratic Eco-Socialism as a Real Utopia: Transitioning to an Alternative World System*. New York: Berghahn.

Bakalaki, Alexandra. 1994. "Gender-Related Discourses and Representations of Cultural Specificity in Nineteenth-Century and Twentieth-Century Greece." *Journal of Modern Greek Studies* 12:75–106.

Baker, Chris, and Pasuk Phongpaichit. 2016. *The Palace Law of Ayuttaha and the Tham-masat: Law and Kingship in Siam*. Ithaca, NY: Cornell University Press.

Balibar, Étienne. 1991. "Is There a 'Neo-Racism'?" In *Race, Nation, Class: Ambiguous Identities*, edited by Étienne Balibar and Immanuel Wallerstein, 17–28. London: Verso.

Balibar, Étienne. 2001. "Outlines of a Topography of Cruelty: Citizenship and Civility in the Era of Global Violence." *Constellations* 8:15–29.

Balibar, Étienne. 2009. "Violence and Civility: On the Limits of Political Anthropology." *Differences* 20:9–35.

Bangkok Post. 2020. "The Mahakan Fort Mistake." 31 October. https://www.bangkokpost.com/opinion/opinion/2011531/the-mahakan-fort-mistake.

Barmé, Scot. 1993. *Luang Wichit Wathakan and the Creation of a Thai Identity*. Singapore: Institute of Southeast Asian Studies.

Barrow, Richard. 2015. "The Bank of Thailand to Launch New 100-Baht Banknote." Richard Barrow in Thailand, 24 February http://www.richardbarrow.com/2015/02/the-bank-of-thailand-to-launch-new-100-baht-banknote/.

Bates, Thomas R. 1975. "Gramsci and the Theory of Hegemony." *Journal of the History of Ideas* 36:351–66.

Belew, Kathleen. 2018. *Bring the War Home: The White Power Movement and Paramilitary America*. Cambridge, MA: Harvard University Press.

Bennhold, Katrin. 2020. "Body Bags and Enemy Lists: How Far-Right Police Officers and Ex-Soldiers Planned for 'Day X.'" *New York Times*, 1 January.

Ben-Yehoyada, Naor. 2016. "'Follow Me, and I Will Make You Fishers of Men': The Moral and Political Scales of Migration in the Central Mediterranean." *Journal of the Royal Anthropological Institute* 22:183–202.

Berliner, David. 2010. "Perdre l'esprit du lieu: Les politiques de l'UNESCO à Luang Prabang (RDP Lao)." *Terrain* 55:80–105.

Bestor, Theodore C. 2003. *Tsukiji: The Fish Market at the Center of the World*. Berkeley: University of California Press.

Blogo. 2008. "Via il menu etnico dalle scuole. Si torna alla carbonara." 21 May. https://www.blogo.it/post/3339/via-il-menu-etnico-dalle-scuole-si-torna-alla-carbonara.

Blok, Anton. 1981. "Rams and Billy-Goats: A Key to the Mediterranean Code of Honour." *Man* (n.s.) 16:427–40.

Bolotta, Giuseppe. 2021. *Belittled Citizens: The Cultural Politics of Childhood on Bangkok's Margins*. Copenhagen: Nordic Institute of Asian Studies.

Bourdieu, Pierre. 1977. *Outline of a Theory of Practice*. Translated by Richard Nice. Cambridge: Cambridge University Press.

Bouté, Vanina. 2011. *En miroir du pouvoir: Les Phounoy du Nord-Laos: Ethnogenèse et dynamiques d'intégration*. Paris: École Française d'Extrême-Orient.

Bowie, Katherine. 2008. "Standing in the Shadows: Of Matrilocality and the Role of Women in a Village Election in Northern Thailand." *American Ethnologist* 35:136–53.

Bracewell, Wendy. 2003. "'The Proud Name of Hajduks': Bandits as Ambiguous Heroes in Balkan Politics and Culture." In *Yugoslavia and Its Historians: Understanding the Balkan Wars of the 1990s*, edited by Norman M. Naimark and Holly Case, 22–36. Stanford, CA: Stanford University Press.

Braudel, Fernand. 1973. *The Mediterranean and the Mediterranean World in the Age of Philip II*. Translated by Siân Reynolds. New York: Harper and Row.

Brownell, Susan. 1995. *Training the Body for China: Sports in the Moral Order of the People's Republic*. Chicago: University of Chicago Press.

Burton, Jack. 2020. "Prawit Defends Police Chief Promoting His Own Son." *The Taiger*, 5 February. https://thethaiger.com/hot-news/politics/prawit-defends-police-chief -promoting-his-own-son.

Burton, John W. 1983. "Same Time, Same Space: Observations on the Morality of Kinship in Pastoral Nilotic Societies." *Ethnology* 22:109–19.

Byrne, Denis. 2009. "Archaeology and the Fortress of Rationality." In *Cosmopolitan Archaeologies*, edited by Lynn Meskell, 68–88. Durham, NC: Duke University Press.

Cabot, Heath. 2014. *On the Doorstep of Europe: Asylum and Citizenship in Greece*. Philadelphia: University of Pennsylvania Press.

Cabot, Heath. 2018. "The Good Police Officer: Ambivalent Intimacies with the State in the Greek Asylum Procedure." In *The Anthropology of Police*, edited by Kevin G. Karpial and William Garriott, 210–29. Abingdon: Routledge.

Caftanzoglou, Roxani [Καυτανζόγλου, Ρωξάνη]. 2001. *Στη σκιά του Ιερού Βράχου: Τόπος και Μνήμη στα Αναφιώτικα* [In the shadow of the Holy Rock: Place and memory in Anafiotika]. Athens: Ellinika Grammata.

Caldeira, Teresa P. R. 2000. *City of Walls: Crime, Segregation, and Citizenship in São Paulo*. Berkeley: University of California Press.

Campbell, J. K. 1964. *Honour, Family, and Patronage: A Study of Institutions and Moral Values in a Greek Mountain Community*. Oxford: Clarendon.

Campkin, Ben. 2013. "Placing 'Matter out of Place': *Purity and Danger* as Evidence for Architecture and Urbanism." *Architectural Theory Review* 18:46–61.

Candea, Matei. 2019. *Comparison in Anthropology: The Impossible Method*. Cambridge: Cambridge University Press.

Carta, Silvio. 2015. *Visual Anthropology in Sardinia*. Oxford: Peter Lang.

Cellamare, Carlo. 2008. *Fare città: Pratiche urbane e storie di luoghi*. Milan: Elèuthera.

Charnvit Kasetsiri. 2019. "Thai Historiography." In *Routledge Handbook of Contemporary Thailand*, edited by Pavin Chachavalpongpun, 26–35. New York: Routledge.

Chatri Prakitnonthakan [ชาตรี ประกิตนนทการ]. 2003. "ป้อมมหากาฬ: อนุรักษ์หรือทำลายประวัติศาสตร์" [Pom Mahakan: Conserving or destroying history?]. *Silapawatthanatham*, February, 124–35.

Chatri Prakitnonthakan. 2012. "Rattanakosin Charter: The Thai Cultural Charter for Conservation." *Journal of the Siam Society* 100:107–32.

Chernela, Janet. 2008. "Guesting, Feasting and Raiding: Transformations of Violence in the Northwest Amazon." In *Revenge in the Cultures of Lowland South America*, edited by Stephen Beckerman and Paul Valentine, 42–59. Gainesville: University Press of Florida.

Chun, Allen. 2017. *Forget Chineseness: On the Geopolitics of Cultural Identification*. Albany: State University of New York Press.

Clastres, Pierre. 1987. *Society against the State: Essays in Political Anthropology*. Translated by Robert Hurley in collaboration with Abe Stein. New York: Zone.

Collingwood, R. G. 1946. *The Idea of History*. Oxford: Clarendon.

Connors, Michael Kelly. 2007. *Democracy and National Identity in Thailand*. Rev. ed. Honolulu: University of Hawai'i Press.

Dakin, Douglas. 1973. *The Greek Struggle for Independence, 1821–1833*. London: Batsford.

Damer, Seán. 1988. "Legless in Sfakia: Drinking and Social Practice in Western Crete." *Journal of Modern Greek Studies* 6:291–310.

Danforth, Loring M. 1984. "The Ideological Context of the Search for Continuities in Greek Culture." *Journal of Modern Greek Studies* 2:53–87.

Danforth, Loring M. 1997. *The Macedonian Conflict: Ethnic Nationalism in a Transnational World*. Princeton, NJ: Princeton University Press.

Davis, Elizabeth. 2012. *Bad Souls: Madness and Responsibility in Modern Greece*. Durham, NC: Duke University Press.

Davis, John. 1977. *People of the Mediterranean: An Essay in Comparative Social Anthropology*. London: Routledge and Kegan Paul.

Davis, John. 1988. *Libyan Politics: Tribe and Revolution*. Berkeley: University of California Press.

Davis, Richard. 1984. *Muang Metaphysics. A Study of Northern Thai Myth and Ritual*. Bangkok: Pandora.

De Genova, Nicholas, ed. 2017. *The Borders of "Europe": Autonomy of Migration, Tactics of Bordering*. Durham, NC: Duke University Press.

Delaney, Carole. 1995. "Father State, Motherland, and the Birth of Turkey." In *Naturalizing Power: Essays in Feminist Cultural Analysis*, edited by Sylvia Yanagisako and Carole Delaney, 177–99. New York: Routledge.

Dellios, Rosita. 2003. *Mandala: From Sacred Origins to Sovereign Affairs in Traditional Southeast Asia*. Robina, Australia: Bond University Centre for East-West Cultural and Economic Studies. http://epublications.bond.edu.au/cewces_papers/8.

Dellios, Rosita. 2019. "Narratives of Security in Asian Geopolitics." *Culture Mandala: The Bulletin of the Centre for East-West Cultural and Economic Studies* 13, no. 2: 19–28.

Denes, Alexandra. 2015. "Folklorizing Northern Khmer Identity in Thailand: Intangible Cultural Heritage and the Production of 'Good Culture.'" *Sojourn* 30, no. 1 (March): 1–34.

Dhani Nivat. 1947. "The Old Siamese Conception of the Monarchy." *Journal of the Siam Society* 36, no. 2: 91–106.

Dhani Nivat. 1955. "The Reconstruction of Rama I of the Chakri Dynasty." *Journal of the Siam Society* 43, no. 1: 21–47.

Diamandouros, P. Nikiforos. 1994. *Cultural Dualism and Political Change in Postauthoritarian Greece*. Madrid: Centro Juan March de Estudios Avanzados en Ciencias Sociales.

Di Bella, Maria Pia. 2008. *Dire ou taire en Sicile*. Paris: Éditions du Félin.

Dietler, Michael. 1994. "Our Ancestors the Gauls: Archaeology, Ethnic Nationalism, and the Manipulation of Celtic Identity in Modern Europe." *American Anthropologist* 96:584–605.

Di Giovine, Michael. Forthcoming. "Galactic Shrines and the Catholic Cult of St. Padre Pio of Pietrelcina." In *Landscapes of Christianity: Destination, Temporality, Transformation*, edited by James S. Bielo and Amos S. Ron. London: Bloomsbury.

Diller, Tony. 2006. "Polylectal Grammar and Royal Thai." In *Catching Language: The Standing Challenge of Grammar Writing*, edited by Felix K. Ameka, Alan Dench, and Nicholas Evans, 565–606. Berlin: de Gruyter.

D'Orsi, Lorenzo, and Fabio Dei. 2018. "What Is a Rite? Émile Durkheim, a Hundred Years Later." *Open Information Science* 2:115–26.

Douglas, Mary. 1966. *Purity and Danger: An Analysis of Concepts of Pollution and Taboo.* London: Routledge and Kegan Paul.

Dresch, Paul. 1986. "The Significance of the Course Events Take in Segmentary Systems." *American Ethnologist* 13, no. 2: 309–32.

Ducourtieux, Olivier. 2013. "Lao State Formation in Phôngsali Villages: Rising Intervention in the Daily Household and Phounoy Reaction." *Asian Studies Review* 37, no. 4: 451–70.

Dumont, Sylvie. 2020. *Vrysaki: A Neighborhood Lost in Search of the Athenian Agora.* Princeton, NJ: American School of Classical Studies at Athens. Also published as *Βρυσάκι: Η Εξαφάνιση μιας Συνοικίας για την Ανακάλυψη της Αρχαίας Αγοράς.* Athens: Melissa, 2020.

Durkheim, Émile. 1960. *Les formes élémentaires de la vie religieuse.* 4th ed. Paris: Presse Universitaires de France.

Dürr, Eveline, and Rivke Jaffe. 2012. "Theorizing Slum Tourism: Performing, Negotiating and Transforming Inequality." *European Review of Latin American and Caribbean Studies / Revista Europea de Estudios Latinoamericanos y del Caribe*, October, no. 93: 113–23.

Durrell, Lawrence. 1957. *Bitter Lemons.* London: Faber and Faber.

Dyal, Mark. 2018. *Hated and Proud: Ultras contra Modernity.* London: Arktos.

Efetio Pireos [Εφετείο Πειραιώς, Piraeus Appellate Court]. 2010. "Πρακτικά και Απόφαση του Τριμελούς Εφετείου Πειραιώς (Κακουργημάτων)" [Proceedings and decision of the three-member appellate court of Piraeus (felonies)]. Decisions 347, 348, 374, 384, 411, 485, 502, 526, 550, 551, 609, 640, 651, 722, 735, 767, 782, 841, 856, 906 ([all] 2009), [and] 9, 213, 342 ([all] 2010), vol. 1 (of 3).

Elinoff, Eli. 2017. "Despotic Urbanism in Thailand." *New Mandala*, 4 May. www .newmandala.org/despotic-urbanism-thailand.

Elinoff, Eli. 2020. "From Blood, Cast in Cement: Materialising the Political in Thailand." In *Political Theologies and Development in Asia: Transcendence, Sacrifice, and Aspiration*, edited by Giuseppe Bolotta, Philip Fountain, and R. Michael Feener, 68–86. Manchester: Manchester University Press.

Elinoff, Eli. 2021. *Citizen Designs: City-Making and Democracy in Northeastern Thailand.* Honolulu: University of Hawai'i Press.

Ellis-Petersen, Hannah. 2019. "Murder on the Mekong: Why Exiled Thai Dissidents Are Abducted and Killed." *The Observer*, 17 March.

Englehart, Neil A. 2001. *Culture and Power in Traditional Siamese Government.* Ithaca, NY: Cornell University Southeast Asia Publications.

Evans, Grant. 2002. "Immobile Memories: Statues in Thailand and Laos." In *Cultural Crisis and Social Memory: Modernity and Identity in Thailand and Laos*, edited by Shigeharu Tanabe and Charles F. Keyes, 154–82. London: RoutledgeCurzon.

Evans-Pritchard, E. E. 1940. *The Nuer: A Description of the Modes of Livelihood and Political Institutions of a Nilotic People*. Oxford: Clarendon.

Evans-Pritchard, E. E. 1949. *The Sanusi of Cyrenaica*. Oxford: Clarendon.

Evans-Pritchard, E. E. 1956. *Nuer Religion*. Oxford: Clarendon.

Fabian, Johannes. 1983. *Time and the Other: How Anthropology Makes Its Object*. New York: Columbia University Press.

"Facts and Details: Lao Royal Family." 2014. http://factsanddetails.com/southeast-asia /Laos/sub5_3a/entry-2943.html.

Fallmerayer, Jakob Philipp. 1830, 1836. *Geschichte der Halbinsel Morea während des Mittelalters*. Stuttgart: Cotta.

Farrelly, Nicholas. 2016. "Being Thai: A Narrow Identity in a Wide World." *Southeast Asian Affairs* 2016:331–43.

Faubion, James D. 1993. *Modern Greek Lessons: A Primer in Historical Constructivism*. Princeton, NJ: Princeton University Press.

Faubion, James D. 2001. *The Shadows and Lights of Waco Millennialism Today*. Princeton, NJ: Princeton University Press.

Feldman, Gregory. 2016. "'With My Head on the Pillow': Sovereignty, Ethics, and Evil among Undercover Police Investigators." *Comparative Studies in Society and History* 58:491–518.

Feldman, Gregory. 2019. *The Gray Zone: Sovereignty, Human Smuggling, and Undercover Police Investigation in Europe*. Stanford, CA: Stanford University Press.

Ferguson, James G. 1994. *The Anti-Politics Machine: "Development," Depoliticization, and Bureaucratic Power in Lesotho*. Minneapolis: University of Minnesota Press.

Fishel, Thamora. 2018. "Relocating Reciprocity: Politics and the Transformation of Thai Funerals." In *Spirited Politics: Religion and Public Life in Contemporary Southeast Asia*, edited by Andrew C. Willford and Kenneth M. George, 143–58. Ithaca, NY: Cornell University Press.

Foran, John. 1998. "Dangerous Populations? Concepts for the Comparative Study of Social Movements in Qajar Iran." *Critique: Journal for Critical Studies of the Middle East* 7:3–27.

Formoso, Bernard. 1990. "From the Human Body to the Humanized Space: The System of Reference and Representation of Space in Two Villages of Northeast Thailand." *Journal of the Siam Society* 78, no. 1: 66–83.

Frenzel, Fabian, Ko Koens, and Malte Steinbrink, eds. 2012. *Slum Tourism: Poverty, Power and Ethics*. London: Routledge.

Friedl, Ernestine. 1962. *Vasilika: A Village in Modern Greece*. New York: Holt, Rinehart and Winston.

Gajek, Esther. 1990. "Christmas under the Third Reich." *Anthropology Today* 6, no. 4: 3–9.

Gallant, Thomas W. 1988. "Greek Bandits: Lone Wolves or a Family Affair?" *Journal of Modern Greek Studies* 6:269–90.

Gallant, Thomas W. 2015. "Revolutions and Regimes of Violence." *Historein* 15:30–40.

Gatopoulos, Derek, and Elena Becatoros. 2020. "Greek Court Rules That Golden Dawn Party Is a Criminal Group." *AP News*, 7 October. https://apnews.com/article/hip-hop -and-rap-trials-athens-financial-markets-greece-8193d867c12224dbc9ba3e2675b8d25c.

Gershon, Ilana. 2011. "Neoliberal Agency." *Current Anthropology* 52:537–55.

Ghertner, D. Asher. 2010. "Calculating without Numbers: Aesthetic Governmentality in Delhi's Slums." *Economy and Society* 39:185–217.

Gibson, Thomas. 2007. *Islamic Narrative and Authority in Southeast Asia from the 16th to the 21st Century*. New York: Palgrave Macmillan.

Giddens, Anthony. 1984. *The Constitution of Society: Introduction to the Theory of Structuration*. Berkeley: University of California Press.

Gikandi, Boniface. 2018. "Raila Odinga: Let's Save Our Nation from Graft, Violence." *The Standard*, 11 August. https://www.standardmedia.co.ke/article/2001291471/raila -odinga-let-s-save-our-nation-from-graft-violence.

Gluckman, Max. 1955. "The Peace in the Feud." *Past and Present* 8:1–14.

Goldstein, Leon J. 1976. *Historical Knowing*. Austin: University of Texas Press.

González, Pablo Alonso. 2016. "Race and Ethnicity in the Construction of the Nation in Spain." *Ethnic and Racial Studies* 39:614–33.

González, Pablo Alonso. 2019. *The Heritage Machine: Fetishism and Domination in Maragatería, Spain*. London: Pluto.

Gramsci, Antonio. 1971. *Selections from the Prison Notebooks*. Edited and translated by Quintin Hoare and Geoffrey Nowell Smith. New York: International.

Gray, John. 2006. *Domestic Mandala: Architecture of Lifeworlds in Nepal*. Aldershot, UK: Ashgate.

Greenfeld, Liah. 1993. *Nationalism: Five Roads to Modernity*. Cambridge, MA: Harvard University Press.

Greenland, Fiona. 2021. *Ruling Culture: Art Police, Tomb Robbers, and the Rise of Cultural Power in Italy*. Chicago: University of Chicago Press.

Guano, Emanuela. 2004. "The Denial of Citizenship: 'Barbaric' Buenos Aires and the Middle-Class Imaginary." *City and Society* 16:69–97.

The Guardian. 2020. "Thai King Reinstates Royal Consort a Year after Disloyalty Claim." 2 September.

Guerrisi, Tiziana. 2008. "Alemanno e il menu etnico: 'Da mal di pancia ai bimbi.'" *La Repubblica*, Rome section, 19 July, 1.

Gupta, Akhil. 1998. *Postcolonial Developments: Agriculture in the Making of Modern India*. Durham, NC: Duke University Press.

Gupta, Akhil. 2012. *Red Tape: Bureaucracy, Structural Violence, and Poverty in India*. Durham, NC: Duke University Press.

Gutmann, Matthew C. 1993. "Rituals of Resistance: A Critique of the Theory of Everyday Forms of Resistance." *Latin American Perspectives* 20, no. 2: 74–92.

Haberkorn, Tyrell. 2016. "A Hyper-Royalist Parapolitics in Thailand." *Bijdragen tot de Taal-, Land- en Volkenkunde* 172:225–48.

Haberkorn, Tyrell. 2018. *In Plain Sight: Impunity and Human Rights in Thailand*. Madison: University of Wisconsin Press.

Hage, Ghassan. 1996. "The Spatial Imaginary of National Practices: Dwelling-Domesticating /Being-Exterminating." *Environment and Planning D* 14:463–85.

Halkià, Alexandra. 2015. "Democracy and Greece-in-Crisis: Contesting Masculinities Take Center Stage." *DEP (Deportate, Esuli, Profughe)* 27:182–91. https://www.unive.it

/pag/fileadmin/user_upload/dipartimenti/DSLCC/documenti/DEP/numeri/n27/14 _fsp_14-Halkia.pdf.

Hamilakis, Yannis. 2007. *The Nation and Its Ruins: Antiquity, Archaeology, and the National Imagination in Greece.* New York: Oxford University Press.

Hamilakis, Yannis, and Eleana Yalouri. 1996. "Antiquities as Symbolic Capital in Modern Greek Society." *Antiquity* 70:117–29.

Handley, Paul M. 2006. *The King Never Smiles: A Biography of Thailand's Bhumibol Adulyadej.* New Haven, CT: Yale University Press.

Hardy, Andrew. 2015. "La muraille de Quáng Ngãi et l'expansion territoriale du Vietnam: Projet pluridisciplinaire de recherche historique." *Comptes rendus de l'Académie des Inscriptions et Belles-Lettres* 2015 (3): 1117–35.

Harms, Erik. 2016. *Luxury and Rubble: Civility and Dispossession in the New Saigon.* Berkeley: University of California Press.

Harney, Nicholas DeMaria. 2020. "Interculturalism, Inequality and Hospitality in Italy." *Ethnos.* https://doi.org/10.1080/00141844.2020.1806898.

Hart, David. 1970. "Conflicting Models of a Berber Tribal Structure in the Moroccan Rif: The Segmentary and Alliance System of the Aith Varyaghar." *Revue des mondes musulmans et de la Méditerranée* 7:93–99.

Heatherington, Tracey. 2010. *Wild Sardinia: Indigeneity and the Global Dreamtimes of Environmentalism.* Seattle: University of Washington Press.

Heine-Geldern, Robert. 1956. *Conceptions of State and Kingship in Southeast Asia.* Ithaca, NY: Cornell Southeast Asia Program.

Helmholz, Richard M. 2016. "The Myth of Magna Carta Revisited." *North Carolina Law Review* 94:1475–93.

Herzfeld, Michael. 1973. "The Siege of Rhodes and the Ethnography of Greek Oral Tradition." *Kritika Khronika* 25:413–40.

Herzfeld, Michael. 1980. "Honour and Shame: Some Problems in the Comparative Analysis of Moral Systems." *Man* (n.s.) 15:339–51.

Herzfeld, Michael. 1982. "When Exceptions Define the Rules: Greek Baptismal Names and the Negotiation of Identity." *Journal of Anthropological Research* 38:288–302.

Herzfeld, Michael. 1984a. "The Horns of the Mediterraneanist Dilemma." *American Ethnologist* 11:439–54.

Herzfeld, Michael. 1984b. "The Significance of the Insignificant: Blasphemy as Ideology." *Man* (n.s.) 19:653–64.

Herzfeld, Michael. 1985. *The Poetics of Manhood: Contest and Identity in a Cretan Mountain Village.* Princeton, NJ: Princeton University Press.

Herzfeld, Michael. 1987a. *Anthropology through the Looking-Glass: Critical Ethnography in the Margins of Europe.* Cambridge: Cambridge University Press.

Herzfeld, Michael. 1987b. "'As in Your Own House': Hospitality, Ethnography, and the Stereotype of Mediterranean Society." In *Honor and Shame and the Unity of the Mediterranean,* edited by David D. Gilmore, 75–89. Washington, DC: American Anthropological Association.

Herzfeld, Michael. 1991a. *A Place in History: Social and Monumental Time in a Cretan Town.* Princeton, NJ: Princeton University Press.

Herzfeld, Michael. 1991b. "Textual Form and Social Formation in Evans-Pritchard and Lévi-Strauss." In *Writing the Social Text: Poetics and Politics in Social Science Discourse*, edited by Richard Harvey Brown, 53–70. New York: de Gruyter.

Herzfeld, Michael. 1992. *The Social Production of Indifference: Exploring the Symbolic Roots of Western Bureaucracy.* Oxford: Berg.

Herzfeld, Michael. 1999. "Of Language and Land Tenure: The Transmission of Property and Information in Autonomous Crete." *Social Anthropology* 7:223–37.

Herzfeld, Michael. 2001. "Irony and Power: Toward a Politics of Mockery in Greece." In *Irony in Action: Anthropology, Practice, and the Moral Imagination*, edited by James W. Fernandez and Mary Taylor Huber, 63–83. Chicago: University of Chicago Press.

Herzfeld, Michael. 2002. "The Absent Presence: Discourses of Crypto-Colonialism." *South Atlantic Quarterly* 101:899–926.

Herzfeld, Michael. 2006. "Spatial Cleansing: Monumental Vacuity and the Idea of the West." *Journal of Material Culture* 11:127–49.

Herzfeld, Michael. 2007. "Small-Mindedness Writ Large: On the Migration and Manners of Prejudice." *Journal of Ethnic and Migration Studies* 33:255–74.

Herzfeld, Michael. 2009a. "The Cultural Politics of Gesture: Reflections on the Embodiment of Ethnographic Practice." *Ethnography* 10:131–52.

Herzfeld, Michael. 2009b. *Evicted from Eternity: The Restructuring of Modern Rome.* Chicago: University of Chicago Press.

Herzfeld, Michael. 2011. "Crisis Attack: Impromptu Ethnography in the Greek Maelstrom." *Anthropology Today* 27, no. 5: 22–26.

Herzfeld, Michael. 2014. "Drunken Noodles and Prostitutes' Pasta: The Intangible Delicacy of Cultural Embarrassments in International Policy Settings." *Ethnologies* 36:47–62.

Herzfeld, Michael. 2015. "Common Sense." In *International Encyclopedia of the Social Sciences*, vol. 4, edited by Neil J. Smelser and Paul B. Baltes, 258–62. Oxford: Elsevier.

Herzfeld, Michael. 2016a. *Cultural Intimacy: The Social Poetics and the Real Life of States, Societies, and Institutions.* 3rd ed. New York: Routledge.

Herzfeld, Michael. 2016b. "The Hypocrisy of European Moralism: Greece and the Politics of Cultural Aggression." *Anthropology Today* 32, no. 1: 11–13; 32, no. 2: 10–13.

Herzfeld, Michael. 2016c. *Siege of the Spirits: Community and Polity in Bangkok.* Chicago: University of Chicago Press.

Herzfeld, Michael. 2017a. "The Blight of Beautification: Bangkok and the Pursuit of Class-Based Urban Purity." *Journal of Urban Design* 22:291–307.

Herzfeld, Michael. 2017b. "Thailand in a Larger Universe: The Lingering Consequences of Crypto-Colonialism." *Journal of Asian Studies* 76:887–906.

Herzfeld, Michael. 2018a. "Anthropological Realism in a Scientistic Age." *Anthropological Theory* 118:129–50.

Herzfeld, Michael. 2018b. "Cultural Intimacy and the Politics of Civility." In *Handbook of Political Anthropology*, edited by Bjørn Thomassen and Harald Wydra, 101–13. Cheltenham, UK: Elgar.

Herzfeld, Michael. 2019. "What Is a Polity? Subversive Archaism and the Bureaucratic Nation-State." *Hau: Journal of Ethnographic Theory* 9:23–35.

Herzfeld, Michael. 2020a. "Lockdown Reflections on Freedom and Cultural Intimacy." *Anthropology in Action* 27, no. 3: 44–50.

Herzfeld, Michael. 2020b. *Ours Once More: Folklore, Ideology, and the Making of Modern Greece.* Rev. ed, epilogue by Sharon Macdonald. Oxford: Berghahn.

Herzfeld, Michael. 2020c. "Seeing like a Village: Contesting Hegemonic Modernity in Greece." *Journal of Modern Greek Studies* 38:43–58.

Heywood, Paolo. 2015. "Freedom in the Code: The Anthropology of (Double) Morality." *Anthropological Theory* 15:200–217.

Heywood, Paolo. 2017. *Making a Difference: Ethics, Activism, and Anthropological Theory.* Oxford: Berghahn.

Hobsbawm, Eric. 1959. *Primitive Rebels: Studies in Archaic Forms of Social Movement in the 19th and 20th Centuries.* Manchester: Manchester University Press.

Hodgen, Margaret T. 1936. *The Doctrine of Survivals: A Chapter in the History of Scientific Method in the Study of Man.* London: Allenson.

Hodges, Matt. 2013. "Illuminating Vestige: Amateur Archaeology and the Emergence of Historical Consciousness in Rural France." *Comparative Studies in Society and History* 55:474–504.

Holmes, Douglas R. 1989. *Cultural Disenchantments: Worker Peasantries in Northeast Italy.* Princeton, NJ: Princeton University Press.

Holmes, Douglas R. 2000. *Integral Europe: Fast-Capitalism, Multiculturalism, Neofascism.* Princeton, NJ: Princeton University Press.

Holmes, Douglas R. 2013. *Economy of Words: Communicative Imperatives in Central Banks.* Chicago: University of Chicago Press.

Holston, James. 2008. *Insurgent Citizenship: Disjunctions of Democracy and Modernity in Brazil.* Princeton, NJ: Princeton University Press.

Holston, James. 2009. "Insurgent Citizenship in an Era of Global Urban Peripheries." *City and Society* 21:245–67.

Hom, Stephanie Malia. 2015. *The Beautiful Country: Tourism and the Impossible State of Destination Italy.* Toronto: University of Toronto Press.

Horn, Robert. 2010. "In Thailand, a Little Black Magic Is Politics as Usual." *Time*, 20 March.

Høyem, Harald H. 2018. "Empowerment and Human Rights: Comparing Two Cultural Heritage Cases in Xi'an, China." In *World Heritage and Human Rights: Lessons from the Asia-Pacific and Global Arena*, edited by Peter Bille Larsen, 87–102. New York: Routledge.

Humphreys, S. C. 1978. *Anthropology and the Greeks.* London: Routledge.

Hutchinson, Sharon, and Naomi R. Pendle. 2015. "Violence, Legitimacy, and Prophecy: Nuer Struggles with Uncertainty in South Sudan." *American Ethnologist* 42:415–30.

in.gr. 2021. "Ο Σασμός βάζει τέλος μετά από δεκαετίες στη βεντέτα τριών οικογενειών στα Ζωνιανά—Τι είναι το έθιμο της συμφιλίωσης" [The *sasmos* put an end to decades of vendetta among three families in Zoniana—What is the custom of reconciliation?]. 23 January. https://www.in.gr/2021/01/23/greece/o-sasmos-vazei -telos-meta-dekaeties-sti-venteta-trion-oikogeneion-sta-zoniana-ti-einai-ethimo-tis -symfiliosis/.

Isaacs, Bronwyn. 2019. "Gloss and Dirt: Bangkok Advertising Production, Labor and Value." PhD diss., Harvard University.

Isaacs, Bronwyn, and Trude Renwick. n.d. "The Political Rituals of Post-Democratic Thailand." Unpublished manuscript, cited with permission.

Ismailbekova, Aksana. 2017. *Blood Ties and the Native Son: Poetics of Patronage in Kyrgyzstan*. Bloomington: Indiana University Press.

Jackson, Peter. 2004. "The Thai Regime of Images." *Sojourn: Social Issues in Southeast Asia* 19, no. 2: 1–39.

Jacobs, Jane. 1993 [1961]. *The Death and Life of Great American Cities*. New York: Random House.

Jiang, Yi-Huah. 2018. "Confucian Political Theory in Contemporary China." *Annual Review of Political Science* 21:155–73.

Jintamas Saksornchai. 2018. "Little Love Lost for Neighbors of Evicted Fort Community." Khaosod English, 31 May. http://www.khaosodenglish.com/featured/2018/05/31/little-love-lost-for-neighbors-of-evicted-fort-community.

Johnson, Andrew Alan. 2020. *Mekong Dreaming: Life and Death along a Changing River*. Durham, NC: Duke University Press.

Jonsson, Hjorleifur. 2014. *Slow Anthropology: Negotiating Difference with the Iu Mien*. Ithaca, NY: Cornell Southeast Asia Program.

Jory, Patrick. 2016. *Thailand's Theory of Monarchy: The Vessantara Jataka and the Idea of the Perfect Man*. Albany: State University of New York Press.

Jory, Patrick. 2021. *A History of Manners and Civility in Thailand*. Cambridge: Cambridge University Press.

Julispong Chularatana and Ittigorn Thongkamkaew [จุลิศพงศ์ จุฬารัตน์, อิทธิกร ทองแกมแก้ว]. "การตรวจราชการหัวเมืองของสมเด็จฯ กรมพระยาดำรงราชานุภาพกับการสร้างความรู้ด้านประวัติศาสตร์และโบราณคดี สยาม ทศวรรษ 2440–2450" [Prince Damrong Rajanubhab's formation of historical and archaeological knowledge in Siam in the decade 1897–1907]. *วารสารอักษรศาสตร์ มหาวิทยาลัย ศิลปากร/Journal of the Faculty of Arts of Silpakorn University* 22:45–61.

Kalantzis, Konstantinos. 2012. "Crete as Warriorhood: Visual Explorations of Social Imaginaries in 'Crisis.'" *Anthropology Today* 28, no. 3: 7–11.

Kalantzis, Konstantinos. 2014. "On Ambivalent Nativism: Hegemony, Photography and Recalcitrant Alterity in Sphakia, Crete." *American Ethnologist* 41:56–75.

Kalantzis, Konstantinos. 2015. "'Fak Germani': Materialities of Nationhood and Transgression in the Greek Crisis." *Comparative Studies in Society and History* 57:1037–69.

Kalantzis, Konstantinos. 2016. "Proxy Brigands and Tourists: Visualizing the Greek-German Front in the Debt Crisis." *Visual Anthropology Review* 32:24–37.

Kalantzis, Konstantinos. 2019. *Tradition in the Frame: Photography, Power and Imagination in Sfakia, Crete*. Bloomington: Indiana University Press.

Kalantzis, Konstantinos. 2020. "Picturing the Imaginable: Fantasy, Photography, and Displacement in the Highland Cretan 'Village.'" *Journal of Modern Greek Studies* 38:59–83.

Kammales Photikanit and Patcharin Sirasoonthorn. 2018. "Reconstruction of Social Ideology through the Power of Music: Case Study of Suntaraporn Band, Thailand." *Kasetsart Journal of Social Sciences* 39:343–50.

Kapferer, Bruce. 1988. *Legends of People, Myths of State: Violence, Intolerance, and Political Culture in Sri Lanka and Australia*. Washington, DC: Smithsonian Institution.

Karp, Ivan, and Kent Maynard. 1983. "Reading *The Nuer*." *Current Anthropology* 24, no. 4: 481–503.

Kavadias, Georges B. 1965. *Pasteurs nomades mediterranéens: Les Saracatsans de la Grèce.* Paris: Gauthier-Villars.

Kazantzakis, Nikos [Καζαντζάκης, Νίκος]. 1968. *Βίος και Πολιτεία του Αλέξη Ζορμπά* [Life and lifeway of Alexis Zorbas]. 6th ed. Athens: Kazantzaki.

Kazazis, Kostas. 1982. "Partial Linguistic Autobiography of a Schizoglossic Linguist." *Glossologia* 1:109–17.

Kenna, Margaret E. 1976. "House, Fields, and Graves: Property and Ritual Obligation on a Greek Island." *Ethnology* 15:21–34.

Kertzer, David I. 1980. *Comrades and Christians: Religion and Political Struggle in Communist Italy.* Cambridge: Cambridge University Press.

Khaosod English. 2020a. "Democratic Revolt Anniversary: Army Honors Royalist Rebels." 24 June. https://www.khaosodenglish.com/politics/2020/06/24/democratic -revolt-anniversary-army-honors-royalist-rebels/.

Khaosod English. 2020b. "Health Minister: 'Dirty' Europeans Pose Virus Risk to Thailand." 13 March. https://www.khaosodenglish.com/news/2020/03/13/health-minister -dirty-europeans-pose-virus-risks-to-thailand/.

Khaosod English. 2020c. "1932 Revolt Plaque, Its Fate Unknown, Now an Icon of Activist Fashion." 26 June. https://www.khaosodenglish.com/featured/2020/06/26/1932 -revolt-plaque-its-fate-unknown-now-an-icon-of-activist-fashion/.

Kharalambidis, Dimitris [Χαραλαμπίδης, Δημήτρης]. 2010. "Θεσμοθέτηση και Ίδρυση της Αρχαιολογικής Υπηρεσίας" [Institutionalization and foundation of the Archaeological Service]. In *Μεταξία Τσιποπούλου*, ed., " . . . *Ανέφερα εγγράφως . . .": θησαυροί του ιστορικού αρχείου της αρχαιολογικής υπηρεσίας* [". . . I reported in writing . . .": Treasures of the historical archive of the Archaeological Service], 13–17. Thessaloniki: Ministry of Culture and Tourism: Archaeological Museum of Thessaloniki. http://nam.culture.gr/images/deam/docs /katalogos.pdf.

Kieti, Damiannah M., and Kennedy O. Magio. 2013. "The Ethical and Local Resident Perspectives of Slum Tourism in Kenya." *Advances in Hospitality and Tourism Research* 1, no. 1: 1–21.

King, Ross, and Kim Dovey. 2012. "Reading the Bangkok Slum." In *Slum Tourism: Poverty, Power and Ethics,* edited by Fabian Frenzel, Ko Koens, and Malte Steinbrink, 159–71. London: Routledge.

Kisnaphol Wattanawanyoo. 2012. "Poverty Tourism as Advocacy: A Case in Bangkok." In *Slum Tourism: Poverty, Power and Ethics,* edited by Fabian Frenzel, Ko Koens, and Malte Steinbrink, 207–14. London: Routledge.

Kitchana Lersakvanitchakul. 2019. "Heritage Destroyed: Why the ASA Is Trying to Raise Consciousness of Preserving our History." *The Nation* (Thailand), 28 December. www .nationthailand.com/lifestyle/30379911.

Knight, Daniel M. 2015. *History, Time, and Economic Crisis in Central Greece.* New York: Palgrave Macmillan.

Koehne, Samuel. 2014. "Were the National Socialists a 'Völkisch' Party? Paganism, Christianity, and the Nazi Christmas." *Central European History* 47:760–90.

Lambropoulos, V. G. 2008a. "Έγκλημα και ατιμωρησία στα Ζωνιανά" [Crime and impunity in Zoniana]. *To Vima*, 25 November. https://www.tovima.gr/2008/11/25 /archive/egklima-kai-atimwrisia-sta-zwniana/.

Lambropoulos, V. G. 2008b. "Εμπόλεμη ζώνη τα Ζωνιανά" [Zoniana a war zone]. *To Vima*, 6 November. http://www.tovima.gr/politics/article/?aid=218463.

Lambropoulos, V. G. 2014. "Άνω του 50% των αστυνομικών ψήφισε Χρυσή Αυγή!" [Over 50% of the police voted for Golden Dawn]. *To Vima*, 26 May. http://www .tovima.gr/society/article/?aid=599952.

Lamprakos, Michelle. 2014. "The Idea of the Historic City." *Change over Time* 4, no. 1: 8–38.

Lamprakos, Michelle. 2015. *Building a World Heritage City: Sana'a, Yemen*. Burlington, VT: Ashgate.

Leach, E. R. 1956. *Political Systems of Highland Burma: A Study of Kachin Social Structure*. London: Athlone.

Lefevre, Amy Sawitta, and Aukkarapon Niyomyat. 2014. "Thailand's Junta Sidelines Pro-Thaksin Police, Governors." Reuters.com, 4 June. https://www.reuters.com/article /us-thailand-politics-reshuffle/thailands-junta-sidelines-pro-thaksin-police-governors -idUSKBN0EG03320140605.

Lekatsas, Panayis [Παναγής Λεκατσάς]. 1970. *Η Μητριαρχία και η σύγκρουσή της με την Ελληνική Πατριαρχία* [Matriarchy and its conflict with Greek patriarchy]. Athens: Kimena.

Lipat-Chesler, Eleanor. 2010. "Beautification, Possession, and Cultural Imagination." Abstract, Society for Ethnomusicology annual meeting, Los Angeles. https://cdn.ymaws .com/www.ethnomusicology.org/resource/resmgr/2010_annual_meeting/abstract _book_final_11.05.10.pdf.

Loizos, Peter. 1975. *The Greek Gift: Politics in a Cypriot Village*. Oxford: Blackwell.

Low, Setha. 1995. "Indigenous Architectural Representations: Mesoamerican and Caribbean Foundations of the Spanish American Plaza." *American Anthropologist* 97:748–62.

Low, Setha. 1996. "Spatializing Culture: The Social Production and Social Construction of Public Space." *American Ethnologist* 23:861–79.

Low, Setha. 2001. "The Edge and the Center: Gated Communities and the Discourse of Urban Fear." *American Anthropologist* 103:45–58.

Low, Setha. 2003. *Behind the Gates: Life, Security, and the Pursuit of Happiness in Fortress America*. New York: Routledge.

Low, Setha. 2008. "The Gated Community as Heterotopia." In *Heterotopia and the City: Public Space in a Postcivil Society*, edited by Michiel Dehaene and Lieven De Cauter, 153–63. London: Routledge.

Low, Setha, and Neil Smith. 2006. "Introduction: The Imperative of Public Space." In *The Politics of Public Space*, edited by Setha Low and Neil Smith, 1–17. New York: Routledge.

MacGillivray, Iain. 2016. "The Impact of Gush Emunim on the Social and Political Fabric of Israeli Society." *E-International Relations*, July 21. https://www.e-ir.info/2016/07/21 /the-impact-of-gush-emunim-on-the-social-and-political-fabric-of-israeli-society.

Machin, Barrie. 1983. "St. George and the Virgin: Cultural Codes, Religion and Attitudes to the Body in a Cretan Mountain Village." *Social Analysis* 14:107–26.

Mac Sweeney, Naoíse, et al. 2019. "Claiming the Classical: The Greco-Roman World in Contemporary Political Discourse." *Council of University Classical Departments Bulletin* 48. https://cucd.blogs.sas.ac.uk/bulletin/.

Mahony, Sorcha. 2018. *Searching for a Better Life: Growing Up in the Slums of Bangkok.* New York: Berghahn.

Malarney, Shaun Kingsley. 1996. "The Limits of 'State Functionalism' and the Reconstruction of Funeral Ritual in Contemporary Vietnam." *American Ethnologist* 23:540–60.

Mamoulaki, Elena. 2017. "Anthropology, History and Academic Ethnocentrism Biases and Limitations in Recognizing and Understanding Solidarity." *Etnofoor* 29, no. 2: 39–58.

Mbembe, Achille. 1992. "Provisional Notes on the Postcolony." *Africa* 62, no. 1: 3–37.

McCargo, Duncan. 2019. *Fighting for Virtue: Justice and Politics in Thailand.* Ithaca, NY: Cornell University Press.

Meskell, Lynn. 2018. *A Future in Ruins: UNESCO, World Heritage, and the Dream of Peace.* Oxford: Oxford University Press.

Misos Taksiko [Ταξικο Μίσος, literally "Class Hatred"]. 2015. "Ο τρομονόμος 187Α με απλά λόγια" [Terror Law 187A in simple words]. *Provo*, 9 March. https://www.provo.gr/187a/.

Missingham, Bruce D. 2003. *The Assembly of the Poor in Thailand: From Local Struggles to National Protest Movement.* Chiang Mai: Silkworm.

Moore, Clive. 2007. "Review of Robbins and Wardlow 2005." *Journal of Pacific History* 42:122–23.

Morgan, Lewis Henry. 1877. *Ancient Society: or, Researches in the Lines of Human Progress from Savagery through Barbarism to Civilization.* New York: Holt.

Moschonas, Spiros A. 2004. "Relativism in Language Ideology: On Greece's Latest Language Issues." *Journal of Modern Greek Studies* 22:173–206.

Muehlebach, Andrea. 2012. *The Moral Neoliberal: Welfare and Citizenship in Italy.* Chicago: University of Chicago Press.

Nagy, Gregory. 1994. "Genre and Occasion." *Mètis: Anthropologie des mondes grecs anciens* 9–10:11–25.

Nathapong Jitrnirat [ณฐพงศ์ จิตรนิรัตน์]. 2005. รหัสชุมชน *(Community Code)* พื้นที่ อัตลักษณ์ ภาพแทน ความจริงและหลังสมัยใหม่ [Community code: Place, identity, and the postmodern alternative image of reality]. Bangkok: Taksin University.

The Nation (Thailand). 2020. "Visual Feast of Flowers for Bangkokians." 29 November. https://www.nationthailand.com/news/30398764?utm_source=homepage&utm_medium=internal_referral.

Navanath Osiri. 2003. "Lak Ban and Lak Muang: The Ideology of Settlement Landscape in Traditional Southeast Asia." *Manusya: Journal of Humanities* 5, no. 3: 29–39.

Ta Nea [Τα Νέα]. 2018. "Για τη Συμφωνία των Πρεσπών—Ιερά πυρά από τους Αγιορείτες" [For the Prespa Agreement: Holy fire from the Mount Athos monks]. 29 June. https://www.tanea.gr/2018/06/29/greece/iera-pyra-apo-toys-agioreites/.

Newsbomb. 2011. "Ζωνιανά . . . 'άβατο' για την αστυνομία!" [Zoniana . . . "inaccessible for the police!"]. 23 August. https://www.newsbomb.gr/ellada/story/74385/zwniana-abato-gia-thn-astynomia.

Niarchos, Thanasis [Νίαρχος, Θανάσης]. 2012. "Ο γιατρός μου και εγώ" [My doctor and I]. *Ta Nea* [*Τα Νέα*], 14–15 July. https://www.tanea.gr/2012/08/06/greece/o -giatros-moy-kai-egw/.

Niezen, Ronald. 2003. *The Origins of Indigenism: Human Rights and the Politics of Identity.* Berkeley: University of California Press.

Nisbett, Melissa. 2017. "Empowering the Empowered? Slum Tourism and the Depoliticization of Poverty." *Geoforum* 85:37–45.

Ockey, James. 2004. "State, Bureaucracy and Polity in Modern Thai Politics." *Journal of Contemporary Asia* 34, no. 2: 143–62.

O'Connor, Richard. 1990. "Place, Power and Discourse in the Thai Image of Bangkok." *Journal of the Siam Society* 78, no. 2: 61–73.

O'Connor, Richard. 2000. "A Regional Explanation of the Tai Muang as a City-State." In *A Comparative Study of Thirty City-State Cultures: An Investigation*, edited by Mogen Herman Hansen, 431–43. Copenhagen: Kongelige Danske Videnskabernes Selskab.

Odermatt, Peter. 1996. "Built Heritage and the Politics of (Re)Presentation: Local Reactions to the Appropriation of the Monumental Past in Sardinia. With commentary by Michael Herzfeld, M. Beatrice Annis, and Orvar Löfgren." *Archaeological Dialogues* 3:95–136.

Ong, Andrew. 2018. "Producing Intransigence: (Mis)understanding the United Wa State Army in Myanmar." *Contemporary Southeast Asia* 40:449–74.

Özyürek, Esra. 2004. "Wedded to the Republic: Public Intellectuals and Intimacy-Oriented Publics in Turkey." In *Off Stage/On Display: Intimacy and Ethnography in the Age of Public Culture*, edited by Andrew Shryock, 101–30. Stanford, CA: Stanford University Press.

P.K. [Π.Κ.] 2018. "Υμνούν τον Χίτλερ και το ναζισμό" [They laud Hitler and Nazism]. Rizospastis, 30 June–1 July. https://www.rizospastis.gr/story.do?id =9906148&textCriteriaClause=%2BMAXAIPOBΓΑΛΤΕΣ+%2BXPYΣH+%2BAYΓ H+%2BKATOXH+%2BKPHTH.

Paik, Christopher, and Jessica Jessica Vechbanyongratana. 2019. "Path to Centralization and Development: Evidence from Siam." *World Politics* 71:289–331.

Palmer, David A. 2003. "Modernity and Millennialism in China: Qigong and the Birth of Falun Gong." *Asian Anthropology* 2:79–109.

Panourgiá, Neni. 2009. *Dangerous Citizens: The Greek Left and the Terror of the State.* New York: Fordham University Press.

Panu Wongcha-um and Patpicha Tanakasempipat. 2019. "Thai Exiles in Fear after Murders and Disappearances." Reuters, 24 May. https://www.reuters.com/article/us -thailand-rights-exiles-insight/thai-exiles-in-fear-after-murders-and-disappearances -idUSKCN1SU0DV.

Papapandoleon, Klio [Παπαπαντολέων, Κλειώ]. 2020. "Η ιστορική απόφαση για τη Χρυσή Αυγή ως ευκαιρία αυτοκριτικής" [The historic decision on Golden Dawn as an opportunity for reflexive critique]. *Singkhrona Themata* 149. https://www .synchronathemata.gr/i-istoriki-apofasi-gia-ti-chrysi-aygi-os-eykairia-aytokritikis/.

Papataxiarchis, Evthymios. 1991. "Friends of the Heart: Male Commensal Solidarity." In *Contested Identities: Gender and Kinship in Modern Greece*, edited by Peter Loizos and Evthymios Papataxiarchis, 156–74. Princeton, NJ: Princeton University Press.

Papataxiarchis, Evthymios [Παπαταξιάρχης, Ευθύμιος]. 2014. "Ο αδιανόητος ρατσισμός: Η πολιτικοποίηση της 'φιλοξενίας' την εποχή της κρίσης" [Incomprehensible racism: The politicization of "hospitality" in the time of crisis]. *Singkhrona Themata* 127:46–62.

Papataxiarchis, Evthymios [Παπαταξιάρχης, Ευθύμιος]. 2017. "Ασκήσεις συμβίωσης στην 'ανθρωπιστική πόλη': Άτυπες εκπαιδευτικές πρακτικές και διακυβέρνηση του 'προσφυγικού' μετά το 2016" [Exercises in coexistence in the "humanistic city": Informal educational practices and governance of the "refugee problem" after 2016]. *Singkhrona Themata* 137:74–89.

Parasiris, Dimitris [Παρασύρης, Δημήτρης]. n.d. *Ζώ: Ζού το Λάκκο: 4000 Χρόνια από το Θάνατο του Δία* [Zo: The animal's hole: 4,000 years since the death of Zeus]. Rethimno: n.p.

Pashley, Robert. 1837. *Travels in Crete.* Vol. 1. London: Murray.

Pattana Kittiarsa. 2005. "'Lives of Hunting Dogs': 'Muai Thai' and the Politics of Thai Masculinities." *South East Asia Research* 13:57–90.

Pavlaković, Vjeran. 2010. "Croatia, the International Criminal Tribunal for the Former Yugoslavia, and General Gotovina as a Political Symbol." *Europe-Asia Studies* 62, no. 10: 1707–40.

Peleggi, Maurizio. 2002. *Lords of Things: The Fashioning of the Siamese Monarchy's Modern Image.* Honolulu: University of Hawai'i Press.

Perera, Nihal. 2012. "Multiple Roots, Cascades of Thought, and the Local Production of Architecture." In *Transforming Asian Cities: Intellectual Impasse, Asianizing Space, and Emerging Translocalities,* edited by Nihal Perera and Wing-Shing Tang, 78–93. New York: Routledge.

Peutz, Nathalie. 2018. *Islands of Heritage: Conservation and Transformation in Yemen.* Stanford, CA: Stanford University Press.

Pinkaew Laungaramsri. 2014. "Contested Citizenship: Cards, Colors and the Culture of Identification." In *Ethnicity, Borders, and the Grassroots Interface with the State: Studies on Southeast Asia in Honor of Charles F. Keyes,* edited by John A. Marston, 143–62. Chiang Mai: Silkworm.

Plantzos, Dimitris. 2012. "The Kouros of Keratea: Constructing Subaltern Pasts in Contemporary Greece." *Journal of Social Archaeology* 12:220–44.

Plika, Maroula [Πλήκα, Μαρούλα]. 2018. "Οι 'γαλάζιες' καταδίκες άργησαν μια μέρα" [The "blue" convictions arrived one day late]. *I Avgi,* 29 June. http://www.avgi .gr/article/10813/9005218/oi-galazies-katadikes-argesan-mia-mera-.

Politis, Nikolaos G. 1871 (pt. 1), 1874 (pt. 2). *Μελέται επί του βίου των νεωτέρων Ελλήνων* [Study of the life of the modern Greeks]. Vol. 1 of *Νεοελληνική Μυθολογία* [Modern Greek mythology]. Athens: Wilberg and Nakis.

Poomchai Punpairoj. 2010. "Recalibrating the New Thai Vernacular Architecture." *Journal of Architectural/Planning Research and Studies* [Thammasat University] 7:65–79.

Porranee Singpliam. 2018. "Women and Nation: Historicizing Thai Femininity from 1960s–1990s." PhD diss., Waseda University.

Pravit Rojanaphruck. 2018. "No Explanation for Anti-Corruption Group's 'Full Marks' for Prayuth." *Khasod English,* September 1. http://www.khaosodenglish.com

/politics/2018/09/01/anti-corruption-campaigner-criticized-for-giving-junta-leader
-full-marks/.

Pravit Rojanaphruck. 2020a. "No Explanation: Democratic Leaders['] Statues Gone
Missing." Khaosod English, 27 January. https://www.khaosodenglish.com/politics
/2020/01/27/no-explanation-democratic-revolt-leaders-statues-gone-missing/.

Pravit Rojanaphruck. 2020b. "Scholar Fears Massive Renovation of Iconic Avenue
May Erase History." Khaosod English, 23 January. https://www.khaosodenglish.com
/news/2020/01/23/scholar-fears-massive-renovation-of-iconic-avenue-may-erase
-history/.

Quagliariello, Chiara. 2021. "Caring for the Others, Managing the Migrants: Local and
Institutional Hospitality in Lampedusa, Italy." In *Migrant Hospitalities in the Mediter-
ranean: Encounters with Alterity in Birth and Death*, edited by Marc Brightman and
Vanessa Grotti, 15–38. London: Palgrave.

Radin, Max. 1947. "The Myth of Magna Carta." *Harvard Law Review* 60, no. 7: 1060–91.

Raendchen, Oliver. 2000. "The Tai *Lak*: Ritual and Socio-Political Function." In
Proceedings, International Conference on Thai Studies (1998: Bangkok, Thailand),
223–29. Salaya, Nakhon Pathom: Institute of Language and Culture for Rural Development. http://sealang.net/sala/archives/pdf8/raendchen1998tai.pdf.

Rakopoulos, Theodoros. 2015a. "Solidarity Tensions: Informality and Sociality in the
Greek Crisis." *Social Analysis* 59:85–104.

Rakopoulos, Theodoros, 2015b. "Which Community for Cooperatives? Peasant Mobili-
zations, the Mafia, and the Problem of Community Participation in Sicilian Co-ops."
Focaal: Journal of Global and Historical Anthropology 71:57–70.

Rakopoulos, Theodoros. 2017. *From Clans to Co-ops: Confiscated Mafia Land in Sicily*.
Oxford: Berghahn.

Rakopoulos, Theodoros. 2018. "The Social Life of Mafia Confession: Between Talk and
Silence in Sicily." *Current Anthropology* 59:167–91.

Razsa, Maple. 2015. *Bastards of Utopia: Living Radical Politics after Socialism*. Bloomington: Indiana University Press.

Reddy, Malavika. 2015. "Identity Paper/Work/s and the Unmaking of Legal Status in Mae
Sot, Thailand." *Asian Journal of Law and Society* 2:251–66.

Reed-Danahay, Deborah. 1993. "Talking about Resistance: Ethnography and Theory in
Rural France." *Anthropological Quarterly* 66:221–29.

Regione Autònoma de Sardigna/Regione Autonoma della Sardegna. 1997. Legge Regio-
nale 15 ottobre 1997, n. 26: Promozione e valorizzazione della cultura e della lingua
della Sardegna. http://www.regione.sardegna.it/j/v/86?v=9&c=72&file=1997026.

Rethemniotiko Vima [Ρεθεμνιώτικο Βήμα]. 2010. "Διάσημοι Κρητικοί Πολιτικοί:
Συνεργάτες των Γερμανών με Αγγλικό . . . Συγχωροχάρτι" [Famous Cretan politicians: Collaborators of the Germans with an English . . . indulgence]. http://www
.liberalparty.gr/files/uploads/RETHEMNIOTIKO_BHMA.pdf.

Reynolds, Craig J. 2006. *Seditious Histories: Contesting Thai and Southeast Asian Pasts*.
Seattle: University of Washington Press.

Robb, Erika M. 2009. "Violence and Recreation: Vacationing in the Realm of Dark Tourism." *Anthropology and Humanism* 34, no. 1: 51–60.

Robbins, Joel, and Holly Wardlow, eds. 2005. *The Making of Global and Local Modernities in Melanesia: Humiliation, Transformation and the Nature of Cultural Change.* New York: Routledge.

Rosaldo, Renato. 1989. "Imperialist Nostalgia." *Representations* 26:107–22.

Rozakou, Katerina. 2012. "The Biopolitics of Hospitality in Greece: Humanitarianism and the Management of Refugees." *American Ethnologist* 39:562–77.

Rozakou, Katerina. 2016. "Socialities of Solidarity: Revisiting the Gift Taboo in Times of Crises." *Social Anthropology* 24:185–99.

Rozakou, Katerina. 2017a. "Non-Recording the 'European Refugee Crisis' in Greece: Navigating through Irregular Bureaucracy." *Focaal: Journal of Global and Historical Anthropology* 77:36–49.

Rozakou, Katerina. 2017b. "Solidarity #Humanitarianism: The Blurred Boundaries of Humanitarianism in Greece." *Etnofoor* 29:99–104.

Rozakou, Katerina [Ροζάκου, Κατερίνα]. 2018. *Από "αγάπη" και "αλληλεγγύη": Εθελοντική εργασία με πρόσφυγες στην Αθήνα του πρώιμου 21ου αιώνα* [For "love" and "solidarity": Volunteer work with refugees in the Athens of the early 21st century]. Athens: Alexandria.

Rozenberg, Guillaume. 2012. Review of Bouté 2011. *Moussons* 20:216–20.

Ruiz, Todd. 2017. "1932 Democratic Revolution Plaque Removed." Khaosod English, 14 April. https://www.khaosodenglish.com/featured/2017/04/14/1932-revolution -plaque-removed/.

Ruiz, Todd. 2019. "Thai Idol Group BNK48 Member Wears Nazi Flag on Stage." Khaosod English, 26 January. https://www.khaosodenglish.com/featured/2019/01/26/thai-idol -group-bnk48-member-wears-nazi-flag-on-stage/.

Rumsey, Alan. 2004. "Ethnographic Macro-Tropes and Anthropological Theory." *Anthropological Theory* 4:267–98.

Sahlins, Marshall. 1992. "The Economics of Develop-Man in the Pacific." *Res* 21:13–25.

Saichon Satayanurak [สายชล สัตยานุรักษ์]. 2002. ชาติไทยและความเป็นไทยโดยหลวงวิจิตรวาทการ [Thai nation and Thainess according to Luang Wichit Wathakan]. Bangkok: Matichon.

Saulnier, Françoise. 1980. *Anoya, un village de montagne crétois.* Paris: Stahl, Laboratoire d'Anthropologie Sociale.

Schneider, Jane C., and Peter T. Schneider. 1994. "Mafia, Antimafia, and the Question of Sicilian Culture." *Politics and Society* 22:237–58.

Schneider, Jane C., and Peter T. Schneider. 2003. *Reversible Destiny: Mafia, Antimafia, and the Struggle for Palermo.* Berkeley: University of California Press.

Schneider, Jane C., and Peter T. Schneider. 2005. "Mafia, Antimafia, and the Plural Cultures of Sicily." *Current Anthropology* 46:501–20.

Scott, James C. 1985. *Weapons of the Weak: Everyday Forms of Peasant Resistance.* New Haven, CT: Yale University Press.

Scott, James C. 1998. *Seeing like a State: How Certain Schemes to Improve the Human Condition Have Failed.* New Haven, CT: Yale University Press.

Scott, James C. 2009. *The Art of Not Being Governed: An Anarchist History of Upland Southeast Asia.* New Haven, CT: Yale University Press.

Shore, Cris, and Susan Wright. 1999. "Audit Culture and Anthropology: The Rise of Neo-liberalism in Higher Education." *Journal of the Royal Anthropological Institute* 5:557–75.

Shore, Cris, and Susan Wright. 2015. "Audit Culture Revisited: Rankings, Ratings, and the Reassembling of Society." *Current Anthropology* 56:421–44.

Shryock, Andrew. 1997. *Nationalism and the Genealogical Imagination: Oral History and Textual Authority in Tribal Jordan*. Berkeley: University of California Press.

Shryock, Andrew. 2019. "Keeping to Oneself: Hospitality and the Magical Hoard in the Balga of Jordan." *History and Anthropology* 30:546–62.

Siani, Edoardo. 2020. "Embodying the Late King: Buddhist Salvation and the Sacrifice of Sovereignty at a Bangkok Mall." In *Political Theologies and Development in Asia: Transcendence, Sacrifice, and Aspiration*, edited by Giuseppe Bolotta, Philip Fountain, and R. Michael Feener, 104–18. Manchester: Manchester University Press.

Silverman, Sydel. 1975. *Three Bells of Civilization: The Life of an Italian Hill Town*. New York: Columbia University Press.

Silverstein, Michael. 2010. "Society, Polity, and Language Community: An Enlightenment Trinity in Anthropological Perspective." *Journal of Language and Politics* 9:339–63.

Sirinya Wattanasukchai. 2018. "At Fort Mahakan, a Birthday That Shuns the Past." *The Nation* (Thailand), 28 April. https://www.nationthailand.com/noname/30344180?utm_source=category&utm_medium=internal_referral.

Sirinya Wattanasukchai. 2020. "City's History Being Lost to Fake Facade of Beauty." *Bangkok Post*, 5 November. https://www.bangkokpost.com/opinion/opinion/2014143/citys-history-being-lost-to-fake-facade-of-beauty.

Smith, Donald E. 1996. "Religion and the Good Polity." *Cardozo Journal of International and Comparative Law* 4:277–93.

Smith, Helena. 2020a. "Golden Dawn Leaders and Ex-MPs Found Guilty in Landmark Trial." *The Guardian*, 7 October.

Smith, Helena. 2020b. "Neo-Nazi Leaders of Greece's Golden Dawn Sentenced to 13 Years." *The Guardian*, 14 October.

Smith, Laurajane. 2006. *Uses of Heritage*. London: Routledge.

Society for Threatened Peoples. 2004. "Campaign against Forced Evictions in the Informal Settlements in Nairobi." 26 April. www.gfbv.it/3dossier/africa/nairob-en-html/.

Solomon, Esther, ed. 2021. *Contested Antiquity: Archaeological Heritage and Social Conflict in Modern Greece and Cyprus*. Bloomington: Indiana University Press.

Sophorntavy Vorng. 2017. *A Meeting of Masks: Status, Power and Hierarchy in Bangkok*. Copenhagen: Nordic Institute of Asian Studies.

Sopranzetti, Claudio. 2012. "Burning Red Desires: Isan Migrants and the Politics of Desire in Contemporary Thailand." *South East Asia Research* 20:361–79.

Sopranzetti, Claudio. 2017. *Owners of the Map: Motorcycle Taxi Drivers, Mobility, and Politics in Bangkok*. Berkeley: University of California Press.

Sorge, Antonio. 2015. *Legacies of Violence: History, Society, and the State in Sardinia*. Toronto: University of Toronto Press.

Souliotis, Yannis [Σουλιώτης, Γιάννης]. 2007. "Αμέτρητες κρύπτες με όπλα και ναρκωτικά στα Ζωνιανά" [Countless hiding places with weapons and drugs in

Zoniana]. *I Kathimerini*, 15 November. https://www.kathimerini.gr/society/304561
/ametrites-kryptes-me-opla-kai-narkotika-sta-zoniana/.

Spivak, Gayatri. 1989. "In a Word: Interview with Ellen Rooney." *Differences* 1, no. 2: 124–56.

St. Clair, William. 1972. *That Greece Might Still Be Free: The Philhellenes in the War of Independence*. London: Oxford University Press.

Stefou, Olga [Στέφου, Όλγα]. 2018. "Ηριάννα και Περικλής: Μια ιστορία . . .
τρομονόμου έφτασε στο τέλος της" [Irianna and Periklis: A tale . . . of terror-law has reached its end]. *In.gr*, 28 June. https://www.in.gr/2018/06/28/plus/features/irianna
-kai-periklis-mia-istoria-tromonomou-eftase-sto-telos-tis/.

Steinmüller, Hans. 2013. *Communities of Complicity: Everyday Ethics in Rural China*. Oxford: Berghahn.

Steinmüller, Hans. 2015. "'Father Mao' and the Country-Family: Mixed Feelings for Fathers, Officials, and Leaders in China." *Social Analysis* 59:83–100.

Stengs, Irene. 2009. *Worshipping the Great Moderniser: King Chulalongkorn, Patron Saint of the Thai Middle Class*. Singapore: NUS Press.

Stevenson, William. 1999. *The Revolutionary King: The True-Life Sequel to The King and I*. London: Constable.

Stewart, Charles. 1989. "Hegemony or Rationality? The Position of the Supernatural in Modern Greece." *Journal of Modern Greek Studies* 7:77–104.

Stewart, Charles, and Rosalind Shaw, eds. 1994. *Syncretism/Anti-Syncretism: The Politics of Religious Synthesis*. London: Routledge.

Stocking, George W., Jr. 1965. "On the Limits of 'Presentism' and 'Historicism' in the Historiography of the Behavioral Sciences." *Journal of the History of the Behavioral Sciences* 1:211–18.

Stocking, George W., Jr. 1995. *After Tylor: British Social Anthropology, 1888–1951*. Madison: University of Wisconsin Press.

Strate, Shane. 2015. *The Lost Territories: Thailand's History of National Humiliation*. Honolulu: University of Hawai'i Press.

Strathern, Marilyn, ed. 2000. *Audit Culture: Anthropological Studies in Accountability, Ethics, and the Academy*. London: Routledge.

Strathern, Marilyn. 2020. *Relations: An Anthropological Account*. Durham, NC: Duke University Press.

Subrahmanyan, Arjun. 2020. "The Unruly Past: History and Historiography of the 1932 Thai Revolution." *Journal of Contemporary Asia* 50:74–98.

Suchit Wongthes [สุจิตต์ วงษ์เทศ]. 2003. "วิกลิเกแห่งแรกในสยามอยู่ริมกำแพงป้อมมหากาฬ" [The first place in Siam where *Likae* was performed is on the edge of the Pom Mahakan Wall]. *Khao Sod*, 27 May, 6.

Sunait Chutintaranond. 1990. "Mandala, 'Segmentary State,' and Politics of Centralization in Medieval Ayudhya." *Journal of the Siam Society* 78, no. 1: 88–100.

Sutton, David E. 1997. "Local Names, Foreign Claims: Family Inheritance and National Heritage on a Greek Island." *American Ethnologist* 24:415–37.

Tambiah, Stanley J. 1976. *World Conqueror, World Renouncer: A Study of Buddhism and Polity in Thailand against a Historical Background*. Cambridge: Cambridge University Press.

Tambiah, Stanley J. 1977. "The Galactic Polity: The Structure of Traditional Kingdoms in Southeast Asia." *Annals of the New York Academy of Sciences* 293:69–97.

Tambiah, Stanley J. 1989. "Ethnic Conflict in the World Today." *American Ethnologist* 16:335–49.

Tambiah, Stanley J. 1990. *Magic, Science, Religion, and the Scope of Rationality*. Cambridge: Cambridge University Press.

Tambiah, Stanley J. 2013. "The Galactic Polity in Southeast Asia." *Hau: Journal of Ethnographic Theory* 3, no. 3: 503–34.

Tanabe, Shigeharu. 2016. "Introduction: Communities of Potential." In *Communities of Potential: Social Assemblages in Thailand and Beyond*, edited by Shigeharu Tanabe, 1–18. Chiang Mai: Silkworm.

Tappanai Boonbandit. 2019. "*Bangkok Post* Reporter's Racially Charged Articles on Hmongs, 'Negroes' Draws Backlash." Khaosod English, 30 December. https://www .khaosodenglish.com/politics/2019/12/30/bangkok-post-reporters-racially-charged -article-on-hmongs-negroes-draws-backlash/.

Tausig, Benjamin. 2019. *Bangkok Is Ringing: Sound, Protest, and Constraint*. Oxford: Oxford University Press.

Taylor, James. 2008. *Buddhism and Postmodern Imaginings in Thailand: The Religiosity of Urban Space*. Farnham, UK: Ashgate.

Taylor, James. 2017. "The Perplexing Case of Wat Dhammakaya." *New Mandala*, March 6. https://www.newmandala.org/perplexing-case-wat-dhammakaya/.

Terner, Vania [Τέρνερ, Βάνια]. 2014. "Οι Ανωγειανοί μας εξήγησαν γιατί ποτέ κανείς στο χωριό δεν θα ψηφίσει Χρυσή Αυγή" [The Anoyans explained why no one in the village will ever vote for Golden Dawn]. Vice.com, 28 May. Updated 21 September 2015. https://www.vice.com/gr/article/3d8gzy/anogeia-evroekloges.

Thak Chaloemtiarana. 2007. *Thailand: The Politics of Despotic Paternalism*. Ithaca, NY: Cornell Southeast Asia Program.

Thiranagama, Sharika. 2018. "The Civility of Strangers? Caste, Ethnicity, and Living Together in Postwar Jaffna, Sri Lanka." *Anthropological Theory* 18:357–81.

Thiranagama, Sharika, Tobias Kelly, and Carlos Forment. 2018. "Introduction: Whose Civility?" *Anthropological Theory* 18:153–74.

Thomas, Kedron. 2016. *Regulating Style: Intellectual Property Law and the Business of Fashion in Guatemala*. Berkeley: University of California Press.

Thomas, Kedron, and Rebecca Galemba. 2013. "Illegal Anthropology: An Introduction." *PoLAR: Political and Legal Anthropology Review* 36, no. 2: 211–15.

Thongchai Winichakul. 1994. *Siam Mapped: A History of the Geo-Body of a Nation*. Honolulu: University of Hawai'i Press.

Thongchai Winichakul. 2000. "The Quest for 'Siwilai': A Geographical Discourse of Civilizational Thinking in the Late-Nineteenth-Century and Early-Twentieth-Century Siam." *Journal of Asian Studies* 59:528–49.

Thongchai Winichakul [ธงชัย วินิจะกุล]. 2001. "ประวัติศาสตร์ไทยแบบราชาชาตินิยมจากยุคอาณานิคม อำพรางสู่ราชาชาตินิยมใหม่หรือลัทธิเสด็จพ่อของกระฎุมพีไทยปัจจุบัน" [Royalist Thai history from the crypto-colonial era to neo-royalism, or, The present-day Thai bourgeois doctrine of paternalism]. *Silapawatthanatham* 23, no. 1: 56–65.

Tongkao Panin, Tanakarn Mokkhasmita, and Chinasak Tantikul. 2015. "Re-constructing the Vernacular? The Search for Contemporary Vernacular Houses in Central Thailand." *NAJUA: Architecture, Design and Built Environment* 290:281–90. https://s004 .tci-thaijo.org/index.php/NAJUA-Arch/article/view/44249.

Triandafyllidou, Anna, and Ifigeneia Kokkali. 2010. *Tolerance and Cultural Diversity Discourses in Greece*. Accept Pluralism Research Project. Fiesole: European University Institute, Robert Schuman Centre for Advanced Studies.

Tsandiropoulos, Aris [Τσαντηρόπουλος, Άρης]. 2004. *Η Βεντέτα στη Σύγχρονη Ορεινή Κεντρική Κρήτη* [The vendetta in modern mountainous central Crete]. Athens: Plethron.

Tsandiropoulos, Aris [Τσαντηρόπουλος, Άρης]. 2007. "Οικονομικός και κοινωνικός μετασχηματισμός στην ορεινή Κεντρική Κρήτη: Μια πρώτη προσέγγυση με αφορμήγ το ζήτημα των Ζωνιανών" [Economic and social reorganization in mountain central Crete: A first approach prompted by the Zoniana issue]. *Ariadni* 13:169–91.

Turner, Victor W. 1969. *The Ritual Process: Structure and Anti-Structure*. Chicago: Aldine.

Ünaldi, Serhat. 2014. "Working towards the Monarchy and Its Discontents: Anti-Royal Graffiti in Downtown Bangkok." *Journal of Contemporary Asia* 44:377–403.

Van Esterik, Penny. 2000. *Materializing Thailand*. Oxford: Berg.

Vernier, Bernard. 1991. *La genèse des sentiments: Aînés et cadets dans l'île grecque de Karpathos*. Paris: Éditions de l'École des Hautes Études en Sciences Sociales.

Vico, Giambattista. 1944. *The Autobiography of Giambattista Vico*. Translated by Max Harold Fisch and Thomas Goddard Bergin. Ithaca, NY: Cornell University Press.

Viqar, Sarwat. 2014. "Constructing Lyari: Place, Governance and Identity in a Karachi Neighbourhood." *South Asian History and Culture* 5:365–83. https://doi.org/10.1080 /19472498.2014.905335.

Voutira, Eftihia. 2016. "The Perversion of the Ancient and Traditional Value of 'Hospitality' in Contemporary Greece: From Xenios Zeus to 'Xenios Zeus.' " In *Migration— Networks—Skills: Anthropological Perspectives on Mobility and Transformation*, edited by Astrid Wonneberger, Mijal Gandelsman-Trier, and Hauke Dorsch, 83–98. New York: Columbia University Press.

Vradis, Antonis, and Dimitris Dalakoglou, eds. 2011. *Revolt and Crisis in Greece: Between a Present Yet to Pass and a Future Still to Come*. Oakland, CA: AK Press and Occupied London.

Walker, Andrew. 2012. *Thailand's Political Peasants: Power in the Modern Rural Economy*. Madison: University of Wisconsin Press.

Wanjiru, Melissa, and Kosuke Matsubara. 2016. "The Slum Toponymy of Nairobi: A Cultural Arena for Socio-Political Justice and Symbolic Resistance." In *History— Urbanism—Resilience: Planning and Heritage*, vol. 4 of *International Planning History Society Proceedings*, 17th IPHS Conference, Delft, edited by Carola Hein, 261–71. http://iphs2016.org/proceedings/.

Watson, James L. 2004. "Presidential Address: Virtual Kinship, Real Estate, and Diaspora Formation: The Man Lineage Revisited." *Journal of Asian Studies* 63:893–910.

Weber, Max. 1905. "Die protestantische Ethik und der 'Geist' des Kapitalismus, II. Die Berufsidee des asketischen Protestantismus." *Archiv für Sozialwissenschaft und Sozialpolitik* 21:1–110.

Weber, Max. 1930. *The Protestant Ethic and the Spirit of Capitalism*. Translated by Talcott Parsons. Foreword by R. H. Tawney. London: Allen and Unwin.

Wenner, Miriam. 2013. "Challenging the State by Reproducing Its Principles: The Demand for 'Gorkhaland' between Regional Autonomy and the National Belonging." *Asian Ethnology* 72:199–220.

Wilcox, Phill. 2021. *Heritage and the Making of Political Legitimacy in Laos: The Past and Present of the Lao Nation*. Amsterdam: Amsterdam University Press.

Wills, Garry. 1978. *Inventing America: Jefferson's Declaration of Independence*. New York: Houghton Mifflin.

Wilson, Edmund. 1982. *Israel and the Dead Sea Scrolls*. New York: Farrar, Straus and Giroux.

Wimmer, Andreas, and Nina Glick Schiller. 2002. "Methodological Nationalism and Beyond: Nation-State Building, Migration and the Social Sciences." *Global Networks* 2:301–34.

Wolf, Richard K., and Frank Heidemann. 2014. "Guest Editors' Introduction: Indigeneity, Performance, and the State in South Asia and Beyond." *Asian Ethnology* 73, nos. 1–2: 1–18.

Wolters, O. W. 2018. *History, Culture, and Region in Southeast Asian Perspectives*. Rev. ed. Ithaca, NY: Cornell University Press.

Woodhouse, Leslie. 2012. "Concubines with Cameras: Royal Siamese Consorts Picturing Femininity and Ethnic Difference in Early 20th Century Siam." *Trans-Asia Photography Review* 2, no. 2: n.p.

Wyatt, David K. 1994. *Studies in Thai History*. Chiang Mai: Silkworm.

Wyatt, David K. 2003. *Thailand: A Short History*. 2nd ed. New Haven, CT: Yale University Press.

Yalouri, Eleana. 2001. *The Acropolis: Global Fame, Local Claim*. Oxford: Berg.

Yanagisako, Sylvia, and Carol Delaney, eds. 1995. *Naturalizing Power: Essays in Feminist Cultural Analysis*. New York: Routledge.

Yannaras, Khristos [Γιανναράς, Χρήστος]. 1972. *Ορθοδοξία και Δύση: Η Θεολογία στην Ελλάδα Σήμερα* [Orthodoxy and the West: Theology in Greece today]. Athens: Athena.

Zambelios, Spyridon [Ζαμπέλιος, Σπυρίδων]. 1859. *Πόθεν η κοινή λέξις τραγουδώ: Σκέψεις περί ελληνικής ποιήσεως* [Whence the vulgar word *traghoudho*? Thoughts concerning Hellenic poetry]. Athens: Soutsas and Ktenas.

Index

Abhisit Vejjajiva, 84
Abu El-Haj, Nadia, 201n11
Acropolis (Athens), 114
activism and activists, 83, 161, 164, 178n93, 190n54; academic, 144; anarchist, 173n18; democracy, 184n68; legislative, 15; solidarity, 78
address, forms of, 88, 105
Administrative Court (Thailand), 25
advertising industry, 139
aesthetic and aesthetics, 137, 184n66, 186n40; architectural, 21; class, 41, 98; governmentality, 184n1; hegemonic, 199n6; hierarchized, 138; Italian, exported, 125; musical, 141; neoclassical, 50, 138; sartorial, 141; of state museums, 134; of Thainess, 41, 139; Western, in Thailand, 16
agency, 5
Agora (Athens), 113, 132; excavations in, 43
airbrushing of historical narratives. *See* historiography
Albania, 55
alcohol, 159
Alikambos, 46
Allen, Susan Heuk, 182n48
altitude. *See* height
anarchism, 173n18, 182n41
ancestor worship, 70, 115
Anderson, Benedict, 2, 4, 199n16
animal theft, 10, 11, 17, 24, 25, 31, 36, 65, 73, 76, 86, 87, 91, 102–3, 105, 121, 124, 125–26, 127, 155–56, 160, 178n89, 185n27, 190n62, 194n35, 196n13
animism, as colonial category, 115
Ankara, 69
Anoya (Crete), 86, 193n26
anthropology, colonial aspects of, 42; criminal, 124
antimaskers and antivaxxers, 165–66
antiquity, claims on, 3, 8, 9, 15, 16, 33, 36, 44, 45, 70, 72, 73, 74, 75, 81, 114, 124, 125, 127, 128, 133, 142, 155, 162–63, 165, 166
Apirak Kosayodhin, 21, 84, 85
Appadurai, Arjun, 81, 158, 184n1
Archaeological Service (Greece), 43, 47, 50, 127–28, 163, 184n66
archaeologists, 99
archaeology: biblical, 201n11; colonial model of, 45; in France, 182n40; as political tool, 43–44, 45, 47, 48, 52; rhetoric of, 144
"archaic" societies, 5

archaism. *See* subversive archaism
architects, 50, 183n63
architecture: classical orders of, 98; compared to etymology, 98; contempt for, 21–22, 48, 49; as heritage, 70; as historical evidence, 161–62; lack of interest in, 50, 183n63; selective treatment of in Greece, 50; Siamese religious and royal, 46; Siamese vernacular, 21, 37–38, 49–50, 83–84, 145, 177n78
Ardener, Edwin, 67, 174n38
aristocracy, European, 102; Thai, 40, 48, 82
army (Thai), 21, 83, 105, 107, 132
Association of Siamese Architects, 22, 83–84, 148, 190n57
Astrinaki, Ourania, 189n46
Atatürk, Mustafa Kemal, 69
atheism, state, 8
Athenocentrism, 32, 36, 47; defied, 143
Athens, 23, 67–68, 113, 114, 127, 128; Academy of (modern), 44, 47, 182n49; ancient, 32, 126, 127, 128, 132. *See also* Exarcheia
Athos, Mount, 192n13
Attachak Sattayanurak, 185n15
audit culture, 198n38
Aulino, Felicity, 171n3, 179n5
authenticity, 11, 27, 41; of local knowledge, 74
authoritarianism, 57, 81, 132, 133, 153, 199n11
authorized heritage discourse (AHD), 16, 103, 176n66
autochthony, 37
avato. See remoteness
Ayutthaya, 80

Bachofen, Johann Jakob, 180n16
Baer, Hans, 173n19
Balibar, Étienne, 104, 192n20, 194n48
banditry, 7, 31, 32, 36, 54, 125, 138, 196n10, 196n13. See also *klefts*; *nakleng*
Bangkok, 57, 113, 131, 198n26; architecture in, 98; as capital, 161; cosmological underpinnings of, 71, 80; landscape of, 48; symbols of, 94. *See also* architecture; *moeang*; Pom Mahakan
Bangkok Metropolitan Administration (city hall), 24, 25, 50, 82, 132, 139–40, 202n28
bankers, as usurers, 77–78
Ban Khrua (Bangkok community), 110–11
baptism sponsorship, 86

guerrillas. See *klefts*

guns, 91, 154, 165; firing of (*balothies*), 36, 54, 86, 89–90, 91, 156, 168; Kalashnikov, 62, 64, 160; trade in, 65. *See also* weapons

Gupta, Akhil, 144–45, 157

Gush Emunim, 7–8, 173n26

"Gypsies" (derogatory label), 109

Haberkorn, Tyrell, 171n3

Hage, Ghassan, 67

hajduks, 33, 180n23

Halkià, Alexandra, 202n27

Hamilakis, Yannis, 35, 192n9

Handley, Paul, 178n93

Hardy, Andrew, 135

Harms, Erik, 191n3

Hatfields and McCoys, 103

hearth, as community core, 58

Heatherington, Tracey, 109, 124, 128, 173n32, 197n22

height, symbolism of, 71, 93–95, 131, 132, 198n28

Heine-Geldern, Robert von, 134

Hellenes (official name for Greeks), 34–35

heritage, 1, 2,16, 30, 60, 145; alternative readings of, 3, 21, 170; authorized discourse of, 103, 176n66; Italian, 10; language of, 3, 5; parodied, 6, 17; refracted, 73; state management of, 138; subnational, 9; subversive versions of, 143, 163, 169; World Heritage Sites, 203n32

Heywood, Paolo, 69

hierarchy: and age, 74, 132, 133; blended with democracy, 58; and civility, 97; geopolitical, 28, 43; implicitly questioned, 57; in Laos, 57; of leaders and followers, 81, 132, 133; royal-inflected, 95, 178n93; social, in Greece, 39, 47–48; structural, of cosmological polity, 56, 57; of Thai identities, 108, 148, 175n53; in Thailand, 25, 32, 39, 40, 48, 49, 50, 57–58, 94–95, 113, 131, 183n61, 183n62, 198n26. *See also* global hierarchy of value

Hindutva nationalism (India), 196n6

history and historiography, 174n42; airbrushed, 12, 13, 14–15, 20, 37, 117, 159, 174–75n51, 175n52, 195n58; alternative, 50; collective, on Crete, 46; contested, 26, 42; European, as model, 45; neo-classicist, 47; official, 12, 20, 21, 35, 37, 38, 40, 71, 75, 127, 154, 159; refracted, 187n28; re-used, 27, 30, 33; rewritten, 31, 80; royal, 46, 48, 183n63. *See also* periodization

Hmong, 109, 182n39

Hobsbawm, Eric, 179n7

Holmes, Douglas R., 190n64, 201n11, 202n21

Holocaust memorial (Thessaloniki), 101

Holston, James, 5

Hong Kong, 75

hospitality, 18, 23, 29, 52, 58, 64, 147, 164; toward bureaucrats (Soqotra), 9; and friendship, 197n24; toward migrants, 188n37; reciprocal, ancient, 188n32; reified as migrant reception, 187n30,

188n33; reverses power relation, 93–94, 105; and segmentation, 76–77, 78

houses and housing, 110; concentric with *moeang*, 56; as economic indicator, 121; monumentalized, 43; preservation and destruction of, 83, 145, 157

Hrê, 135

humiliation: national, 39, 40, 54, 77, 166, 178n87, 181n33; rejected, 170; of villagers, 18, 41, 55–56, 164

humor, 105, 150; lack of, in bureaucracy, 84, 103

icons (religious images), 73

identity, cultural: attribution and formation of, 58, 105, 109; forms of, linked to specific polities, 131; national, 60; shared, 131; Thai concepts of, 185n22

illegality and illegalization, 150, 160, 161. *See also* law

images, 198n3; battle of, 142; national, 162; regime of, 138

impermanence, 57

impunity, 15, 105, 175n57, 202n27

inaccessibility. *See* remoteness

indigeneity, 111, 126, 130, 163, 194n44; Cretan, 138; in Guatemala, 196–97n13; in India, 196n6; in leadership, 37, 83; in scholarship, 74

individualism, 102, 166, 170

inequality, 25, 152. *See also* egalitarianism

inheritance practices, 32

integralism, 166, 170, 202n21, 202n26

Iraklio (Crete), 75

irony, 54, 57, 135

irredentism, 118

Isan, 108, 141

Islamic caliphate, 71

Ismailbekova, Aksana, 184n5

Israel, 8, 70–71, 173n26, 201n11

Italy, 6, 46, 67, 122, 199n6; Catholicism in, 69, 74, 115, 173n19; civility in, 98, 125 130, 197–98n25; colonial, 188n38; fascism in, 16, 127; *italianità* as essence of, 131; migrants in, 197n18, 197–98n25; nationalism in, 45, 124, 127, 128, 197n18; politics in, 69; soil of, 10, 52; subversive archaism in, 7; urbanity of, 196–97n17; violence in, 125. *See also mafia*; Orgosolo; Rome; Sardinia

Jackson, Peter A., 138

Jain, Ravindra K., v

Jefferson, Thomas, 34

Jewish settlers. *See* Gush Emunim

Jews in Greece, 189n42

Johnson, Andrew Alan, 118, 119

Jonsson, Hjorleifur, 161

Jordan, 2, 55, 73, 187n28, 187n30

Jory, Patrick, 81, 190n53, 198n26

Judaism, Ultra-Orthodox, 70–71; Orthodox Christianity represented as form of, 72

judiciary, Thai, 25. *See also* impunity

justice, retributive, 6

meat, consumption of, 155–56

media, 29, 42, 60; attitudes to Greek state of, 101; attitudes to Pom Mahakan of, 24, 61, 64, 136, 142; and narcotics trade, 194n40; in Thailand, 200n25; treatment of Zoniana, 159–60. See also vilification campaigns

Mediterranean and Mediterraneanism, 197n24

merchants as mediators, 53

merit-making, 58, 71, 158, 190n61, 198n26

Meskell, Lynn, 203n32

methodological statism, 112, 120, 194n47

metonymy, 59. See also concentricity

microcosm, community as, 26

middle class. See bourgeoisie

migrants, 78, 94, 103, 108, 188n37, 188n39, 197n18, 197–98n25, 199–200n20

Milopotamos, 23, 53, 54, 61, 138

minorities, 27, 46, 60, 134–35, 139, 182n39, 193n27; assimilated, 109; competing claims of, 8; excluded, 68, 108, 158; favored, 110–11; included, 41, 133, 164; languages of, 141; rights of, 199–200n20; status of, 16

Minos, Minoans, 35, 36, 46, 128. See also Linear B

Mitsotakis, Konstantinos, 86, 90, 187n20; and son Kyriakos, 187n20

modernity, modernism, modernization, 49, 80, 104, 112, 113, 119, 139; absence of, 43; antimodernity, among ultrarightists, 165, 166; bourgeois, 159, 162; bureaucrats as agents of, 3; Chinese, 8; and diversity, 100; exploited, 147; Greek and Italian, compared, 127; planning, 38; political uses of, 86–87; relation to heritage, 11, 33, 124, 138; relation to monarchy, 117; resisted, 125; Thai, 180n21; unmodernity, anxiety of, xiv, 158

moeang, xiv, 56, 57, 71, 74, 114, 196n8; alternative, 81; ambiguities at the edges of, 118; Chiang Mai as, 113; compared to nation-state, 113; compared to polis, 182n51; ethnic Tai, 113, 117; flexibility of, 170; as heritage, 170; hierarchy within, 94, 132; in Laos, 57; as nation-state, 80; northern Thai, 186n1; as polity, 113; Pom Mahakan as, 117, 118, 159, 161, 185n20; rupture with, 119; rural, 186n9; segmentary properties of, 80, 183–84n65, 194n45; spectral presence of, 119. See also mandala

monarchy: absolute, 117; as heritage, 70; British, German roots of, 34; Greek, 14, 15, 40, 175n61; Greek and Thai compared, 14, 15, 45; and abolition of, 14, 20, 34, 180n25; Bavarian roots of, 34; Thai, 13, 14–16, 37, 40, 46; as embodiment of virtue, 25. See also lèse-majesté

monks, 58, 70, 71, 101, 133, 158, 165

Montenegro, 55

monument, 57; focus on, 45, 85; houses as, 43; monumentalization, 154

moral community, xvi, 95, 104–5, 113–14, 195n50, 195n51, 195n52; city as, 113, 161

morality, 25, 28, 92, 142, 150; "double," 69; higher, claimed, 93, 94; immorality, community accused of, 149; of legal system, challenged, 25; and moralism, 29; political, 29, 184n7; and status, 71. See also corruption; karma

moral panic, 24, 67

Morgan, Lewis Henry, xv, xvi, 32, 177n79, 179n12, 180n16

Mormons. See Latter-Day Saints, Church of

museum, 2, 11, 29–30, 35–36; living, 154; National (Bangkok), 13, 45, 145; national (in general), 42; Pom Makahan community, 21, 134, 143, 144, 145; private, in Bangkok, 177n77; Rattanakosin (Bangkok), 20

music, 2, 11, 16, 141, 142, 159

Muslims, Chinese, 111; Thai, 41, 110, 148; Sri Lankan, 70

Mussolini, Benito, 99, 124, 127, 165. See also fascism

Myanmar, 70, 165

Nairobi. See Kibera

nakleng (bandit style), 38, 138, 180n31, 198n3

naming practices, 32–33

narcotics: absent, 159; decried, 194n40; suppressed, 146; trade in, 17, 24–25, 65, 87, 106, 121–22, 165; use of, 21, 149; war against, 21. See also cannabis cultivation

nationalism, 2, 4, 41, 44, 126; ambiguity and ambivalence in, 142; core paradox of, 30; cultural, 45, 143; decried, 68; ethnonationalism, 15, 26, 27, 38, 41, 74, 79, 81, 100, 109, 111, 112–13, 159, 166, 170, 182n40, 202n25; European, 45; and iconicity, 199n16; methodological, 97, 120, 194n47; narratives of, 42; and religion, 69, 70, 71; resentment as trigger in, 202n22; and scholarship, 27; of subversive archaists, 163. See also nation-state

nation-state, xiii–xvi, 1, 4, 130, 166; Balkan, 31; building of, 67; colonial dissemination of, 97; as cosmological, 81; disaggregated, 44–45; European, as model, 45–46, 183–84n65; fractures within, 1, 55; fragility of, 4; frontiers of, 118; as guardian of national virtue, 99; militarism in, 139; modernity of, 3, 112, 157, 158; as a polity, 69, 80, 97, 101, 186n1; rigid, 112; segmentary aspects of, 119; and temporality, 161; Thai, 37; traditionalism of, 5

nativism, 39

Nazism, 72, 165, 173n19, 182n39, 189n42, 202n28; neo-Nazism, 165

neoclassicism, 46, 47, 50, 71, 76, 99, 138, 188n32

neoliberals and neoliberalism, 59–60, 91, 100, 191n71, 194n48; Neoliberals (Greek political party), 86, 87, 187n20, 191n71

Neo-Orthodoxy, 70, 71, 186n10

Nepal, 57

New Democracy (Greek political party), 86, 87, 101, 187n20